BORN TO BE KING

THE EPIC OF THE INCARNATION

BORN TO BE KING
THE EPIC OF THE INCARNATION

Dom Bernard Orchard
OSB

EALING ABBEY SCRIPTORIUM
London
1993

British Library Cataloguing in Publication Data
Orchard, B. (Bernard—see also under Orchard, J.B.) *1910-*
Born to be King: The Epic of the Incarnation.
1. Bible. N.T. Gospels—Devotional
I. Title
232

ISBN 09522104 0 1 (paperback)
ISBN 09522104 1 X (hardback/papercased)

First published in Great Britain 1993

The Scripture quotations contained herein are from the
Revised Standard Version (Catholic Edition, 1966) and
B.Orchard, *A Synopsis of the Four Gospels* (1982).

Cum permissu superiorum O.S.B.

Published by EALING ABBEY SCRIPTORIUM,
a trading sub-division of Ealing Abbey (Reg. Charity),
Charlbury Grove, London W5 2DY.
Orders to:
Overton, 74 Castlebar Road, London W5 2DD.
Fax No: 081-991 2587.

Typeset in Century 11/13pt by Scriptmate Editions.
Printed in Great Britain at The Alden Press, Oxford.
Booksprint, 30 Clerkenwell Close, London EC1R 0AT.

———

The cover illustration is a photograph taken at Tiberias of the sun
rising over the Sea of Galilee.

Foreword

This book is my own personal contribution towards Pope John Paul's appeal for the promotion of Evangelization during this last decade of the twentieth century. For Evangelization is nothing but making known to the whole world the person of Jesus Christ, 'the image of the invisible God, the first-born of all creation...the head of his body the Church...in whom the fulness of God was pleased to dwell...who has reconciled to himself all things... making peace by the blood of his Cross' (Col 1:15-20). It is moreover the fruit of a lifetime of meditation and research,[1] initially inspired by my revered teachers, Abbot John Chapman and Abbot/Bishop Christopher Butler, both of Downside Abbey, my former Alma Mater.[2]

Its purpose is to edify and to sustain all orthodox Christians, whether Catholics or Greeks or Anglicans or Evangelicals, at a time when the ideas of the Enlightenment appear to be in the ascendent. It is specially directed to aid all teachers of the Faith, whether clergy or religious Brothers or Sisters or missionaries or lay teachers or heads of families. It seeks to be entirely faithful to the teaching of the new Universal Catechism, and is based

---

1   For a popular introduction to the relationships between the Four Gospels see B. Orchard, *The Evolution of the Gospels,* CTS London 1990, 2nd edition Ealing Abbey 1993. Some of my other recent books and articles of interest in this context: *Matthew, Luke and Mark,* Koinonia Press, Ealing Abbey 1976; *Synopsis of the Four Gospels in Greek,* T & T Clark, Edinburgh 1983; *Synopsis of the Four Gospels in English,* Mercer UP, Macon Ga. 1982; *The Order of the Synoptics* (Orchard and Riley), Mercer UP, Macon Ga. 1987; 'Dei Verbum and the Synoptic Gospels', *Downside Review,* July 1990.

2   J. Chapman, *Matthew, Mark and Luke,* London 1937; B. Butler, *The Originality of St Matthew,* Cambridge 1951; W. R. Farmer, *The Synoptic Problem:* A Critical Analysis, London/New York 1964.—For the present state of the scholarly discussion cf. *The Interrelations of the Gospels,* ed. D. L. Dungan, Leuven UP 1990; J. Wenham, *Redating Matthew, Mark & Luke,* London 1991.

on my Synopsis of the Four Gospels in Greek, and also on the English version of the same, of which a new edition is now in preparation. All quotations are taken either from my own translation of the Gospels or from the Revised Standard Version (Catholic Edition, 1966).

It is impossible to evaluate all the help I have received from so many quarters over so many years; but I wish especially to thank my own Community of Ealing Abbey and the many persons who have read early drafts of my text and offered helpful comments, including an Oblate of our Community without whose personal dedication to the project it might never have been completed.

The whole work is dedicated to the Blessed Virgin Mary, the Mother of God, from whom at Medjugorje in 1988 I sought sanction for its undertaking and guidance in its composition in order to make sure that what I have now written may be neither more nor less than what is pleasing to her and her glorious Son, who is the Truth itself.

Ealing Abbey   Bernard Orchard OSB
Feast of the Assumption BVM 1993

Contents

PART I: THE HIDDEN LIFE

PART II: THE PUBLIC LIFE

PART III: THE LIFE OF GLORY

Part I

The Hidden Life

1

The Time of Preparation

For the Christian, the fundamental fact is the existence of the Supreme Being, of the God, who alone exists of himself and is infinite in all perfections. We also believe that God is a Spirit, that is, totally detached from everything else that exists, and that he made the world and all that is in it, both matter and spirit out of nothing by his Word. In Jesus it was revealed that in the One God there are three equal Persons—the Father, the Son, who is the Word, and the Holy Spirit, each possessing in a different relationship the one infinite Being of God—and that everything that has come to be has been made by the Father, through the Son, in the Holy Spirit. The opening verses of the Book of Genesis proclaim this clearly:

In the beginning God created the heavens and the earth.

This supports the Church's teaching that God is Existence itself—the One who cannot not exist, the one Source of all life and all energy both spiritual and physical. This God, in one sense, is a perfect society, that of the Father, the Son and the Spirit, who live in a union of mutual love—utterly self-contained and independent of his creation—yet totally unselfish in the human sense. For reasons we can only guess at, this God, whom the Jews were to call Yahweh—making him, or rather accepting him, as the God of their nation—this God, who is infinite in power and majesty, of his own free-will (for God is the only truly free being) determined to create (i.e. to make out of nothing by

his Word alone) other beings entirely dependent on him for existence and for everything. Moreover our God is detached from
time; he is outside time, for time is simply the measure by which
human beings fix the duration of things created by God.

The ancient tradition informs us that the first creation of God
was the nine categories of angelic spirits, an uncountable multitude, whom he endowed with intelligence and will. There are
myriads of each category, and within each category every single
one is entirely different from all the others; and all are endowed
with wonderful talents. According to the tradition recorded by
Dionysius, these nine categories of angels are named as follows:
the Seraphim, the Cherubim, and Thrones; Dominations, Virtues, and Powers; Principalities, Archangels, and Angels. The
same tradition adds that as the Lord God only desires homage
given freely and willingly, he tested their willingness to adore
him before permitting them to enjoy the sight of his glory and
beauty. A certain portion of them refused to worship and serve.
The leader of those who said: 'I will not serve' has come to be
known as Satan—the Adversary, the Devil. Having refused
homage to the God who created them, these proud Spirits condemned themselves to total frustration because they were
created to worship their Creator, and having failed of their own
free will to do so, they are forever turned in on themselves and
can find no satisfaction except in trying to make others like
themselves. Since all these Spirits have enormous intellectual
power, their test happened in a flash and at the beginning of
their creation, and all are now fixed forever according to the
particular decision each freely made with regard to God. This is
because in his boundless wisdom God created spiritual beings
who were like himself in possessing freedom of choice. Their
choice—once made—was irrevocable, because they knew exactly what they were doing. In this way, for reasons we can only
surmise, the Lord God allowed an evil disharmony to enter into
the universe he created, even before the creation of man took
place.

It is at this stage in the unfolding of the history of creation that Genesis opens with the second stage of God's plan, the creation of the visible world that we know, which was to become the theatre in which the human race was to appear and operate. Although the ancient Israelite tradition asserted that the Book of Genesis was the work of Moses—who flourished in the 13th century before Christ—it would seem rather that his name became attached to it, and to the Pentateuch as a whole, because he collected up and wrote down some of the stories about the origins of his people. Other elements of this Book, including its first chapter, are now believed to be the work of some author or scribe who lived at the time of the Exile, c. 587 BC. But the two most important things to remember about the Book of Genesis is firstly that it presupposes a profound philosophical and theological view of the meaning of human life and of the universe, and secondly that the Holy Spirit is its author, jointly and severally, with the human writers.

The first chapter of Genesis embodies the following doctrines that determined for all time the fundamental attitudes of the Israelites towards God and the world, and towards one another, both men and women: namely, the creation of the world out of nothing by the sole word of the Lord God, who regarded the Israelites as his people, as we shall see from later chapters of the same book. It teaches that the world did not always exist, and that Spirits, angels good and bad, existed before the world was created; it teaches that all earthly phenomena, i.e. all things that can be seen, were made by God for man's good and for his enjoyment, including the sun and moon and stars, which according to Genesis were to help him to tell the time; it teaches that first in order of God's intention was the creation of Adam, the first man, but that Eve, the first woman, was created next as his equal to make him happy, provide him with a companion to share his life and remove his loneliness; it teaches that both man and woman are made in the image of God, are unique among God's creatures and superior to all the animals. As St Augustine pointed out, this image is seen chiefly in the human soul and in its powers of memory, understanding and will.

God created man in his own image, in the image of God he created him; male and female he created them. (Gen 1:27)

To them was given by God dominion over all the other creatures of the earth. The entire story of the creation is presented as if God, like a workman, had worked for six days and then rested on the seventh day. By using this literary artifice the inspired author made it clear that the week with its six days of work and its Sabbath rest is a matter of divine institution and is to be scrupulously observed by the human race in its activities.

The explanation of the meaning of human existence continues in the second and third chapters of Genesis. They make it clear that the earth in its present form is not meant to be the permanent home of mankind but a place of testing, for like the angels the human race is not to be granted happiness and fulfilment without first passing a worthiness test. Again, the equality and the complementarity of men and women is emphasized in the description of the woman being taken from the rib of man:

Adam said: This at last is bone of my bones and flesh of my flesh; she shall be called Woman, because she was taken out of Man. (Gen 2:23)

The next two verses leave no doubt that woman was made for man, and man for woman; and that, when first created, all their physical, mental and moral powers were at peace within them. There was no element in the constitution or psychology of the first man and woman that was discordant or disruptive or out of harmony with God or the universe in which he had placed them. They are complementary to each other.[3] However, Adam and Eve, the first pair of human beings, before they begat any

3   Note that my treatment of Adam and Eve is based on Catholic doctrine. The Catholic Church has always taught and teaches that the human race is descended from one pair, whom Genesis names Adam and Eve, and that their disobedience was the cause of the fall and the loss of eternal life. The widely accepted modern theory of the evolution of the human species from lower forms of life, such as the apes, is without true scientific foundation, because there is no evidence to prove that any species can evolve into another species. It seems to me far easier and more scientific to believe in the existence of an omnipotent life-giving creator of infinite intelligence than to attribute the variety of creation to the development of life and spirit from inanimate matter.

children, had first to face the same trial as the angels and to demonstrate their willingness to obey the commands of God in the light of faith, without seeing why they should obey.

Note that the Christian tradition is that both Adam and Eve from the very first moment of their existence were endowed with sanctifying grace and all the virtues needed to exercise it. The test that the Lord God devised for them is described for us in the form of an allegory: God had placed them in ideal surroundings in the Garden of Eden; they were at harmony with him and with each other; and there were no internal impulses within them to make them want to act contrary to the law of their own being and the laws of the universe. So God permitted Satan, the leader of the wicked angels, to prepare a test for them by encouraging them to query the command God had given them when putting them into Paradise:

> The Lord God commanded Adam, saying: You may freely eat of every tree of the garden; but of the tree of the knowledge of good and evil you shall not eat, for in the day that you eat of it you shall die. (Gen 2:16-17)

Chapter 3 of Genesis describes how Eve allowed herself to be tempted by Satan, in the guise of a serpent, into eating of the fruit of this tree, and persuaded her husband to share her disobedience. It was also a sin of pride; and the immediate effect of it upon Adam and Eve was to discover that they had cut themselves off from the grace of God, that their powers of mind and body were no longer controlled by his sanctifying grace and were now unruly. Genesis 3:7 ('The eyes of both were opened and they knew that they were naked') makes specific mention of their realization of their loss of control over themselves and over their relationships with other people, with everybody in fact. Henceforth mankind was to find itself alienated from God and his creation; and Adam and Eve found themselves deprived and severely punished. From now on they and their children were denied access to the tree of life, that is to say, the tree of the knowledge of good and evil, and they had no way of recovering their pristine state of innocence. The Devil was as happy as that sad creature could be; but the gates of Paradise which had been waiting to receive Adam and Eve were now definitely closed against them, so horrific was their sin. Before their fall there had been no weakness, no concupiscence as such within them, i.e. no internal inclination to sin against any of the commandments. Their sin was the result of pride, taking the Devil's word for it that they knew better than God himself about the knowledge of good and evil.

But God allowed this to happen to them in order that he might reveal to the human race some of the immense depths of his love for the creatures that he had made in his own image. And so in the very moment in which he pronounced sentence on Adam and Eve, he gave the first hint of the next stage of his plan, of what is called the Redemption, when he said:

> I will put enmities between you and the woman, and between your seed and her seed. It shall crush your head and you shall lie in wait for its heel. (Gen 3:15)

This passage is the first announcement of the future good news of the Gospel, because it conveys the notion of the victory of the woman's seed over the Serpent, the woman being understood in later Tradition as a type of Our Blessed Lady. However, the full plan of God for undoing the effects of the sin of Adam remained unknown and hidden for thousands of years. And then in the time of Abraham, God took the next step in its implementation. Since in the time of Jesus every Jewish child was taught about God's dealings with the human race in terms of the stories recorded in the Bible, no apology need be made here for the following brief summary of the history of Israel as it would have been related by Mary and Joseph to the boy Jesus; and incidentally I am not concerned either to defend or to explain the historicity of these narratives, since Jesus himself treated them as the Word of God.

We simply do not know how long a time elapsed between the fall of Adam and Eve and the call of Abraham; some say many thousands of years, others even a million or so. Between these two events the chapters of Genesis just hint darkly about the depravity and wickedness of the human race now that it lacked the grace of God to keep it healthy and pure; and their constant theme is its enslavement to sin and to misery:

> Now the earth was corrupt in God's sight, and the earth was filled with violence. And God saw the earth, and behold it was corrupt; for all flesh had corrupted their way upon the earth. (Gen 6:11-12)

And so in pre-historic times God destroyed in the great flood all the inhabitants except for Noah, who 'found favour in his eyes', thus showing that there were still a few good men left to serve God (6:9 ff). With Noah, God made a fresh start with the recalcitrant human race; but the effects of original sin still persisted; and at the tower of Babel God scattered the inhabitants of the earth in all directions as a punishment for their pride and arrogance (11:1-9). Then, some time about the beginning of the 20th century before the Christ, God mysteriously called a certain man, Abram, who had migrated with his father Terah from Ur of the Chaldees in Mesopotamia to Harran, saying to him:

> Go from your country and your kindred and your father's house to the land that I will show you. And I will make of you a great nation, and I will bless you, and make your name great, so that you will be a blessing. I will bless those who bless you, and him who curses you I will curse; and in you shall all the families of the earth be blessed. (Gen 12:1-3)

This blessing is repeated in 18:18; and in 22:18 it is added that this blessing is to be through his seed, as a reward for having been willing to sacrifice his son Isaac in obedience to God's command.

There are several important comments to be made here:

a) Abram is 'justified', that is to say, God dwells with him and he is admitted to God's favour because of his faith in God's promise of an heir to his body, his son Isaac, and of the further promise of a future deliverer of the human race, i.e. the Messiah. This promise, first given in very general terms, will be made more and more explicitly to special persons, as the history of the Chosen People unfolds in the sacred Scriptures of the Old Testament.

b) We see here God's choice of a particular person, Abram, his name being soon changed to Abraham, meaning 'Father of many nations', as he will become the Father of all those who believe in the promise.

c) God the omnipotent Creator chose to make himself the 'tribal' God of the descendants of Abraham and to become their national God and their special protector and guardian.

d) It was an essential part of God's design that he would lavish on this people of his an ever clearer idea of his nature and power, gradually revealing himself to them by means of 'prophets', men who were special instruments of his revelation of himself and of his messages to his Chosen People.

e) In this way the Lord God was preparing the right circumstances, the right environment, the right home, and even the appropriate 'cradle' for the coming of the Anointed Prince first intriguingly hinted at in Gen 3:15. In other words, the Lord God was preparing with infinite forethought, from the time of Abraham over a period of nearly two thousand years, a series of moves to make sure that everything and everyone was ready for the coming of the great king, so that when he came, he too would have at his command all that was necessary for the initiation of the final stage in the world's redemption that would be inaugurated by him. Even so, as we shall see, the actual way in which the Messiah came into the world took everyone by surprise.

The next stage in the development of God's plan was the barter of Jacob's son Joseph as a slave, the exciting and romantic story of his rise to power in Egypt, and the eventual settling of the twelve sons of Jacob in Egypt in the land of Goshen. Joseph has been rightly regarded by the Christian Church as a type of our Saviour because he not only relieved his own family but the Egyptians too.

After some four hundred years of unrecorded stay in that land, we are told in the Book of Exodus of the birth of Moses, of his adoption by the daughter of Pharaoh, and of his re-call from exile at the age of eighty to lead his people forth from Egypt—

from the human and political point of view an impossible task, but one which God made possible by himself leading them through the Red Sea into the desert of Sinai. There Moses was instructed by God to give his people a moral code, the Ten Commandments, a solemn liturgy with which they were to worship the God who had delivered them out of the power of Pharaoh, a priesthood to take charge of the cult, and above all a covenant, i.e. a solemn agreement made between the Lord God and his people at Mt Sinai. God promised to protect them, to cherish them and to make them victorious over all their enemies provided they adhered to him and worshipped him alone. He made it clear to them that if they turned to pagan gods, he would let them fall into the hands of their enemies, as was unfortunately to happen over and over again in the course of the next 1200 years and more. Their first defection was their failure to trust God to lead them to victory over the inhabitants of Canaan, the land promised to Abraham some 700 years before (as the deliverance from Egypt seems to have taken place round about the year 1225 BC). Consequently, they were left to wander about in the desert for forty years until all that faithless generation had passed away and died, including Moses himself. We may also note in passing that this wandering in the desert was a parable of the life of men on earth; for none can reach the Promised Land of heaven until they have at last passed through death. Only Joshua, another type of the future Saviour (Joshua is simply a variant of the name Jesus), and Caleb, the two chief lieutenants of Moses, were privileged to live long enough to lead the people into the Promised Land.

Each generation of the Chosen People was in fact to register some sort of failure to keep their covenant with God; and God allowed each generation to suffer the consequences of failure by becoming in one way or another subject to their enemies, in order to teach them that all sin is a form of slavery. But God never entirely deserted his people, because there was always a 'holy remnant' among them who were preserved, and upon whom the Lord was able to build for the future.

The high point of the earthly kingdom of the Israelites came in the reigns of David and Solomon; and it fell to Solomon, David's son, to build in Jerusalem, which David had made his capital city, the splendid Temple in which at length the worship of the true God could be carried out with appropriate dignity and splendour. According to the tradition, king David himself composed a number of psalms in honour of God, for use in the Temple liturgy. It was to David also that the prophet Nathan gave the most explicit prophecy as yet of the future birth of the Messiah, one of whose titles was to be 'the Son of David'. Nathan said to David:

> When your days are fulfilled I will raise up your offspring after you, who shall come forth from your body, and I will establish his kingdom... And your house and your kingdom shall be made sure for ever before me; your throne shall be established for ever. (2 Sam 7:12-16)

However, in the reign of Solomon's successor, Rehoboam, the kingdom of Solomon was divided; and ten tribes set themselves up as the Northern kingdom of Samaria, leaving only Judah and Benjamin as the Southern kingdom with Jerusalem as its capital. A further consequence was the setting up of a schismatic temple in Samaria in opposition to the true Temple of God in Jerusalem. The wickedness of the rulers of the Northern kingdom soon led to its being abandoned by God; and it fell captive to the Assyrians in 721 BC, in spite of many warnings from Isaiah and other prophets. The Southern kingdom got into an equally miserable state from the spiritual point of view; and after its refusal to listen to the warnings of the prophet Jeremiah it too perished, Jerusalem being sacked in 586 BC, and its king and nobles being deported to Babylon.

But God always brings good out of evil; and the captivity of the leaders of the Jewish race in Babylon for some seventy years was a time of repentance and grace, led by the prophet Ezekiel. Dreams of the restoration of the glorious kingdom of Solomon faded away; but, in the face of the reality of being captives in a foreign land, the religion of Israel spiritualised itself. All during their exile the Jews had mourned the loss of their glorious Temple and its beautiful liturgy—for there alone could true sacrifice be offered to their God. In consequence, they developed instead the practice of coming together every Sabbath for prayer, the reading of the Scriptures and listening to commentaries thereon. In this way the Synagogue came to be instituted; and the weekly meeting later became the special feature of Jewish worship in every city in which they settled. Thus the Exile and Dispersion of the Jews led to a great revival of faith among them everywhere. About 520 BC Cyrus, king of Persia, gave permission for the return of the first batch of exiles; and over the next hundred years there was a steady trickle of repatriates. By then their belief in the one true God had been finally restored; and from that time onwards their monotheism was established beyond any further temptation towards idolatry.

After the return from the Exile the Jews no longer had a king; the Persian emperors had abolished the power of the Davidic dynasty, Zerubbabel being the last of the royal descendants of David to act as ruler of the returned exiles. They then evolved into a theocracy ruled by the high priesthood, which in course of time became more and more secular in its outlook. So the descendants of king David, the heirs of the promise to David, retired into private life, and entered into the anonymity of the rest of the population. Of course, these descendants of David retained their pride in their ancestry, and carefully guarded their genealogical tree.

After the Exile, which was completed by about 420 BC, the Lord God sent no more prophets to remind the Jews of their destiny and of their moral and religious responsibilities. Instead, the purity of their faith came to be maintained by the class of scribes and rabbis, laymen who made a special study of the Law of Moses and the Prophets. The threat to the spiritual life of the Jews that came from the spread of Hellenistic culture was met by them in two ways: firstly by the growth of the sect of the Pharisees, who became the principal defenders of the purity of their ancient religion, and secondly, by deliberately isolating themselves from social contacts with pagans and foreigners, contacts being restricted to formal business relations and no more. Nevertheless the Jews, the proud people of God, like the other nations eventually became subjects of the pagan Roman empire in 63 BC, and their holy priesthood was degraded and corrupted. Finally in the years immediately preceding the birth of Christ even the priesthood lost its independence and became subject to an upstart tyrant, Herod the Great, who ruled as a client-king by favour of imperial Rome.

This was the situation in Judea and Galilee in the early years of the emperor Augustus Caesar when Mary and Joseph grew up and got engaged. However, as we learn from the Gospel of Luke, there were still many faithful and holy Jews waiting for the coming of the Messiah, some of whom were to be chronicled in the Gospels of Matthew and Luke.

2

The Birth Narratives

1) The Sources

An eleventh century saint, Peter Damian, is related to have remarked that it was both unnecessary and wrong for Christians to seek for details about the life and family of Jesus that the Gospels have not recorded. This however was not the view of some 2nd century inquirers who composed the so-called 'apocryphal' Gospels, seemingly in order to satisfy the curiosity of those Christians who could not refrain from speculating about the 'hidden' family life of Jesus.

One such Gospel, first mentioned by Origen in the third century and known as the 'Proto-Evangelium of the Apostle James', provided the Eastern Church with a good deal of information about the parents of the Blessed Virgin; but it cannot be trusted and reads to us moderns like pious fiction. Perhaps the only certain facts that can be derived from this document are the names of her parents, which are given as Joachim and Anne; and if we may follow the ancient Church guideline of *lex orandi lex credendi*, we are justified in holding that, if nothing else, at least their true names have been preserved by the ancient tradition, for nowadays the universal Church prays to Joachim and Anne on 26th July. The same tradition also claims that Joachim was a lineal descendant of king David. It is a dogma of faith that their daughter Mary, destined to be the mother of Jesus, was conceived immaculate, that is to say, that from the first moment of her conception by her parents she was preserved from all stain of Original Sin in virtue of the foreseen merits of Christ, her redeemer as well as the redeemer of the rest of the human race. The Church has solemnly declared that the flesh that was to provide the physical body of the Saviour could not at any time have been under the dominion of Satan, the fallen angel. This is all we know of any value about the family into which Mary was born, for the Holy Spirit, who was the co-author and the inspirer of the whole New Testament, did not sanction the sacred writers saying anything more than what we find in the two birth narratives of Matthew and Luke. Of course we know a good deal about the life of Jewish people at the time of the birth of Jesus; and this knowledge may be judiciously used to throw further light on the Gospel narratives.

The circumstances leading to the composition of the Gospel of Mark did not require him to make any special reference to the early life of Jesus; whilst John in his prologue, though having the birth narratives of Matthew and Luke at his disposal, decided to concern himself solely with the eternal generation of the Son. Hence we find that only Matthew and Luke independently describe the infancy of Jesus, each according to the respective needs of his first readers. Though many modern biblical critics deny the historical character of these narratives there are no solid reasons for denying their authenticity and historicity.[4]

---

4   See notes 1 and 2 above. The relationships between the four Gospels and their respective dates of composition together with the resulting questions about their apostolicity and historicity are still highly debatable issues today among critical scholars. They differ sharply over the length of time that elapsed before the Gospels were committed to writing. The majority of scholars, basing themselves on the 'Markan Priority Hypothesis', prefer to hold that the Gospels as we have them did not reach their final form until the post-70 era and thus have been the compositions of post-apostolic communities. However, the solid tradition of the Church has never ceased to affirm that all were composed before AD 70, except perhaps the Gospel of St John. The view taken in this book, based on the Two-Gospel Hypothesis, is that Mt is not only the first Gospel to have been written but was also published before AD 44, and that Mt and Jn are the accounts of the apostolic eyewitnesses of Jesus' words and actions, whilst Lk and Mk are guaranteed by apostolic eye-witnesses. Cf. Orchard & Riley, *The Order of the Synoptics*.

2) *The Matthean Source*

The purpose of the Gospel of Matthew was to provide the harassed body of Christians, who made up the Jerusalem Church (as described in the *Acts of the Apostles*), with a proper defence of the authenticity of Jesus the Messiah, their Lord and Master, against the calumnies of the Jewish authorities. These authorities, led by the high priestly families who controlled the destinies of the Holy City, were to attack the memory of Jesus in several ways. In particular they ruled out his claim to be the Messiah on two grounds, namely that he was merely an illegitimate son of Mary, and that no prophet could come from his home-town of Nazareth. Therefore, in answer to these charges, the birth narrative of Jesus in Matthew limits itself to proving, firstly, that Joseph, the true husband of Mary, was indeed a lineal descendant of king David; next that he, Joseph, had officially adopted Jesus as his son, which he had done according to Jewish Law by naming him at his circumcision (thus making him a true Son of David); and thirdly, that Mary had in fact conceived Jesus by the power of the Holy Spirit, thus revealing that Joseph could not have fathered the child, because he had never 'known' her and had not at that time even taken her to his home, as the ceremony of marriage required for its completion. Furthermore, our account clearly states that Mary was a virgin when she conceived by the Holy Spirit and that in her case was fulfilled the prophecy of Isaiah 7:14 (according to the Septuagint text[5]) that the Messiah would be born of a virgin.

Other prophecies of the Old Testament fulfilled in the infancy of Jesus were that of Micah (5:2) who had foretold that the Messiah would be born in Bethlehem, that of Hosea (11:1) that he would in some mysterious way come from Egypt (as he did as a result of the flight into Egypt), that of Jeremiah (31:15) foretelling the grief of the mothers of the slaughtered Innocents

---

5 The quotations of the OT prophecies in the Gospels are from the Septuagint because the Apostles thought it necessary to transfer their allegiance from the original Hebrew text of the Bible to the Greek Septuagint version, since it alone could serve their missionary needs in the Greco-Roman world where Greek was the *lingua franca*.

of Bethlehem, and finally the prophecy of Isaiah (9:1-2) that the Messiah would appear like a beacon light in Galilee (cf. Mt 2:23, 4:13-17). Thus we learn that Matthew's account of the birth of Jesus is deliberately restricted to refuting the calumnies of the Jews regarding his origins; but it was adequate at the time for the first Jerusalem community which would have either known Jesus personally or seen or heard about him during his public ministry, which had alerted every living Israelite to his presence in the land. And so we find that the Gospel of Matthew was a manifesto particularly geared to the immediate needs and problems of the Mother Church of Jerusalem, needs which influenced the choice of many of Matthew's stories. It was also very largely apologetic in content, in view of the beleaguered nature of its Christian community. At the same time it displayed a remarkable underlying understanding of the future world-wide mission of the Church which confirmed its position as the fundamental document of the Christian Church in the Apostolic Age.

3) The Lukan Source

For some years, while Paul was conducting his three missionary journeys (AD 46-58) the Gospel of Matthew was the only recognized account of the life and teaching of Jesus available to the Church. But its Jewish colouring and perspective made it somewhat off-putting to Greek converts to Christianity. Paul himself would have discovered that its Hebraic character and contents also failed to provide the material to answer some important questions that his Greek converts were asking him about Jesus. The opportunity to undertake the composition of another Gospel that would relate the life and teaching of Jesus more immediately to the needs of his Gentile converts came when Paul found himself a prisoner of the governor down at Caesarea, with his disciple Luke in attendance, about the year AD 57-58. At that time it was less than thirty years after the resurrection, and there were still many living eye-witnesses of the life of Jesus, including some of the original twelve Apostles. Thus many of the resources that Luke required to re-write and

spiritual endowments.

When the story opens in the Gospel of Luke, Mary is already engaged to marry Joseph. The engagement of a Jewish couple was a solemn affair for both families, because it marked the conclusion of the sometimes protracted negotiations between the two families regarding the terms of the marriage contract and the price the bridegroom would pay for his bride. It was normal to allow some time to elapse between the completion of the agreement and the actual wedding, which was celebrated by a feast and by the bridegroom publicly leading his bride through the streets to his own dwelling. It was during this interval that Gabriel appeared to Mary. A girl became marriageable at the age of twelve, so that Mary was probably still in her teens when she became engaged to Joseph. We have no idea of the age of Joseph himself; but there are good reasons for thinking that he was a virile young man, a proper match for Mary, and the counterpart of the chaste Joseph who was the saviour of his family in Egypt (Gen 39:1 ff) and not the old man usually depicted by the apocryphal Gospels of the Infancy.

Since John the Baptist sensed from his mother's womb that he was destined to be the precursor of the Most High (as we are entitled to assume from the fact of his leaping in her womb at the voice of Mary already carrying the Saviour), we may be permitted a fortiori to assume that the Blessed Virgin from the first moment of consciousness knew intuitively that she belonged exclusively to the Lord God who had created her. Though without previous intimation of the fact, she had been mysteriously prepared by divine providence from before time began to be at one and the same time the Virgin Daughter of Sion, the Bride of the Most High and the Mother of God-become-Man. Hence she could never envisage any man as her husband and soul mate, for it was not in her constitution to do so. Joseph too had been similarly prepared to become at God's request her chaste husband and to be all that the husband of such a woman should be, in order to sustain her in her unparalleled role and in all the complexities of their unique partnership as her lifelong companion and friend and as the perfect human father of the boy Jesus.

It is for reasons like these that many theologians hold that those Fathers of the Church, who spoke of Mary's vow of virginity, were right to understand her declaration to Gabriel 'I know not man' in precisely this sense. If this is so, then it becomes necessary to assert that already before their engagement took place she must have persuaded Joseph to accept her on the clear understanding that he would always respect her virginity and himself agree to remain celibate all his days. For Jewish custom at that time required a daughter to have the prior consent both of her parents and her future husband for such a vow. Yet neither Mary nor Joseph need have had any definite idea of God's real purpose in inspiring them to adopt this special marital relationship. Although this view of their marriage runs counter to the ideas of modern western society, it seems the logical way of interpreting the data of Luke's Gospel.

Thus the appearance of the angel Gabriel to announce that God was going to ask Mary to conceive a son by the Holy Spirit could not but perturb her profoundly, and Joseph too. There seems to be no solid reason for doubting that the angel appeared to her in bodily form; she needed the evidence of her senses to be sure that she was not dreaming. And since the angel's message concerned the future manifestation of God himself in human flesh, it was appropriate for him to appear to her in visible form. Nevertheless, it is also perfectly possible to hold that the vision was rather an interior one, just like the star that was to appear to the Magi.

Luke does not say that she was perturbed by the sight of the angel but only by the message that he brought, 'Rejoice, thou, full of grace, the Lord is with you'. The greeting is virtually the same as that to Gideon; in neither case is the addressee referred to by name; but Gideon is described as a 'mighty man of valour' (Jg 6:12), and Mary as 'full of grace', because she is to give birth to him who is Grace itself. The Greek word *kecharitomene* means more than 'the highly-favoured one' of many modern translations, and fully justifies the ancient Catholic rendering 'full of grace', i.e. the one to whom the fullness of grace has been given, the one who would literally bring forth salvation itself. Mary had been endowed with all the mental and spiritual gifts and all the knowledge, virtues and charisms necessary to fulfil the task entrusted to her and to understand its magnitude. Although by subsequent meditation her brilliant intelligence would continue to plumb the depths of God's munificence ever more profoundly, yet because of her breeding and endowments she was able, despite her youth, to rise with equanimity of heart and mind to the invitation of her Creator.

Mary's knowledge of the Scriptures was already profound as her 'Magnificat' was soon to testify; and she would have recalled the passage from Zephaniah (3:14):

> Rejoice and exult with all your heart, O daughter of Jerusalem... fear not... The Lord your God is in your midst.

The Fathers of the Church were to apply this passage to Mary, declaring her to be the 'Daughter of Sion', holding her in her own person to represent the whole 'Israel of God'. Mary could see that Gabriel's greeting must in some way apply to herself; and she was perturbed by the limitless vista that it opened out for her. Whilst she was mastering her emotion and pondering on the meaning of his greeting, the angel explained:

> Fear not, Mary; for you have found favour with God. And behold you will conceive in the womb and bear a son and you will call his name Jesus. For he will be great and shall be called the Son of the Most High, and the Lord God will give him the throne of David his father; and he will reign over the House of Jacob for ever, and his Kingdom shall have no end.

And Mary said to the angel:

> How shall this be, since I know not man?

The angel's words show us that Jesus is to be both her son and the Son of the Most High God at the same time; and this son is to inherit the everlasting kingdom promised by the prophet Nathan to king David. However, Mary cannot yet visualize in practical terms how this conception can take place, as can be seen from the fact that she has voluntarily declared herself to be a virgin, though she does not doubt that God can and will do what he says. And so the angel intimates that God would resolve this dilemma for her, by adding:

> The Holy Spirit will come upon you and the power of the Most High will overshadow you; wherefore also the Holy One born of you will be called Son of God.

In these words of Gabriel we have for the first time in Holy Writ the explicit revelation that in the one God there are three persons, the Father, the Son and the Holy Spirit. The Son of God, her Son-to-be, is indeed 'the Holy One'. What a great act of faith Mary has been invited to make! She is asked to put her trust in God and allow herself to become the human instrument of the plan of the Most High God to bring into the world the Messiah prophesied repeatedly since the time of Abraham. She, a maiden seemingly unconscious of her immaculate conception, is to be set at the centre of world-history; she is to be the 'cynosure of all eyes'. She needed incredible courage and insight, as well as perfect faith, to have the strength of mind to say 'Yes' to the daunting destiny God had planned for her. At the same time she would not only have been aware of her promise to marry Joseph, but also of the dilemma confronting him, his problem being how to separate without scandal from a woman who was now betrothed to the Holy Spirit and who for that reason presumably could never even become his virgin-wife.

St Bernard was effectively to argue in his famous sermon on the annunciation, that the salvation of the world actually depended at that moment on her free consent to the divine plan and will. She makes that decision by responding in profound faith and with great joy to the Lord's request, wholeheartedly saying: 'Behold the handmaid of the Lord; may it be so with me according to thy word'. The future salvation of the world is now assured.

Through another revelation (this time to Joseph, Mt 1:18f) Mary is soon to learn that their dilemma would be neatly resolved by the Holy Spirit arranging to respect both Joseph's promise to take her as his wife and her promise to him. As the spouse of the Holy Spirit and the mother of the Messiah she was also to become the virgin-wife of Joseph, whose protection she would need to defend her child and herself from all his enemies.

Thus Mary was destined by God always to be a virgin and Joseph likewise. Our historian Luke has confirmed that both Mary and Joseph fully understood their respective roles in the events he describes, nothing less than the re-marriage of heaven and earth, the eternal God again uniting himself to the humanity that had separated itself from him at the time of the fall of Adam and Eve. Mary is indeed the Second Eve—God comes to earth in a marvellous and incredibly humble way. Joseph's forbearance made it possible for Mary to cope with this unique relationship.

Through our traditional Christian faith we know that as soon as Mary gave her consent to the Incarnation, the conception of Jesus by the Holy Spirit took place. His human soul (indissolubly united to his Godhead) was instantly created; and the new life of the Man, who is also God, now began to pursue the normal course of every human life conceived in the ordinary human way. One corollary that may be drawn from this record is that the conception of Jesus is the exemplar of all other conceptions; and that human life, the human soul, is always present from the first moment of its conception, and not after some days or weeks as some biologists have argued.

At the conclusion of his visit the angel gives Mary the sign of the miraculous conception of her kinswoman Elizabeth to help her to realize that what was happening to her was just one part of the magnificent and all-embracing plan of God, the 'mystery hidden from past ages'.

6) Joseph's Dilemma (Mt 1:18-25)

As with all other women Mary knew that it would be some little time before she would physically feel the holy embryo taking shape in her womb; but she had a unique complaisance in her new condition together with a firm hope and a depth of love for her newly conceived infant that surpassed all understanding. Since her soul and all her human faculties were untouched by the stain of Original Sin, and since she was also free from all actual sin, her judgement was perfect and totally unclouded. Though the Lord had just exalted her above all other women in a unique embrace, he had at the same time given her a supreme test of her faith by presenting her with a daunting dilemma for Joseph and a very bleak immediate future for herself. By freely committing herself to God's will in such a way that she no longer belonged to Joseph but had become in all truth the Bride of Almighty God and the untouchable Ark of the Covenant, it was impossible for her ever to contemplate surrendering her body to him in the way implied by the impending marriage procession to Joseph's home. She could only see that they would have to separate.

Mary was also eminently considerate; and we may be sure that she arranged for Joseph to learn from her own lips as gently as possible her firm decision to break it all off at once. Though it seems highly probable that Joseph had already prepared himself for a celibate marriage, the news of her conception by the Holy Spirit must have come to him as a tremendous shock. Nevertheless, sudden though it was, he could have no doubt that what she told him was true; and being a holy man of God he immediately bowed to God's will and sought to find the best way to implement their joint decision. But there could be no escape from his duty to put her away at once privately and with the least fuss. During the following night he struggled fruitlessly to find a solution that would spare her from slander and shame. When last he fell asleep through sheer weariness, having resolved that on the morrow, however distasteful and unpleasant it might be, he must find a valid excuse for the cancellation of everything, he suddenly saw in a dream an angel of God who riveted his attention by saying:

> Joseph, son of David, do not fear to take Mary your wife, for that which is conceived in her is of the Holy Spirit; she will bear a son, and you shall call his name Jesus, for he will save his people from their sins.

The dilemma was thus resolved to his intensive relief and joy.

He now saw it as his duty to complete the marriage ceremony as soon as possible by complying with the ancient custom of leading Mary in procession to his house. The speedy wedding meant that Jesus would be born almost exactly nine months after the ceremony, thus causing the neighbours no scandal since naturally they would regard Joseph as the child's father. This would protect her good name and prevent her from being stoned as an adulteress. Before God however Joseph, by taking her, expressed his acceptance of Mary's divine pregnancy and his own role as her virgin-husband and as the protector both of her virginity and of the babe whose foster-father he was to be. By insisting therefore on Joseph making Mary his life-companion in marriage—celibate and virginal though their relationship was to be—the Holy Spirit thus not only provided support for her and the boy and protection to enable the Holy Family to escape massacre and take refuge in Egypt, but also the foster-father who was needed to complete the family background for the proper education of this unique child.

7) *The Virgin Mary visits her Cousin Elizabeth (Lk 1:39-56)*

The immediate and hasty completion of the marriage ceremonies left Mary free to visit Elizabeth, surely with Joseph as her escort, since Jewish custom allowed newly weds a long 'honeymoon' style reprieve before settling down to normal life. Her real purpose however was of course to congratulate Elizabeth and jointly to reflect on the blessings they had just received from the Lord. Luke tells us that when Elizabeth heard Mary's greeting the infant in her womb leaped for joy at the sound, thus signifying his sanctification by Jesus whilst still in the womb. Elizabeth herself is likewise filled with the joy of the Holy Spirit and exclaims:

> Blessed art thou among women and blessed the fruit of thy womb.

And, testifying to the divinity of the babe in Mary's womb, Elizabeth continues:

> And whence is this to me that the Mother of my Lord should come to me? For behold when the sound of your greeting came to my ears,

the infant in my womb leapt for joy! And blessed is she that has believed that there will be fulfilment for the things spoken to her by the Lord.

With these words she commends Mary's great faith and total trust in the Lord, the ultimate reason for her selection for the honour done to her.

After Elizabeth had blessed Mary as the mother of the Messiah, Mary in her turn bursts out into a marvellous song in praise of the Lord God of Israel, the God of her fathers, for what he has done for her; indeed, 'her spirit exults in God her Saviour'. Because of her recognition of her nothingness in his sight, he has taken her and raised her up, and to him alone is the glory for doing so. And she knows, through the power of prophecy given her, that because of her divine motherhood she will be famous and blessed for all time and in all generations. She realizes that he has done 'great things' for her, he the All-Holy One; though all the same his 'mercy', his tender Love, is lavished on all who fear him, that is, on all who obey him, and freely acknowledge his love and power. On the other hand he cannot abide the proud and conceited who refuse to acknowledge that they have received everything from him; these arrogant people he will bring to nothing. He will humble to dust the pride of kings and rulers and replace them with the humble, those who know that they have nothing that they have not received from him. Consequently he will reward the humble poor with spiritual food and riches, and reduce to beggary the proud and wealthy; but above all he has remembered the promise he made to look after his own people, the House of Israel, the promise he made to Abraham and to his descendants for ever.

It is St Luke who has recorded these wonderful sentiments which have come to be known as the 'Magnificat'. It is a poem that is entirely Semitic in character and there is no good reason to doubt, as some have done, that it is Mary's own composition. It seems to be modelled on the Canticle of Hannah (1 Sam 2:1-10), with which Mary must have been familiar. There are also a number of allusions that reveal her familiarity with the Psalms.

The visitation is therefore to be seen as the essential corollary of the annunciation. For Mary receives the tangible confirmation of her faith in the Incarnation when Elizabeth recognises the physical as well as the spiritual presence of the Messiah in her womb. At the same time, through Mary her Son's future precursor and herald is sanctified by the Holy Spirit in the womb of his mother Elizabeth; and the two sons are so to speak introduced to each other through their mothers. Moreover, Joseph, who must have remained with his newly wed bride for the duration of the visit, found his confidence in Mary fully vindicated by the words of Elizabeth and his role as the foster-father of the Messiah confirmed. Finally, the two women, the central figures of this cosmic drama, are given the leisure and the freedom to support and encourage each other until John is born three months later.

8) *The Birth of John (Lk 1:57-80)*

St Luke seems to indicate that the friends and neighbours of Elizabeth were unaware of her pregnancy, because she had continued to hide herself right up to the moment of John's birth. Nevertheless as soon as they heard about it they rejoiced for her sake that at last she had got the son she had longed for. All male Jewish children were circumcised as a sign of being admitted to God's Covenant with Abraham, the rite being performed on the eighth day by the father. The family had already decided that the boy ought to be called Zechariah after his father; but at this point his mother, remembering what the angel had told him, intervened to say that his name was to be John. Because the father of a Jewish family always had the final say, they made signs to Zechariah for his decision; and after he had written down on the wax tablet 'His name is John', which means 'Gift of God', his dumbness departed; and his voice was miraculously restored 'and he spoke blessing God', uttering the canticle of the 'Benedictus'. All guests at the circumcision were convinced that this child was to have an extraordinary destiny. Zechariah, moved by the Holy Spirit, told them what it was to be, proclaiming that these events were the sign that the God of Israel was bringing to pass the long prophesied completion of the Covenant that would lead to the redemption of the human race through a descendant of the royal house of David. In the second part of his canticle (vv. 76-79) he prophesied that this baby son of his was to become the herald of 'the Orient from on High', i.e. of the Messiah, whom he spoke of as 'the Most High', the title of the Lord God of Israel himself.

Luke concludes his account by telling us that John was to grow up in seclusion and to spend his early manhood 'in the deserts' until the time when the Spirit of the Lord moved him to begin his mission to prepare the Chosen People for the coming of the Messiah in person.

9) The Birth of Jesus (Lk 2:1-20)

All was now ready for the entrance of the Messiah into the world. As we have seen, the Lord God had been preparing it for nearly two thousand years, the preparation culminating in Jesus' conception by the Holy Spirit and the remarkable events surrounding the birth of his herald John. Yet after all the foretelling of the ancient Jewish prophets, when the moment arrived, the One Who was to Come, the Son of the Most High, was to slip into the world so quietly and silently that his birth had to be made known by means of a vision of angels to a group of shepherds on a hillside outside Bethlehem.

> While silence held all things in the middle of the night and the night was in the middle of its course, thy omnipotent Word, O Lord, came down from its heavenly throne. (*Office of the Vigil of the Epiphany*)

It was some time in the middle of the reign of Augustus Caesar (31 BC-AD 14), probably about the year 8 BC, that Jesus was born at Bethlehem. Politically he was the subject of Herod the Great, who himself was a client king, owing his throne to Augustus. Luke is our authority for informing us that despite Mary's condition Joseph felt obliged to take her on the four or five days' journey from Nazareth to Bethlehem to fulfil the requirements of a census of the whole world ordered by Augustus, a measure with which Herod the Great thought it prudent to conform.[7]

Now although Joseph, as we have seen, was a direct descendant of king David in the male line, it would appear that his own immediate relatives no longer had any connection with that royal city; and therefore, having no one to stay with, he and Mary had to take whatever accommodation they chanced to find. Joseph was, of course, very much aware of the imminent birth of her child; and it is not hard to imagine his anxiety to find suitable shelter. As the public caravansary was full, the only place he could find for the birth of the child in decent seclusion was in a stable normally occupied by cattle. So there—without any ceremony—the king of the universe entered the world; and for want of a proper cradle Mary his mother laid him in a manger or trough in which fodder for the cattle was usually placed. Luke tells us (2:7) that Mary herself wrapped Jesus in what the ancient English translations call 'swaddling cloths', the bands of cloths in which every newborn babe was wrapped. Her action indicated that the birth was very easy, since she herself was able immediately afterwards to care for the babe. It must have been a perfectly normal birth with Joseph her husband alone being present to help her.

We know that all this happened by the deliberate design and foreknowledge of the God of Israel, who wished the life of his Son to demonstrate that wealth is no advantage for entry into the Kingdom of God, and that faithful obedience to the will of his heavenly Father is the sole key for entrance. This baby was to grow up into the man who would become the Saviour of the world, winning its deliverance without any worldly aids, solely by the power of his Spirit.

---

7 No record of such a Roman census during the reign of Herod the Great has yet been found, and exegetes argue that he would in any case not be bound to impose such a census on his own subjects. Nevertheless it is unwise to impugn the accuracy of Luke, who is found to be accurate whenever he can be checked, a statement that cannot always be made about Josephus, the ancient Jewish historian (cf. *Appendix* §4).

Nevertheless his birth, unnoticed by all the people attending the census, was already a cause of great joy to the angels of heaven, who first announced it to the shepherds in the field below the village of Bethlehem, the traditional date being 25th December in mid-winter, a cold period even in Palestine.[8] As usual, God preferred to relay his message to the world through the agency of unsophisticated people, who would not distort the tidings given them. The announcement of the birth of the Saviour was very dramatic. The 'angel of the Lord'—he is not named—appeared to the shepherds on the hillside in the middle of the night and 'the glory of the Lord shone around them', so that they were filled with awe and ready to absorb the most important and joyous announcement ever made to the human race. These unlettered men were privileged to receive the Good News on behalf of the Chosen People of God; and the angel said to them:

> Today there has been born to you the Saviour, who is Christ the Lord, in the city of David. And this is the sign for you: you will find the babe clothed and lying in a manger. (Lk 2:11f)

And then the skies opened and the shepherds beheld 'a multitude of heavenly beings praising God and singing: "Glory to God in the highest and upon earth peace to his favoured ones".' The sight was unforgettable and without a moment's delay, the shepherds hastened to obey the command of the angel. The directions given them for finding the babe were definite enough; he would not be found in either a house or in the caravansary, but in a stable at that moment perhaps unoccupied by cattle.[9] With their local knowledge the shepherds soon worked out where the babe had been born and found everything just as the angel had said. They were, it seems, the first to worship him; and they then hastened to tell everyone what they had seen and heard; and all wondered and debated

---

8   The actual date of the birth of Jesus is unknown; nor is it known for certain why the Church selected 25th December as his 'official' birthday.

9   St Francis of Assisi was the first to popularise the legend that on the night of the birth of Jesus the Holy Family shared the stable with the ox and the ass (cf. Is 11:7).

over the meaning of these events. This babe was a real human being; and he was most clearly approved of by the heavenly vision. But nobody could as yet envisage what it all meant; this was a mystery still hidden in the future. They could not know that not far away another babe, John, was growing up who would some thirty years later be the one to begin to unlock the mystery of the person and mission of Jesus. The shepherds then returned to their daily task, praising God and quite sure that they had been given a revelation, the meaning of which they were confident would be made clear in God's own time.

St Luke adds that Mary kept all these things, pondering them in her heart (Lk 2:19). Cardinal Newman in his famous sermon on the theory of developments in religious doctrine commented as follows on these words:

> Mary is our pattern of faith, both in the reception and in the study of divine truth. She does not think it enough to accept, she dwells upon it; not enough to possess, she uses it; not enough to assent, she develops it; not enough to submit the reason, she reasons upon it; not indeed reasoning first, and believing afterwards, with Zechariah, yet first believing without reasoning, next from love and reverence, reasoning after believing.

Newman concludes that

> she symbolises to us, not only the faith of the unlearned, but of the doctors of the Church also, who have to investigate, and weigh, and define, as well as to profess the Gospel.

It must have been through her agency that these memories at last reached the evangelist Luke some fifty or more years later.

On the eighth day after birth Jesus was circumcised according to the Jewish custom ordained in the Law of Moses, thus becoming a covenant member of the House of Israel (Lk 2:21). Traditionally, it was the father's privilege to perform this operation and at the same time to name the child to confirm his paternity. Joseph therefore accepted paternity of Jesus with all its obligations, adopting him as his own son (Mt 1:24-25). Mary and Joseph stayed on in Bethlehem for obvious reasons and no doubt found more suitable accommodation when the census had been completed. At all events, Joseph had found a house for the family before the Wise Men arrived about a year later. By then both Mary and Joseph realised that they had unwittingly fulfilled the prophecy of Micah (5:2) that the Saviour would be born in Bethlehem, the city of David.

3

The Childhood of Jesus

1) The Presentation in the Temple (Lk 2:21-38)

According to the Mosaic Law (Lev 12) a woman who had given birth to a male child was considered to be ritually unclean for forty days, which meant that during that time she could not touch anything sacred or enter the Temple courts. At the end of the forty-day period the mother would present herself at the Temple; and she and her husband would offer the prescribed gift, which was a lamb if they were well-to-do, and two pigeons if they were poor. At the same time, they would 'buy back' their baby son by a ritual gift of five silver shekels to the priests. This was because at the time of the Exodus the first-born sons of the Israelites were spared by the destroying angel and so were held by the Lord to be his own property until 'bought back'. Jesus of course already belonged totally to God and could not be 'bought back'. Nevertheless, we may assume that Joseph paid the five shekels on his behalf to avoid scandal, just as Jesus was to arrange for Peter to pay the Temple tax on his behalf. Mary and Joseph not only performed these duties; but they also did a thing that was not prescribed in the Law, namely they 'presented their Child to the Lord', which seems to mean that they dedicated him to the Lord in the same way that Hannah dedicated Samuel in 1 Sam 1:22f, thus publicly acknowledging that their Child was to have a unique mission in life in the service of the Lord God.

St Luke now records that under the inspiration of the Holy Spirit there were present in the Temple at that moment two other devout Israelites who gave testimony on behalf of the 'faithful remnant' of the People of Israel to the presence of the Messiah now come for the first time to his Father's House. The first mentioned is Simeon, a holy old man who had been informed by the Holy Spirit that he would be allowed to live long enough to see the Messiah. Led by the same Holy Spirit he came into the Temple while the parents of Jesus were performing the prescribed rites. Mary permitted him to take the babe into his arms and he uttered this blessing (the *Nunc dimittis*):

> Now thou dost release thy servant, O Master, according to thy word, in peace. Because my eyes have seen thy salvation, which thou hast prepared before the face of all the peoples, the light for the revelation of the Gentiles and the glory of thy people Israel.

With these words Simeon foretells that the baby Jesus will be the salvation and the light of all the nations and the peculiar glory of the people of Israel. This unexpected eulogy quite amazed both Mary and Joseph. Simeon then turned to them and blessing them said to Mary also:

> Behold this Son of yours is set for the rise and the fall of many in Israel and for a sign spoken against. And a sword shall also go through your own soul, so that out of many hearts thoughts may be revealed.

The meaning of this prophecy is that the word of revelation brought by Jesus will pass through Israel like a sword and will compel men to reveal their secret thoughts. Nevertheless, since Mary is the Daughter of Sion, who brings the child to the Temple, she too felt this sword pass through her soul in her representative capacity. Simeon's prophecy foreshadows the opposition that Jesus would have to endure and the suffering and anguish that were to test the faith of Mary to the uttermost as the life of her Son unfolded before her eyes, starting with the murder of the Holy Innocents and the Flight into Egypt. Simeon is to be seen as the representative of a great number of contemporary Israelites, pious, obscure and unobtrusive men and women, who kept the Law faithfully and lived a contemplative life, earnestly praying for the coming of the Messiah 'to restore the kingdom to Israel', as the Apostles were to say to Jesus at the time of his ascension.

There were many like-minded women who also worshipped continuously in the Temple. One of them was Anna the daughter of Phanuel who belonged to the tribe of Asher, whose territory was at the northernmost extremity of the land of Israel. She had been a widow for a very long time and was now at least eighty-four years of age, and spent all her waking hours in the Temple. She had heard the utterances of Simeon, and, being gifted likewise with the charism of prophecy, spoke about Jesus to all in the Temple precincts. The words of these two worthy representatives of the people of Israel ensured that the first visit of the infant Messiah to his Temple should be made known to and welcomed by some at least of the holy remnant of the people of Israel.

2) *The Visit of the Magi and Flight into Egypt (Mt 2:1-23)*

We now come to an incident in the early life of Jesus that is related only by Matthew; Luke, who knew our Gospel of Matthew, makes no mention of the flight into Egypt at all, thus ignoring entirely a period of some four to five years in the childhood of Jesus. But then there was no need for him to repeat what the evangelist Matthew had already adequately recorded. So we learn from Matthew that about a year after the birth of Jesus the Holy Family was still in Bethlehem. Then a remarkable event occurred that was to change their whole life. The child Jesus had grown into a toddler; and everything was going on nicely when all of a sudden a party of distinguished visitors came to the village and knocked at their door. The tradition says that they were three in number, because they brought with them three gifts, gold, frankincense and myrrh. They proved to be a deputation from the East, and had been guided to the door by a special star which they claimed to have first seen in their own country, and which had led them to Jerusalem in their search for the king promised of old to the Jews. We know nothing about the origin or ancestry of these noblemen, except that they regarded themselves as ambassadors of the peoples of the East, come to present their homage to the king whose birth had been mysteriously revealed to them by the Lord God in their own land. Perhaps they were Easterners attracted by the Jewish religion, Gentile 'God-fearers', who had studied the stories of the Pentateuch and been selected by the Holy Spirit and given their revelation and their mission. These 'Magi', as our Gospel calls them, were clearly men of substance and education. Their arrival in Jerusalem following this star (which it seems was visible to them alone)[10] had caused a great stir, for they brought this extraordinary request to the authorities: 'Where is he who has been born king of the Jews?' Herod, the ruling monarch, was swiftly informed and took immediate steps to summon the chief priests and the scribes in order to check up on all that was known about the coming of the Messiah. These authorities at once realised that if there was substance in the revelation the Magi purported to bring, it would mean that the long expected Messiah was already among them, about to appear and set up the Kingdom of God. One well-known prophecy, the oracle of Balaam, had spoken of a star that will herald the coming of the Messiah:

> I see him, but not now; I behold him, but not nigh; a star shall come forth out of Jacob, and a sceptre shall rise out of Israel. (Num 24:17)

More important still, a prophecy of Micah actually specified the city where the Messiah was to be born, and the scribes quoted it to Herod:

> And you, O Bethlehem, in the land of Judah, are by no means least among the rulers of Judah; for from you shall come a ruler who will govern my people Israel. (Mic 5:2)

Herod the king was by then very old and very cunning, a suspicious and ruthless tyrant. He did not care whether the news was true or false; he simply saw it as a threat to his throne

---

10 Matthew writes that the star was seen by the Magi, but does not indicate that it was seen by any others. It appears to be a sign manifested exclusively to them, and so it is beside the point to try to link it with any physical star or comet.

and was determined to eliminate it as soon as possible. It seemed to him and to his advisers that if in fact this person had already been born, he was in all probability as old as the first appearance of the star to the Magi, the Wise Men. From this he reckoned that the child was still under two years of age. So Herod devised a simple strategy. He would pretend that he was himself anxious to welcome the Messiah, and accordingly sent the Magi to discover his exact location in Bethlehem, so that he, Herod, might himself then be able to come down and adore the infant. The Magi did not, we may suppose, suspect Herod's evil intentions and went off down to Bethlehem, some five miles to the south of the Holy City. The star they had followed now reappeared to them, and brought them with great joy to the end of their long quest, leading them to the very house in which Mary and Joseph and the babe were now living. They were not embarrassed to find the Messiah to be still a little boy; and in the light of the Holy Spirit who had brought them safely to Jesus, they gave him divine honours, and proffered their gifts of gold, frankincense and myrrh. These gifts represented their act of faith in his kingship (the gold), in his priesthood (the frankincense), and in his humanity and mortality (the myrrh, a spice associated with embalming). In this way, the nations of the world were now associated with the holy remnant of the Jews in recognising the future redeemer of the world.

God's providence then allowed the Magi to depart without knowing that their contact with Herod was to be the indirect cause of the slaughter of the babes of Bethlehem and the exile of the Holy Family. However, they were warned in a dream not to return to Herod but to go home with their Good News by a different route, in order to save them from the ordeal of further interrogation by Herod. The very night of their departure Joseph was told in another dream to get up at once and to take the child and his mother down to Egypt to escape Herod's vengeance. No doubt the latter's spies were monitoring the visit of the Magi to Bethlehem; and when they failed to take the road back to Jerusalem to acquaint him with the identity of the child, he acted with brutal speed. Fortunately, when his cavalry thundered down into Bethlehem the following morning, Mary and Joseph and the child were out of reach on the road south into Egypt. Since Herod had not succeeded in discovering the child's identity, he proceeded to order the slaughter of all the boys under two years of age in Bethlehem to make sure that Jesus was among them. It is estimated that some twenty or so little boys were murdered. Thus this wicked tyrant was to inaugurate the life of the Messiah on earth with an insensate act of violence, a blood-bath that could only be redeemed by a Messiah who was also God, and who alone could therefore make atonement by his own death for all the crimes of men against God and their fellow men and against him as representing them all. The evangelist Matthew reminds us that this terrible deed had its Old Testament counterpart in Rachel's mourning for her exiled children from her tomb in Ramah of Benjamin:

> A voice was heard in Ramah, wailing and loud lamentation, Rachel weeping for her children. And she refused to be comforted, because they are no more. (Jer 31:15)

Perhaps the one good thing that at the time came out of these sad events was the safeguarding of the privacy of the Holy Family. For the stay in Egypt may have lasted as long as four or five years; and when Jesus and his parents finally returned to Israel after the death of Herod, Joseph never took them back to Bethlehem but settled again in Nazareth where there was nothing to connect them with either the angel's song to the shepherds or with the Magi and the massacre at Bethlehem. Thus Jesus was enabled to have a childhood free from the pressures of publicity.

3) The Temple Visit of the twelve-year old Jesus (Lk 2: 41-52)

We learn from Luke that Mary and Joseph faithfully visited the Temple in Jerusalem every year at the feast of the Passover; but there is no record that Jesus went with them until he reached the age of twelve, i.e. until he entered on his thirteenth year. At this age it became his privilege, as a Son of Israel, to fulfil in person all the precepts of the Law of Moses."[11] However, it was also the age at which an Israelite lad decided on his future career; and so for Jesus this visit was a very important occasion. Was he to follow the trade of his foster-father Joseph, or was he to come up to the Holy City and attach himself to some learned rabbi and in due time himself become a teacher of the Law? His behaviour on this occasion suggests very strongly that the career he wanted to follow was indeed that of a teacher of the Law. The Book of Sirach clearly affirms that this was by far the most prestigious calling that a Jewish boy could aspire to:

> The wisdom of the scribe depends on the opportunity of leisure... How can he become wise who handles the plough... whose talk is about bulls?... So too is every craftsman and master workman... All these rely upon their hands... Yet they are not sought out for the council of the people, nor do they attain eminence in the public assembly... they cannot expound discipline or judgement. But they keep stable the fabric of the world, and their prayer is the practice of their trade. On the other hand he who devotes himself to the study of the Law of the Most High, will serve among great men and appear before rulers; he will reveal instruction in his teaching, and will glory in the Law of the Lord's covenant. (Sir 38:24ff)

It would therefore seem that Jesus must have meditated upon this passage from the Book of Sirach and recognized its application to his own situation. Already aware of the mission to which his heavenly Father had destined him, he did not want to spend all the time of preparation for it in the carpenter's workshop; his dialogue with the learned teachers in the Temple revealed that he had the ability to teach even the cleverest and most learned teachers in Israel; and it aroused his desire to adopt the career of a teacher of the Law.

St Luke does not tell us how, at the conclusion of this visit, the misunderstanding arose between Jesus and his parents who unknowingly left him behind in Jerusalem, assuming that he was somewhere in the caravan returning to Nazareth; he simply relates it as a fact. Their grief and self-reproach when they

---

11 The current Jewish custom of the 'Bar-Mitzvah' is of much later origin.

found him missing at the end of the first stage of the journey was most painful; and they returned to the Holy City the very next day in search of him. At last on the third day they found him safe and sound and busily engaged in profound theological dialogue with the teachers in the Temple. They were overwhelmed with relief at the sight of him; but his mother Mary could not understand why he had failed to rejoin the caravan without at least notifying them of his intention. She said:

> Son, why did you do this to us? Behold, your father and I are in great distress seeking you.

These words are not to be understood as a reproach; it is a moving plea for the explanation she knows he can give. Jesus however was, as always, entirely at peace with himself and with his neighbours, and answered her quietly:

> Why did you seek me? Did you not know that I had to be in my Father's house?

He was telling them that they had no reason to worry about his absence, since they ought to have realized that if he was not with them, he could be in no other place than in the house of his heavenly Father. By now they ought to have known him well enough to be sure that his sense of duty and obligation both to them and to his heavenly Father would not allow him to stray from either the one or the other. Indeed, in the strictest sense, he had two terrestrial homes, that of Mary and Joseph at Nazareth and also the Temple in Jerusalem, the only place in the world at that time where the Lord God his Father had declared himself to be located. He was now a responsible adult in his own right, being entitled, and having the power, to determine his own future place and niche in the world. They had failed by inadvertence to notice that on this journey he had 'grown up', that he had reached the age of discretion and was now visibly the master of his own destiny and must prepare himself for his future mission according to his Father's will. He knew, but they did not, that salvation would issue forth from the Temple of his Body. However, since neither Mary nor Joseph as yet understood his logic, out of his love for them, he submitted his own will and meekly returned with them to Nazareth.

Jesus was aware that at this moment his parents were simply unable to imagine him doing anything else but follow in the footsteps of Joseph the carpenter. So he made a deliberate and conscious sacrifice of the career that he knew himself to be best fitted for. In yielding to their wishes he saw it to be his heavenly Father's will that he should continue in a life of obscurity and poverty and hard manual work until the then distant moment when John the Baptist would proclaim his advent. So the Messiah was to undergo some twenty-five years of humdrum physical toil in the humble home of Mary and Joseph, in a village, whose inhabitants seem to have been noted for the narrowness of their outlook, and in a monotony relieved only by his parents' love and piety. This restricted way of life was to be, under God's providence, the milieu for the preparation for his public ministry; its narrowness must often have galled him though it never affected his liberty of spirit.

Some time during those years Joseph passed away; and Jesus became the support and guardian of his mother. Although in the second and third centuries many apocryphal legends speculate about this long period, usually known as the 'hidden life', none of them are credit-worthy; and in fact we know nothing about it. All we are entitled to do is to relate what the evangelists have recorded, viewed in the light of what scholars have ascertained, about his family and childhood companions.

4) The Brethren of the Lord

Before we pass on to narrate the public life of Jesus, we ought first to say a word about the family in which he grew up from childhood to manhood. We have recorded all that we know for certain about his relationships with Mary and Joseph in his early years; but there has been no mention so far either of his grand-parents or of his uncles and aunts, his cousins, and nephews and nieces. That he was in his childhood surrounded by a considerable number of blood relations seems to be certain from several references to 'the brethren of the Lord' in the New

Testament writings (cf. Mt 12:46f = Lk 8:19f = Mk 3:31f; Jn 7:3f; Ac 114; 1 Cor 9:5; Mt 13:55 = Mk 6:3). In Israelite usage the terms 'brothers' and 'sisters', unless qualified, simply meant 'male relatives' and 'female relatives' (cf. 1 Sam 20:29; 2 Kg 10:13 LXX).

It would seem, however, that the NT writers were no longer interested in his family once they had established his royal descent from king David. Only the writers of the apocryphal gospels, composed probably in the latter part of the second century, were interested in providing further details, nearly all of which are agreed to be totally unreliable.

The ancient Christian tradition about the brethren of the Lord is that they were just his relatives. In the first place, it has always been the unwavering tradition and an article of faith that Mary the mother of Jesus was always a virgin, both before her betrothal to Joseph and subsequently until her assumption into heaven. The Gospels insinuate this very clearly; but do not offer proofs sufficient to satisfy the requirements of modern historical criticism, which ignores the rule of faith. From the teaching of the Church we know for certain that Jesus had no brothers or sisters; he was the only child of Mary who conceived him by the Holy Spirit. God was his Father and Joseph his foster-father. As we have already intimated, the faithful celibacy of Joseph is guaranteed by the Church all the time he was married to Mary, although one or two of the ancient Fathers thought that he might have had other children from a former wife (who would have died before he married Mary). But the view seems to have now finally prevailed in the Church that the true tradition about Joseph is that he also was a life-long celibate. Matthew's genealogy reveals that Joseph was of the royal line of David. The Gospels, however, do not tell us anything about the ancestry of Mary although she too was probably of David's line. In the eyes of the villagers of Nazareth Jesus was of course Joseph's child; but in reality the prophecy that Jesus was the Son of David was adequately fulfilled by Joseph naming Jesus at his circumcision. The legal adoption of Mary's child by Joseph made Jesus really and truly 'Son of David' in the eyes of the Law of Moses.

As to the blood relations of both Mary and Joseph, the position appears to be this. There is good reason for thinking that Mary's parents were named Joachim and Anne, as mentioned earlier on; but there is no sure record of the existence of any other members of her family except for her kinship to Elizabeth the wife of the priest Zechariah, the father of John the Baptist (Lk 1:36). Thus John the Baptist was a first or second cousin of Jesus. Nevertheless, Luke seems to imply that John had no direct contact with Jesus until the time of the latter's baptism (cf Lk 180; Jn 1:31), since they lived several days' journey apart; but here again we cannot be sure for they might have met in Jerusalem at one of the three great feasts, Passover, Pentecost, or Tabernacles.

We have however some relatively certain information about the family of Joseph. Hegesippus, a highly esteemed second century Christian writer, who lived in Rome and was in a position to know, asserted that Joseph had a brother called Clopas (a name which St Jerome believed to be the Greek form of the Aramaic *Halphai*, Gk: *Alphaeus*). According to Hegesippus, Clopas had a wife named Mary, who was the sister-in-law of the Blessed Virgin; and it seems that they had four boys, namely, James and Joses, Simon and Jude. But it is also possible that Joseph had another brother in addition to Clopas, and that one or two of these boys may rather have been sons of this brother. And of course the sisters referred to in Mk 6:3 would have been their sisters or cousins. The *Alphaeus* of Mk 3:18 is thought by some to be identical with Clopas. Others think that Clopas is identical with the 'Cleophas' of Lk 24:18.

All these young people would have been either close or distant cousins of Jesus, and the companions of his childhood and boyhood. We know nothing further of any value about their social relationships except that they were able to treat him familiarly and even to chide him (Jn 7:3-4). Therefore the only thing we can be certain about is that although Jesus was an only child, he had a number of young relations, male and female, on Joseph's side of the family, who lived in or near Nazareth. In those days, of course, there was no social mixing of adolescent boys and girls in Jewish society, as social custom required a strict segregation of girls of marriageable age.

As to the social standing of the relations of Jesus, the priestly status of Zechariah assured his family an honourable place in local society, while the royal blood of David that Joseph inherited would be a matter of common knowledge to everyone; and thus the dignity of his family was also assured. We may also be sure that while the family of Jesus may have been poor, it was not indigent; and there is no reason to doubt that it shared in a modest way the relative prosperity of Galilee at that time. As craftsmen Joseph and Jesus would have had a recognized status in their local community.

SUGGESTED RELATIONSHIPS IN THE FAMILY OF JESUS

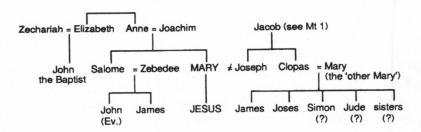

The above chart offers just one possible set of relationships in the family of Mary and Joseph; there is the possibility of Joachim, Anne and Elizabeth (and Jacob too) having brothers and sisters with their own sons and daughters who would be uncles and aunts of Jesus and who would in their turn have begotten children who would be his cousins, i.e. his 'brothers and sisters'.[12]

12 Cf. John A. T. Robinson, 'How small was the Seed of the Church?', *Essays in Honour of Bo Reicke*, 1984.

Part II

The Public Life

4

Social , Political and
Religious Forces at Work in
AD *28*

Palestine in the time of Jesus was an agrarian society. About 90% of the population worked on the land and provided food for the other 10%. The ruling class was not more than 5% of the total and included the royal family of Herod the Great and his numerous progeny, the dozen or so families that were attached by blood to the high priesthood, together with a number of rich Pharisees and Sadducees. Below the ruling class there was another 5% of the population who acted as a link between the rulers and the agricultural workers. There was no middle class; and skilled artisans in wood and metal including carpenters and weavers and workers in all the arts were regarded as 'retainers' of the nobility and rulers. Finally there was a class of 'hangers-on', people who made their living as best they could and who often joined the brigands and outlaws. Naturally, the majority of skilled workers lived and worked either in Jerusalem or in large towns like Caesarea on the coast or at Sepphoris, a few miles north of Nazareth. Merchants, of course, lived in the big cities and formed a small international group among whom were the bankers. In addition, the fishermen on the Sea of Galilee formed a number of small and close-knit communities. Taxation was very heavy; there was a double system, dues paid to the Romans through the tax-farmers they employed, and dues paid to Herod Antipas; and in addition there was the half-shekel for the Temple upkeep.

The Galilee in which Jesus grew up and worked was in many respects unlike the other parts of Palestine at that time. Its ruler was a son of Herod the Great, Herod Antipas I, to whom however the Romans would not grant the title of king, for this would have given him too much autonomy. It was a turbulent province, very sensitive about its independence, and incidentally the cradle of the extreme movement of the Zealots. The Galileans spoke a distinct dialect of Aramaic with a special accent, which was remarked on and often mocked by the more sophisticated Judeans. In the eyes of the Jerusalem Pharisees they were looked upon as uncouth extremists and more or less heretical. These attitudes had grown up over the years because communications with Jerusalem were difficult owing to a hostile and heretical Samaria being in between. Although the Galileans were intensely loyal to the Temple worship and devoted to the Jewish faith, there was a strong prejudice against them in Judea, to which the remark of Nathanael bears witness: 'Can anything good come out of Nazareth?'

When John the Baptist began his preaching (c. AD 27) in preparation for the coming of the Messiah, the situation in Jerusalem was somewhat complicated, and it is necessary to go back to the time of the Maccabees in order to understand it. Judas Maccabeus had won independence for his people from Syria by 160 BC, and his successors, the Hasmonean dynasty, managed to retain it for about a hundred years. The Jews knew themselves to be the People of God; and so in theory the priesthood of Aaron was their temporal as well as their spiritual authority. Their political independence could only be maintained by force of arms and even then only so long as the great powers round them, Egypt, Syria and Rome, were too preoccupied fighting each other to take away their freedom. Could a theocracy really work in these circumstances? Could the priesthood remain independent of the generals and the military aristocracy? These questions created a great division in Jewish society. On the one hand, there was the military aristocracy which wanted to control the high priesthood in the best interests, as it thought, of an independent nation, thus politicising the priesthood. On the other hand there grew up the party of the Pharisees, who believed that the high priesthood should be distinct from and independent of the political government. The military aristocracy came to form the party of the Sadducees, who accepted only the Pentateuch as the inspired writing of Moses. But the Pharisees, who based their teaching not only on the Pentateuch but on the rest of the inspired Books and also on the Law of the Ancients, that is to say, on the Unwritten Law as well as on the Written, believed that the priestly power should be kept apart from the political and wanted the country to be governed by a council of Elders, the Sanhedrin. Through it the Pharisees hoped to wrest control of the high priesthood from the Sadducees.

However, the priesthood came to be in the gift of the pagan Roman power when the Romans conquered Palestine in 63 BC. Subsequently, Herod the Great (40—4 BC) eliminated the Hasmonean dynasty, established a dictatorship and got control of the election of the high priest. From then on the high priests were chosen and deposed as frequently as Herod or the Romans thought fit. During the ministry of Jesus, Caiaphas was the high priest appointed by the Romans, though the Jews still looked to his deposed father-in-law Annas. The Saducean party in the time of Jesus was principally composed of the dozen or so families who had at one time or other held the high priesthood. All these drew from the Temple, in one way or another, their power, their prestige and their wealth, and were bound to be opposed to the reforms that any Messiah would introduce. By this time too the teaching of the Law and its spiritual practice had passed from the priesthood into the hands of a new class of lay teacher, the scribes, who had become the official interpreters of the Law.

The Pharisees however were the section of the intelligentsia that retained the respect and the support of the ordinary people. They were more ardent nationalists than the Sadducees who were inevitably supporters of the Roman occupying power; and their authority came from their insistence on the fundamental principle that the Torah, the Jewish way of life, must be kept pure from all political contamination or compromise, and must dominate every aspect of daily existence.

These were the people and the movements that Jesus would have to confront when the time came for him to stand forth as the Messiah. It is not hard to see that both parties would find their own interests conflicting with his mission to establish a new kingdom of righteousness. The Pharisees had most in common with him; but their long religious dominance over the people had bred in them a pride which made it hard for them to step down and submit to the authority of a man who had never graduated in the Temple schools and who was also a despised Galilean.

5

The Opening of the Ministry in Judea

1) The Arrival of the Lord's Herald (Mt 3:1-17 = Lk 3:1-38)

Luke recorded the coming of John with meticulous accuracy because he considered it to mark the beginning of the era of salvation. And so he gives us the names of the principal rulers, both secular and religious, who controlled the destiny of the Holy Land at that time; and the information that he gives us is extremely precise.

According to Luke, Tiberius was in the fifteenth year of his reign as emperor and sole ruler of the Roman empire. The kingdom of Herod the Great (39-4 BC) had been divided into four parts (tetrarchies) at his death, one to each of his four surviving sons. The most important part, Judea and Samaria, had been taken away from Archelaus and put under the direct rule of Rome, who appointed a succession of procurators (or prefects), the current one being Pontius Pilate. The other three parts were under the other three sons, namely, a younger Herod (Herod Antipas), Philip and Lysanias. The Romans had also interfered from time to time with the appointment of the high priest. Annas had been appointed in AD 6 and deposed in AD 15; and after several others had been appointed and dismissed, his son-in-law Joseph, called Caiaphas, had been installed in AD 18. He was still the official high priest in the time of Jesus, though it seems that the Jews really considered Annas to be the legitimate holder of the office.

In spite of the detail provided by Luke it is not possible to be quite certain about the date of the beginning of John's preaching, because we have no sure means of telling which year Luke took as the first of Tiberius' reign. Did Luke follow the historian Suetonius (*Tib. Vitae* 21) and date the first year of Tiberius from the beginning of his co-regency with Augustus in AD 12 (or even a year earlier according to another authority)? Or did he date it from the death of Augustus on 19 August AD 14? And if he dated it from the death of Augustus, we would still need to know which of four different contemporary calendars he was reckoning by, viz. the Julian, or the Jewish, or the Syrian-Macedonian, or the Egyptian calendar, anyone of which could have been legitimately employed.

After weighing all the probabilities it seems best to accept the year AD 30 as the year of the crucifixion (though this is still disputed) and to make the Passover of AD 28 the first of the three Passovers of the public life of Jesus. In this case the ministry of John would have begun not later than AD 27. And from this it would also follow that the first year of Tiberius' co-regency would have been AD 12, in Luke's reckoning.

And so when John began to preach, the homeland of Jesus was divided into four distinct political regions, Judea, Samaria and Idumea, which were directly governed by Pontius Pilate the Roman procurator, Galilee and Perea, a region on the eastern side of the Dead Sea, ruled over by Herod Antipas, and two outer territories ruled over by Philip and by Lysanias respectively. The Roman military presence was not much felt as the troops were stationed mostly at Caesarea, with only a cohort or so in Jerusalem. The Romans were mainly interested in the tax-yield of these provinces and as a matter of policy did not interfere in the spiritual life of the Jewish population. The spiritual authority of Annas and Caiaphas was however recognised by the Jews in all four provinces. From about the beginning of the century there had been a great revival of religious fervour, especially in Galilee where a large number of new synagogues had been constructed. Economically speaking, despite occasional food shortages the country as a whole was relatively stable, prosperous and hard-working. The time was ripe for the message of John.

In recent years the question has been raised whether John the Baptist ever had any connection with the supposedly Essene community that flourished at Qumran between AD 6 and 73 at a site on the north-western shore of the Dead Sea in the desert of Judea. But there is, in fact, no hint in the Gospels to suggest that either John or his message was influenced in any way by the Qumran community; and in the opinion of most scholars it is improbable that he had anything to do with it. Of course, he must have known of its existence; but its sectarian character and its narrow and exclusive outlook were alien to his spirit.

Luke dates the opening of the Messianic era in the following way:

> Now in the fifteenth year of the reign of Tiberius Caesar, Pontius Pilate being the governor of Judea and Herod tetrarch of Galilee, and Philip his brother tetrarch of Iturea and the region of Trachonitis, and Lysanias tetrarch of Abilene, under the high priest Annas and Caiaphas, the Word of the Lord came upon John the son of Zechariah in the desert. (Lk 3:1 -2)

The Messiah had been born in Bethlehem more than thirty years before. For all that time he had remained unknown to the world and silent; and the portents that had attended his birth had been forgotten by all save his immediate family. His childhood and early manhood had been spent in obscurity and insignificance. But the ripples caused by the astonishing events connected with his birth and the visit of the Magi seem to have been at the root of the general expectancy then abroad that messianic times were at hand. During this period two false Messiahs had appeared one after the other with the avowed intention of expelling the Romans from Judea; but each in turn had perished ignominiously with his followers. Furthermore, the apocalyptic literature that was being written and circulated at this period encouraged the belief that the end times were drawing near.

The sudden appearance of John, the son of Zechariah, in the region of the river Jordan, preaching a baptism of repentance for the remission of sins, revived messianic expectations and caused an electrifying reaction among all classes of Jews in Judea and Galilee. The message of John was clear and simple: 'Repent, for the Kingdom of Heaven is at hand.' Every Jew understood that he was referring to the kingdom of the Messiah, the Anointed Prince, who had been promised by the prophets one after the other ever since Nathan's prophecy to king David (2 Sam 7). And Matthew, Luke and Mark each quote in this connection the prophecy of Isaiah (40:3-5), and the equally striking prophecy of Malachi (3:1-2). Matthew tells us that this John was the voice of the one who cried out in the desert:

Prepare the way of the Lord, make straight his paths... and all flesh shall see the salvation of God. (Is 40:3-5)

Jesus himself will later (Lk 7:27) quote the message of Malachi:

Behold, I send my messenger to prepare the way before me, and the Lord whom you seek will suddenly come to his Temple. (Mal 3:1)

It should have been clear to all (as indeed it was to discerning men of good will) that this Kingdom was not a worldly political kingdom like the Roman empire, for the values it stressed were those of sorrow for sin and the necessity of turning back to God with obedience to his commandments. In the concluding chapters of his prophecy, Isaiah spoke of the coming of the Lord as the reign of justice and peace, as a time when all peoples and all nations would come to Mt Sion to praise the Lord and to glorify the God of Israel (Is 60-66). And John himself was a personification of Elijah the prophet, an ascetical figure whose character and personality had been nourished in solitude and in the hardships of the desert of Judea. John wore the coarsest materials obtainable in a desert environment—a long tunic made of camel hair fastened by a leather belt—and his food was locust-beans and wild honey, just what could be gathered in the desert without contacting civilisation.

John's message announced that the Messiah king himself was about to appear in Judea in order to set up this glorious kingdom of justice, truth and peace. And he emphasised that in some way, as yet unexplained, the Lord God of Israel would himself be present with his Messiah. Hence all who heard the message must take immediate steps to purify their hearts and consciences. A radical change of heart, repenting of all sin, was John's uncompromising demand to which the people responded in overwhelming numbers.

> Then went out to him all the inhabitants of Jerusalem, and all Judea and all the region of the Jordan, and were baptized in the Jordan by him confessing their sins. (Mt 3:5-6)

So successful was John that some of those who came were inclined to think that he himself must be the Messiah. But he quickly disabused them of this notion by saying:

> I indeed baptise you in water unto repentance, but he who comes after me is mightier than I, whose sandals I am not fit to carry; he will baptize you with the Holy Spirit and with fire. (Lk 3:16)

John's teaching was very practical and adapted to the obligations of his audience. To those better off, he said: 'He who has two tunics, let him share with him who has none'. To the tax collectors, he said: 'Do not exact more than you are authorised to take'; and to the soldiers, he said: 'Do not either rob or pillage or threaten the local inhabitants'. On the other hand he had stern words of warning for those Pharisees and Sadducees who came to his baptism not out of conviction but out of human respect, whose repentance, the Spirit told him, was not sincere: 'Offspring of vipers! Who pointed out to you to flee from the wrath to come? Bear fruit therefore worthy of penance...' (Mt 3:7). It seems likely that these Pharisees were among the last to come forward to be baptized, perhaps even after Jesus had begun his ministry in Galilee, as the very same phrase is found on his lips towards the end of his ministry, after it had become clear to him that their hostility to him was irreversible (cf. Mt 23:33). Anyhow, they thought it wise in the circumstances to conform and so they submitted to John's rite hypocritically, while remaining determined to oppose the Messiah whom John had pointed out. For to accept John's word would have involved a change of heart that they were not prepared to make. Their arrogant reliance on being the Chosen People would be proved vain since God could, and would, raise up others (the Gentiles) to replace them.

2) The Baptism of Jesus (Mt 3:13f = Lk 3:21f = Mk 1:9f); his Ancestry

All this time Jesus had been watching the progress of John. Then, much to John's surprise, Jesus came and presented himself for baptism. Here was the very man, for whose coming he had been preparing the people, asking to be prepared for his own coming! This was preposterous. How could Jesus humble himself in this way? He of all men certainly did not need repentance as he was totally sinless. But Jesus insisted saying: 'Let it be now, for so it is fitting for us to fulfil all justice'. By this statement Jesus implied that as a true Jew he claimed solidarity with all his contemporaries; he would have no special treatment. It was a sign of his sublime humility and of his self-effacement. In fact, it was all part of his preparation for his future ministry. And as he, the 'One who is to come', went down into the water, John heard the voice of the Father saying: 'This is my Beloved Son, in whom I am well pleased'; and at the same time he saw the Holy Spirit descending on Jesus in the visible form of a dove. By this sign the Triune God formally expressed approval of Jesus and commissioned him to go forth to save and redeem the world.

This auspicious event concluded the period of preparation. Now Jesus was ready to commence his public ministry. Luke tells us that he was then 'about thirty years of age', the age of maturity for the priesthood according to Jewish tradition. In fact, if we are right in assuming that he had been born about 8 BC, he would have been between 35 and 40 years of age at the time of his baptism.[13]

---

13 Luke's statement that Jesus was 'about thirty' is not to be pressed. The age of thirty years was the age of maturity for assuming responsible office (Num 4:3; 2 Sam 5:4). It means that he was at least thirty, and possibly older. Nor ought we to forget that his enemies said of him: 'You are not yet fifty...' (Jn 8:57). It may also be of interest to note that many theologians are of the opinion that Jesus' baptism was also the moment when the Sacrament of Baptism was instituted and the waters of Christian baptism were given their saving power.

Matthew (1:1-17) has related the ancestry of Jesus from Abraham (to whom the Lord God had promised that his descendants would be more numerous than the stars of heaven) through king David, from whom Jesus inherited the proud title 'Son of David', down to Joseph, thus proving his claim to be the Messiah of the Jews. On the other hand, Luke writing for the Gentiles traces his family tree back to Adam, the first parent, in order to emphasize that Jesus is the Saviour of all peoples of all times and all places (Lk 3:23-38).

3) The Temptations of Jesus (Mt 4:1f = Lk 4:1f = Mk 1:12f)

The first task that the Messiah had to undertake, now that he had been given the signal by his heavenly Father to begin his earthly mission, was to engage in a direct confrontation with Satan, the old Devil, who had held the whole human race in slavery ever since the fall of Adam and Eve. He set out to do so without delay, thus fulfilling Psalm 39[40]:8-9:

> Then I said, Lo, I come; in the roll of the book it is written of me; I delight to do thy will, O my God. Thy law is within my heart.

The evangelists tell us that the Holy Spirit himself led Jesus out into the desert of Judea to meet Satan, whom Jesus was later to describe as 'the Prince of this World'. Satan is identical with the Serpent, the Devil, who deceived our first parents in the Garden of Eden, persuading them to disobey the express command of God not to eat of the forbidden fruit. Thus they lost their state of original innocence and all the spiritual blessings with which God in his love had endowed them, proving themselves unworthy to remain in the Paradise in which God had set them. Above all they had lost the privilege of 'walking with God' and the assurance of eternal happiness, because entry into heaven was barred to them.

Ever since that time, uncountable ages ago, mankind has inherited and shared not only the universal penalty of death but the same vitiated nature, and the constant liability to sin and error, and the dire social consequences of that sin. There was no one capable of restoring the human race to God's favour, because all mankind was suffering the same disgrace. There was need of a man even greater than Adam before his Fall, someone who enjoyed the full favour of God, someone who could speak and act on behalf of the whole human race, someone able to fulfil the promise God had made to restore mankind to his friendship, someone who could face the Devil without flinching, someone who could resist all his wiles, someone who could overcome him without difficulty and render him powerless. The God-Man alone could win victory over Satan through his humanity, by his human will supported only by divine grace.

Jesus was that Person, and knew himself to be that Person, which explains his eagerness to meet Satan and to vanquish him in single combat. On the success of that battle would depend the salvation of the world; for if Jesus won, he would be able to free all who sought his help. For his part, Satan was anxious to test and destroy this new man whose opposition constituted a grave threat to his hold on the rest of the world. Just as Moses had been instructed by God through forty days and nights of prayer and fasting to prepare himself for promulgating the Law of God from Mt Sinai (Ex 24:18; 34:28), so now Jesus, the New Adam, will prepare himself in identical fashion to promulgate the new law of love that will complete and perfect the old.

Prayer and fasting were to be his chief weapons in his warfare against the powers of darkness; and he also knew that to win this contest he had to use his human strength and talents to the full, because he had to accomplish the redemption of the human race by the power of his human body and soul alone, aided of course by the grace of God. A unique contest indeed! The Son of God who at the same time was fully Man, alone and unaided, fighting with his human faculties strengthened by God's grace against one of the most powerful angels ever created by his Almighty Father. This was the arena and condition for the confrontation to which he was subjected by his heavenly Father, one which the God-Man could only win by firmly adhering to his Father's will in every detail and by the ultimate sacrifice of his life. No wonder that at the end, when he was victorious and had caused the Devil to depart leaving himself totally untouched, he was all the same totally drained of energy and in need of the ministry of angels to help him recover.

In this contest, the Messiah steps into the arena as the One who claims mankind as his prize, so that Satan is forced to defend his hold over the human race. The Devil makes three attempts to discover if the Lord's Anointed is capable of resisting his cunning enticements. So he tempts him first to indulge in lust (i.e. bodily pleasure or self-indulgence), next to a sin of pride, and finally to succumb to the drive to domination and power.

The first temptation was to get him to satisfy his physical needs and desires in an irrational way. Any yielding of Jesus to the solicitation to turn the stones into bread to assuage his great hunger would have shewn some lack of balance and so of the proper trust and submission to the will of God. Jesus will have none of it. He replies:

Not by bread alone shall man have life, but by every word proceeding from the mouth of God. (Dt 8:3)

Next, the Devil, remembering that the Jews were looking for a Messiah who would lead them to victory over the Roman army of occupation, suggests that if Jesus would make a dramatic appearance by arranging to throw himself off the Temple's pinnacle in front of the crowds, trusting in the Lord to send his angels to bear him up, they would all follow him blindly to a famous victory. Jesus replies:

Again it stands written, Thou shalt not tempt the Lord thy God. (Ps 90[91]:11-12) As a final test then of this peerless figure whose depths he cannot fathom, Satan offers him mastery over the whole world, if only he will fall down and adore him—a half truth analogous to the one he used to deceive Eve in the Garden of Eden. Jesus replies:

Go away, Satan; for it stands written, the Lord thy God shalt thou worship and him alone adore. (Dt 6: 13)

Thus we see that the integrity of his human nature was proof against the most specious and attractive offers that Satan could make in the shape of these three temptations that cover the whole gamut of human desires. Since the human soul of Jesus is furnished with the holiness of God and is the dwelling place of the Holy Spirit it could not be shaken from the path of rectitude, however great the external allurement. The Devil had tried his utmost and could do no more; for where God's grace dwells, Satan cannot enter. As St John was later to write:

> All that is in the world, the lust of the flesh and the lust of the eyes and the pride of life, is not of the Father but is of the world. (1 Jn 2:14)

And Jesus has overcome the world.

Finally we learn that the Devil left him, but only, as St Luke adds, 'until an opportune time ', when Satan would enter into Judas and make a last open attempt to overthrow God's plan for the Messiah. The New Adam had succeeded in resisting all the efforts of Satan to corrupt him; and so he now stands out as the sole incorrupt sanctuary of God in the created world. The first part of his mission had now been successfully accomplished; but there now awaited him the still more difficult one of drawing to himself the human race corrupted by the Devil, that is to say, the task of laying a firm foundation in this depraved world for the entry of the nations into the kingdom of his Father, which is the Church he came to found.

4) 'The One Who is to Come' (Jn 1:19-51)

The three Synoptic Gospels start to record the public ministry of Jesus only from the moment he entered Galilee after having heard of the imprisonment of John the Baptist, thus following a thematic rather than a chronological order of events. And so it is only in the Gospel of St John that we find the clues to explain why Jesus failed in his attempt to begin his ministry in the Holy City and to set up his headquarters there.

When he had recovered from the ordeal of the temptations, it seems that Jesus took up his residence near to where John was baptising at the ford near Jericho. John had been preaching for a year or more and had gathered around him a group of disciples whom he was training in preparation for the coming of the Messiah. Among them were four fishermen from Galilee, Peter, Andrew, James and John.

By this time the authorities in Jerusalem, who seem to have remained deliberately aloof from the Baptist, decided that they must make a serious effort to find out the real purpose of John's preaching. So they sent down from the Holy City an official delegation of priests and Levites from the Sanhedrin to investigate, with instructions to spare no effort to get to the bottom of what was going on. This delegation questioned John closely and elicited from him that he was neither the Christ nor Elijah nor the prophet mentioned by Moses (Jn 1:19ff). And in response to their insistence that they were required to submit a clear and concise report to those who had sent them, he declared that he was indeed the herald of the Lord God himself, whose coming had been prophesied in the fortieth chapter of the prophecy of Isaiah. John said:

I am the voice of one crying in the wilderness: 'Make straight the way of the Lord'. And he further added:

In your midst there stands one whom you know not, he who comes after me, the thong of whose sandal I am not worthy to loose.

This was indeed arresting and exciting news—that somewhere in the crowd surrounding John was the mysterious personage whom John had been commissioned by the God of Israel to reveal to the people. And to indicate that this was no fairy story, the evangelist John locates it factually by recording that this statement was made in Bethania beyond the Jordan (Jn 1:28).

The delegation remained at the ford in order to catch sight of the person to whom John was referring. The very next day John saw Jesus coming towards him and in the presence of the delegation pointed him out to them, saying:

See the Lamb of God who takes away the sin of the world... He who sent me to baptise in water, he said to me, "The one upon whom you see the Spirit descending and remaining upon him, this is he who baptizes in the Holy Spirit." And I beheld and witnessed that this is the Chosen One of God.

The members of the delegation were left in no doubt that the mission of John was from God and that he was claiming to point out to them the Messiah himself. Having thus seen with their own eyes the man, Jesus of Nazareth, whom John had identified in so solemn a manner, the delegates were able to return to Jerusalem and report their findings to the authorities there.

But John's task was not yet completed. For on the following day he undertook to point out Jesus in identical terms to two of his own disciples, who were in fact John, our future evangelist,[14] and Andrew the brother of Simon Peter. Their immediate reaction was quite different from that of the delegation of the Jews, which had felt obliged to withhold all comment and simply to report back to those who had sent them. These two disciples of John at once decided to go after Jesus and to find out for themselves who indeed he was. Jesus turned and asked them: 'What are you seeking?' In reply they inquired: 'Rabbi, where do you live?' He said: 'Come and you will see'. So they came and saw where he was staying and remained with him the whole day. That day spent with Jesus convinced them that he was indeed the Messiah. On their return to their own lodging, Andrew went to his brother Simon and simply stated: 'We have found the Messiah'. Then he brought him to Jesus, who looking on Simon declared: 'You are Simon, the son of John; you shall be called Cephas' (which means 'Rock', *Petros* in Gk, and anglicised as Peter). Thus did Jesus prophesy about Peter the first time he set eyes upon him.

The next day Jesus purposed to set out for Galilee, perhaps because he had received an invitation to attend a certain wedding in Cana, where he knew that he would again meet his mother Mary. But before he left he invited two other disciples of John the Baptist to join him. One was Philip, who came from Bethsaida, the same village as Peter, on the north-east shore of

14 I accept the identification of John the son of Zebedee with the Beloved Disciple and with the evangelist. Among modern exegetes, I note that Peter F. Ellis, while refraining from identifying the Beloved Disciple with the evangelist, is yet convinced of the unity of authorship of the Gospel of John (cf. P.F. Ellis, *The Genius of John*, Collegeville 1984).

the Sea of Galilee; the other was Philip's friend Nathanael. But whereas Philip was in no doubt that this Jesus of Nazareth was the one of whom Moses wrote in the Law and the Prophets, Nathanael knew that Nazareth was too unimportant to have been mentioned in the ancient Scriptures; and his first response was hostile: 'Can anything from Nazareth be good?' So Philip invited him: 'Come and see'. When Philip brought Nathanael to Jesus the latter made a prophecy about him saying: 'See an Israelite indeed in whom there is no guile'. And when Nathanael (probably the future Apostle Bartholomew) in amazement asked Jesus how he knew him, Jesus explained: 'Before Philip called you, when you were under the fig-tree, I saw you'. Whatever the implications of this statement, the words of Jesus were sufficient to convince Nathanael of the divine knowledge and authority of Jesus, for he exultantly proclaimed: 'Rabbi, you are the Son of God, you are the King of Israel'. The response of Jesus was emphatic: 'Greater things than these will you see. Amen I say to you, you will see the heavens opened and the angels of God ascending and descending upon the Son of Man'. And so Nathanael too like the others was won over to follow Jesus without delay.

Two things are especially remarkable about these first encounters of Jesus with his future apostles. Firstly, their immediate realisation that they were in the presence of one to whose spiritual authority they were wholeheartedly drawn to submit. Secondly, Jesus from the first moment of his encounter with them makes use of the power of prophecy that he possesses. Perhaps the only thing difficult to understand is why it took them so long, and a special grace, fully to realize his divine sonship, despite their early affirmation of his Messiahship. With these first recruits Jesus sets out for Galilee and the wedding at Cana.

5) The Wedding at Cana (Jn 2:1-11)

After the Baptist had pointed out Jesus as the Messiah both to the delegation from the Holy City and to his own disciples, Jesus decided once more to spend a few days in Galilee before going up to Jerusalem for the feast of the Passover. Although the import of John's revelation of Jesus' identity seems at the time to have been imperfectly understood by his disciples, it was otherwise with the chief priests and the Sanhedrin, the Council of Seventy, as we shall shortly learn.

The first event of his short stay in Galilee was his attendance, with these new disciples of his, at a wedding at the village of Cana, a few miles north-east of Nazareth. A late tradition affirmed that Mary was an aunt of the bride—in which case the latter would have been one of his cousins. But this seems to be no more than speculation suggested by the warm welcome given to Jesus and his new followers, and by the proprietary interest taken by Mary in the success of the feasting. At any rate, Jesus and his disciples seem to have been invited because of his mother's connection with the bridal couple.

It was Mary, now in her fifties, who first notices that the wine is running out; and she draws the attention of Jesus by saying quite simply: 'They have no wine'. She is not offering any solution, nor does she ask for a miracle; she just states the fact. To our modern ears the reply of Jesus seems to be a rebuff. For he says: 'Is your concern mine too, O Woman? My hour has not yet come' (Literally: 'What is it to me and to thee, O Woman?'). 'His hour' has a twofold meaning, firstly 'the hour' of his public ministry when he will be working many miracles in confirmation of his messiahship, and secondly 'the hour' of his passion (Jn 12:27).

It is however more difficult to comprehend why he addresses her as 'O Woman'. According to custom this was indeed a respectful address; but nevertheless even in those days it was somewhat strange for a son to address his mother in precisely these terms. It indicated that at that moment he was looking on her in anticipation as the Second Eve, the future Queen of Heaven and the Mother of the Church, the position that she would attain after his resurrection when her place as the supreme advocate in virtue of his divine merits would be confirmed and made known to all. So Jesus is giving her to understand that at this moment his scope of action is restricted by his heavenly Father's plan, according to which he cannot be involved publicly in such a manner as fully to reveal himself, for the reason that his 'hour' has not yet come. Mary's role, too, in God's plan of salvation as principal intercessor for the Church has in any case to await the hour of her Son's triumph and may not be anticipated either! However, she obviously does not consider that she has been rebuffed, for at once she instructs the attendants standing around: 'Do whatever he tells you'.

Jesus then grants her unspoken wish in the most generous way possible. Six great stone barrels or casks are standing there full of water ready for the ritual ablutions of the Jews, each about the size of a nine-gallon cask. Jesus orders the servants to fill their jugs with water from these barrels and take them to the chief steward; and he stands by while they fill them to the brim. They then carry them off; and when the chief steward tastes the water become wine and finds that it is the best wine of the celebration, he congratulates the bridegroom on providing the best wine last of all: 'Every man puts out the good wine first, and after they have got drunk, the inferior. But you have kept the good wine until now'. The chief steward, of course, does not know its origin, though the servants who have drawn it do; and they must have been astounded at the wonderful miracle Jesus had just performed right under their noses.

And so at one and the same time without attracting any attention Jesus prevented a crisis at the feast, rejoiced his mother, and yet satisfied his Father's command not to work any public messianic sign before he presented himself to the chief priests at the Temple in Jerusalem. This personal yet secret and anonymous gift to the young couple is also to be understood as his blessing upon every true marriage, and furthermore as his approval of such joyful festivities and of the proper use of wine as refreshment. The miraculous change of the water into wine—'the water saw its Maker and blushed', as the poet wrote—had the further purpose of revealing his power to change one substance into another by his word alone and at a distance. By this miracle the faithful of later generations have been helped to believe in the power of his word to change the bread and wine of the Eucharist into his body and blood. Finally, St John confirms that this miracle was his first 'sign'.

Before leaving the scene of this story it is important to linger a little longer over two matters that this first miraculous sign has brought to our notice: The sign of the New Adam and the New Eve, and the reason for Jesus' cryptic and abrupt response to his mother's notification that the wine had failed.[15]

The introduction of this story into the career of Jesus at this point when he is on the threshold of his saving ministry is intended to draw our attention to the saving role of the New Adam and the New Eve. Just as mankind's fall from grace began with a married couple, so Jesus was to begin his redemptive work by 'saving' a married couple from disgrace. And by addressing Mary as 'O Woman', he is attributing to her the role of the woman in Gen 3:15, who will crush the head of the serpent. She is thus presented in the Gospel of John as the New Eve who co-operates with Jesus in his work, and as the mother of all the Living, because she is the mother of Jesus, to whose spiritual body all mankind is to belong. Her role as principal intercessor will be confirmed by him as he is dying on the Cross.

We now come to the remark that has proved a stumbling block to many exegetes: 'What is it to me and to thee, O Woman?' It is often regarded as a form of rebuke for her interference. It is nothing of the sort, although it is definitely a protest. But it is not a protest directed against her, but one directed against the situation which her remark has unwittingly created for him. It results from the understandable shrinking of his human nature from her initiating the 'hour' of his redemptive work. It is a sign of the distress of his human nature as he anticipates his surrender to the events that will lead to his passion, and of his human desire to be spared all the agony.

---

15   Fr. Philip Scott OCSO, in his book entitled *A Virgin called Woman* (1987), has provided an illuminating commentary on this passage of St John's Gospel.

Jesus had been proclaimed by the Baptist as the Lamb of God, the atoning victim for the sins of the world; and now, by the disposition of providence and by John the greatest of the prophets, he was about to enter upon the ministry which he already knew would lead to Calvary (Jn 19:17). He comes to Cana fully conscious of all this; in fact he is now no longer a private person, no matter how much he would like to go on without taking up the fated burden. Nothing had so far happened to force him to declare himself by action; but when his mother told him of the threat to the young couple's celebration, Jesus divined that the appointed moment was upon him; the 'Woman' was unintentionally confronting him with his destiny. By changing the water into wine he was privately taking the first irrevocable step towards his passion, death and resurrection. His protest and his declaration were a revelation to her of his involvement in the situation as Messiah and not as the carpenter's son; and she now knew that she was no longer talking to her 'boy' Jesus but to the Messiah in person. Furthermore it also dawned on her that he was inviting her to realize that her role as the New Eve and as the mother of all the redeemed was about to begin. He was awaiting her consent to his mission and to hers, which she gave when she said to the servants: 'Do whatever he tells you'.

What he meant was to protest to her (by that very fact giving her a role in the drama) that she was getting him involved that much sooner in the train of events that would end on Calvary (Jn 19:26). Calling her 'Woman' was his way of declaring her role as helpmate, a changing of her name as fateful as the changing of that of the fisherman Simon into Cephas (Jn 1:42). His protesting to her implied that her personal consent (on her own and on mankind's behalf) was required. His words told her that what he now envisaged was the beginning of his redemptive mission; his protest came from his full awareness of what that meant, and was no more and no less mysterious than his words to his heavenly Father: 'What shall I say? Father, save me from this hour?' (Jn 12:37).

The dilemma for Mary was that her son was the victim needed both to win her salvation and to save his people from their sins (Mt 1:21). We normally expect any mother to sacrifice her own well-being and life for the sake of her child. Here a mother had the same choice: her child's life or her own redemption and ours. Her motherly instinct would have demanded from her to forget about her own redemption and to save her son's life. But the redemption of mankind required her to sacrifice the life of her divine Son. Her way of saying 'Yes' was to tell the servants to obey his instructions. In this sense, she is surely the 'co-redemptrix'.

For Jesus his pain was due not least to the fact that she who was dearest and closest to him was in a way sending him to the Cross. Hence the poignancy of the protest, which implied: 'Do you of all people wish this on me, O Woman?' And the poignancy of her reply: 'Yes. Whatever he shall say to you, do ye'. Both he and she were bound by obedience; he to his heavenly Father, she to the God of her fathers, as was Abraham when he prepared to sacrifice his son Isaac. Such a turning away from his own inclination has already been noted in the case of his foregoing the opportunity of training as a scribe in the Temple out of obedience to his parents (Lk 2:41f).

A few days after the wedding celebrations, having in this manner done homage to his mother's wishes without compromising in any way the official commencement of his public career, he set out for Jerusalem in order publicly to inaugurate his saving mission.

6) The Cleansing of the Temple[16]
(Mt 21:10f = Lk 19:45f = Mk 11:11f = Jn 2:13f)

As we have seen, the devout Jew in the time of Jesus made

---

16 In my opinion, John, writing after the Synoptics, correctly places the Cleansing of the Temple at the opening of Jesus' ministry. The evangelist Matthew, followed by Luke and Mark, places it with the rest of the 'Jerusalem material' at the end of his Gospel for reasons of literary convenience. See my articles 'The Rejection of Christ', and 'The Persecution of Christ' (*Downside Review* 1938/9).

three pilgrimages each year to the Holy City to worship in the Temple, the only place in the world sanctioned by the Lord God of Israel for offering sacrifices to him according to the Law of Moses. The first and most important of the three was that of the Passover, early in April,[17] to thank God for the first fruits of the forthcoming harvest and to praise him for the gift of their country. Jerusalem and its narrow streets were then thronged with the immense concourse of pilgrims with their families from all parts of the inhabited world. The fact that it was forbidden to charge pilgrims for accommodation in the Holy City was no doubt an incentive; but in any case at this time its normal population of 50,000 was so swollen (probably trebled) that people had to sleep outside in the open air on the slopes of Mt Olivet, which they could safely do as the climate was by then dry and warm.

Herod the Great had only recently rebuilt the Temple and its courts on a magnificent scale. The 'courses', or companies, of priests were all lined up ready to cope with the thousands of lambs brought by the pilgrims to be sacrificed at the altar of the Temple in preparation for the Passover meal at home on the evening of the 14th Nisan. At the same time they all paid their tithe of a half-shekel to the priests and also purchased their 'peace offering'. At this time the Temple area became one huge market and a vast amount of money flowed into it, making it in effect also the economic and financial centre of the nation.

The Temple was in addition the nation's intellectual centre, for as soon as the pilgrims had fulfilled their religious duties, they came back to listen to the teaching of the famous doctors of the Law belonging to the two rival schools of Hillel and Shammai, who publicly debated questions of the day. Every rabbi had his own pitch in the colonnades to the east and south of the Temple esplanade. Each had his own students and these in due time after a number of years could themselves become masters in Israel. Jesus had never graduated in this way; and so when

---

17 On the dating of the Passover, see J.B. Orchard, 'The Two-Year Ministry Viewed and Reviewed' (*Downside Review*, Vol 57, 1939, pp. 334-339).

later on he came back to teach in the Temple, the people wondered at the wisdom and knowledge he displayed in spite of never having been apprenticed to a rabbi.

The news brought back to Jerusalem by the delegation of Pharisees and priests following their visit to John at the Jordan was as dramatic and startling as the news of the birth of the Messiah that had been brought more than thirty years earlier by the Magi. On that occasion Herod the Great and his courtiers had been greatly perturbed by the news of the birth of a possible rival in the shape of a helpless babe; but now the religious authorities learnt that they would have to face a grown up man— a Galilean and allegedly a king—able to speak for himself!

During that thirty-year interval Herod the Great had died and a Roman governor had been installed; but the spiritual authority, the high priest with his Council of Seventy, the Sanhedrin, still functioned, though with diminished prestige. The chief priests were now the political appointees of the pagan Roman governor and in the mind of the devout people in Israel they were simply the caretakers of the spiritual leadership until such time 'as a trustworthy prophet should arise' (1 Macc 14:41). They were now badly shaken by the news that the holy prophet John the Baptist had actually identified and personally pointed out to their delegation the man whom he believed to be the Messiah; he affirmed that he was a carpenter from Nazareth whose name was Jesus, son of Joseph. Furthermore, if they had long memories, his age might have given them to think that if one went back thirty years to the time of the Magi, it would correspond to that of the baby king whom everyone believed had been murdered by Herod's soldiers. They therefore expected that this man, impostor or genuine, would be a formidable claimant; and they rightly surmised that he would come up for the next Passover with his supporters to make his bid for power in the presence of the crowds of devout pilgrims, and they were exceedingly afraid.

Jesus would have fully understood the magnitude of his task and the problem of getting himself recognised by all those worldly clergy, the high priests, Annas, his son-in-law Caiaphas, and their family together with eminent scribes, Pharisees and other Elders, who controlled the Sanhedrin, the supreme authority over all Jews everywhere, including in the Diaspora. For many years these high-priestly families and their friends had enjoyed the fruits of power by favour of the Romans and had clung on to them by various shady means, not least by extensive bribery. The thought of having to yield their position of authority and influence unconditionally to this unknown Galilean craftsman from Nazareth was utterly abhorrent to them and was to be resisted at all costs! They had conveniently forgotten, of course, that their true role was to have the nation in a state of readiness at all times for the Coming of the Messiah, which the prophet Malachi had foretold would be sudden and unexpected. Here was a totally unknown person, one with no political influence—and so with little or no 'clout'—about to demand the keys of the Temple! It was surely impossible and ridiculous to consider his claims seriously... but John was nevertheless a man of God, and perhaps after all the man from Nazareth might be what John claimed for him. As we shall learn later, only two members of the Sanhedrin, Nicodemus and Joseph of Arimathea, were to have the integrity and the courage to recognize and accept the word of John that Jesus was the Messiah; but at the time they too were afraid to speak out.

What then was the high priest and the other chief priests to do about this man when he turned up? There were three possible courses. Firstly, an impartial investigation of his claim. If they seriously wanted to cross-question Jesus himself, all they had to do was to invite him to meet the Council face to face, as they were ultimately to do during his 'trial' when Caiaphas solemnly asked him to identify himself in their presence. But since they were soon to find out that Jesus, like the Baptist, was genuine, such a scrutiny would certainly result in their official recognition that he too was from God, and they would have been obliged to submit to his authority and take his orders. Secondly, they could reject him outright as a person of no significance. But in view of John's testimony this would be dangerous since the Baptist was believed by the ordinary people to be a prophet of God. Thirdly, they could dissemble, keep aloof, temporize, and deny him as many facilities as they dared, in the hope that he would either go away or in some way play into their hands and so enable them to eliminate him altogether in due time. From their point of view the safest course would be to remain silent, to obstruct, to wait and see, and hope for an opportunity of getting rid of him by diplomacy or even by force, if necessary.

Jesus on his part was equally determined to assert his authority, now that he had been publicly commissioned by his heavenly Father at his baptism in the river Jordan. To do otherwise would be to betray his mission. After his victory over Satan in the desert the way was open for him to enter his Father's House to inaugurate the Kingdom of God and to call upon the Jewish nation to hearken to him there in the Temple, the appropriate place from which to begin his appeal to the world.

Instead of giving him a courteous welcome, conjoined with a formal scrutiny of his messianic claim, the chief priests adopted the third alternative and gave strict orders to the Temple officials to ignore and as far as possible ostracise him. We learn from Mark (11:11) that when he first arrived for the Feast, he calmly went round unaccompanied, surveying and inspecting everything according to his Messiah's prerogative, noting that the Temple area had been turned into a market-place for buying and selling the many kinds of animals and materials that worshippers needed for the different types of sacrifice. The noise and the bustle and the squabbling that went on were exceedingly disedifying and derogatory to the respect due to the Lord God. However, since the Temple officials were under orders to refuse any instructions given by Jesus, he decided to take the Law into his own hands and himself do what the Levites should have done under his orders.

So he came into the Temple the next day carrying a small symbolical whip of cords, and to the amazement of all drove the buyers and sellers out of the Temple precincts, at the same time scattering the coins and tables of the money-changers all over the Temple pavement, exclaiming as he did so that he would not permit his Father's House to become a market-place for trading (Jn 2:16). A messianic act indeed!

Jesus could not have touched the chief priests on a more sensitive issue, for the revenues from the activities of the money-changers and the stands occupied by the sellers of the Temple requisites brought a vast sum of money not only into the Temple treasury but also into the pockets of the clergy. Jesus would never be forgiven for this astoundingly bold initiative, even though the marketing would be resumed the next day as if nothing had happened. As a result his opponents learned a number of important things about him. In the first place he showed that he was no respecter of high rank as such and would not permit himself to be intimidated. Secondly, they recognized that he possessed a moral integrity and hatred of greed that would endear him to the people. And thirdly, as he did not possess any armed following, he could be ignored and dismissed quite easily. But he had dared to challenge and expose the corruption existing in the supreme spiritual authority in the Holy City and so constituted a grave threat to their position. On the other hand the crowds who thronged the Temple and watched his action seem to have been delighted, for the evangelists have recorded that after this incident 'many believed in him'. The blind and the lame, who were always around begging from the worshippers, came to him and he healed them; while the young people present were thrilled at his action and behaviour, and kept on crying out in his honour: 'Hosanna to the Son of David', thus recognising him as the Messiah (Mt 21:14-17; Jn 2:26).

The chief priests and the scribes watched incredulously as Jesus followed up his 'cleansing' of the Temple with the performance of miracle after miracle of healing in the Temple precincts; and they listened with ever increasing exasperation as the children continued to cry out in his praise. For the moment they were too demoralized to say anything more than: 'Don't you hear what these children are saying about you?'

Jesus' reply was to give his full approval to their refrain: 'Hosanna to the Son of David'. 'Yes', he replied, 'Don't you recall the words of the Psalmist: 'Out of the mouths of babes and sucklings, I will establish praise. If these do not cry out, the very stones will do so!' To which they had no answer, for not even the children were going to be intimidated by the displeasure of the chief priests from proclaiming him to be the Messiah.

Jesus returned to the Temple the next day, and it may well have been on this occasion that he withered the fig-tree as an existential symbol of the consequences for the nation of the opposition of the chief priests and the elders of the people (Mk 11:20ff).

When he took up a position in the Portico of Solomon to begin teaching, they seized their opportunity to challenge his authority and attempted to restore their prestige in the eyes of the people. They approached him and demanded: 'By what authority are you doing these things? And who has given you this authority?' (Mt 21:23 = Jn 2:18). All Jesus needed to do in reply was to remind them that John the Baptist, who had been universally accepted as a prophet of God had borne adequate witness about him to their recent delegation. This would put the onus on them; if they accepted the witness of John they must automatically accept him. So he asked them: 'I too will ask you one question; which if you tell me, I too will tell you by what authority I do these things. The baptism that was John's, whence was it? From heaven or from men?'

This direct question put the chief priests on the horns of a dilemma. If they were to say 'From heaven', they knew he would counter, 'Why then do you not believe John and accept me?'. But this they had already made up their minds not to do. On the other hand, if they were to say: 'The baptism of John is from men and not from God', the people would stone them as liars, for everyone held John to be a prophet. Their only escape seemed to be to plead ignorance. So rather than accept the consequences of telling the truth, they replied: 'We do not know'. Jesus knew, and they knew, and the people also knew, that they were lying;

and from that moment they had to stand by their lie. And Jesus, having shewn up their lie, proved that he recognized their hypocrisy by adding a final word: 'Neither do I tell you by what authority I do these things' (Mt 21:25-27).

Thus the first official appearance of the Messiah at his Temple was a complete disaster so far as obtaining from the Temple authorities the recognition that was due to him. His sense of outrage at the dishonour done to his heavenly Father's House and his brief exercise of his supreme authority had made them his sworn enemies; they would now seek by every means in their power to destroy him, since he posed a mortal threat to their accustomed way of life. Those means they possessed; for they had the physical force available if required and also enjoyed the support of the Roman government; though any action against him might take some time to bring about if he had popular support. In fact, in the sphere of public relations Jesus was soon to achieve an enormous success with the crowds; and, in particular, the Galileans who had been present at the Passover festivities in Jerusalem were enthusiastically in his favour, while he was to enjoy a strong undercurrent of support even in Judea and in Jerusalem itself.

However, Israel was a theocratic society controlled by the high priestly families, and a citizen's rights depended on his membership of one of the synagogues, which were all under their jurisdiction (Jn 9:22). Before long the chief priests would decree that anybody openly adhering to Jesus would be excluded from the synagogue, and thus lose his civil rights. Such hostility on their part was going to make it exceedingly difficult for Jesus to get his message across, above all in the capital city. In fact, from the opening day of his public ministry, his activity was monitored, and his movements were spied on (Jn 4:1, 5:16-18; Lk 5:18f). Before many months had passed, as his reputation grew, the whole Sanhedrin came to realize that nothing short of his total elimination could save them from being overwhelmed by the 'Jesus Movement'. There were of course some upright and faithful men even among the seventy members of the Sanhedrin; but so powerful was its opposition to Jesus that Nicodemus, one of the Seventy, dared not be seen in his company, and therefore had to visit him secretly by night. The paradox of the human life of Jesus is that he lived it simultaneously on two distinct planes, i.e. the plane of the Godhead, where he shared the life of Father and Holy Spirit, and the earthly plane in which he moved just as freely and naturally as any other human being. Hence he was able to cope with human problems in the same way and on the same terms as we ourselves have to. In the present context he already understood that his life would soon be at risk and that he would have to re-think his strategy if he was to succeed in his mission. It was because he had fully appropriated to himself the human condition (which he himself had created) that Jesus was able to meet all contingencies and dangers in a completely human way and so able to 'change his strategy' to meet irreversible opposition and yet triumphantly to attain his final aim by the sacrifice of his own human life. Aquinas put the matter in a nutshell when he wrote that Jesus was at one and the same time a *comprehensor* and a *viator*, i.e. as God he comprehended the totality of reality; and as man he saw it partially as a human traveller.

It is therefore impossible to avoid the conclusion that as soon as Jesus made his claim clear, the chief priests made up their mind to shut him out whatever the cost, and to suppress his mission by every means in their power. The fact that they were prepared to go to the length of having him slaughtered in the alleged interest of the nation meant for Jesus that he in his turn could succeed in saving his people only by persevering even to his own death. He knew that, given the implacable obstinacy of his enemies, the pursuit of his claim to be the Messiah would almost certainly involve the sacrifice of his own life. And so in response to their request to show them a divine sign for his action in sweeping out all the buyers and sellers, he gives them what they ask for by way of an enigmatic prophecy which foretells the consequences of their refusal to co-operate with him in the salvation of the Jewish nation. The sign will be his own sacrificial death and, coupled with it, the end of the old Temple, which will be replaced by the new Temple of his own glorified body. 'Dissolve this sanctuary', he said, 'and in three days I will raise it up' (Jn 2:19), meaning the 'sanctuary of his own body'. Come what may, Jesus was going to fulfil the plan of his Father; no power on earth could stop him. And if he could not fulfil it without first dying for it, then he would fulfil it by his resurrection from the dead!

7) The Visit of Nicodemus (Jn 3:1-4:3)

It thus came about that for security reasons Jesus never slept a night in the Holy City, but always withdrew at nightfall to Bethany on Mt Olivet. Here one evening after dark he was visited secretly by Nicodemus, a rabbi and a Pharisee who was also a member of the Sanhedrin. Nicodemus now confessed to him that the whole Sanhedrin knew that he was indeed a teacher come from God because of the many wonderful signs he had worked in the Temple. Jesus therefore took the opportunity to offer him some insights into the nature of the kingdom that he had been commissioned to establish.

As Nicodemus was an erudite student of the Scriptures Jesus tests him by solemnly addressing him with the words:

> Amen, amen, I say to you, unless a man be born again from above, he cannot see the Kingdom of God.

Jesus assumed that Nicodemus had got some notion of what he meant by this Kingdom of God; but in fact he had not got an inkling, as his reply showed: 'How can a man be born again when he is old? Can he enter a second time into his mother's womb and be born?'

One might have thought that Nicodemus would have grasped that the kingdom preached by John the Baptist was not an earthly nation state, since the only kind of passport required for it was the confession of one's sins and the firm intention, signified by baptism, of leading a good life in conformity with the Law of Moses. It is also fair to assume that Jesus himself must have already made it clear to his audiences in the

Temple that his Kingdom was no rival of, and posed no threat to, that of Caesar or even to the political theocracy in Israel. The new Kingdom is opposed to one thing only—to sin, which is opposition to God. The Kingdom of Jesus is a kingdom of the Spirit, and is as free as the air from earthly trammels. So he simply repeated more emphatically than before that everyone must be born again of water and the Holy Spirit, or he will not be able to enter the Kingdom of heaven. And when Nicodemus continued to demur, Jesus told him that he was not fit to be a teacher in Israel until he had learnt what it meant to be born of the Spirit; nor can Jesus begin to teach him 'heavenly things' since he does not even believe the earthly things that Jesus has told him. As we shall see, to aid Nicodemus and others like him, Jesus will soon invent for his Galilean listeners a great number of parables to illustrate different aspects of the Kingdom. But before letting him go, Jesus imparts a startling revelation and a fateful prophecy that provides the clue to the way in which the Kingdom will be set up. For he concluded the interview by the words: 'No one has ascended into heaven but he who descended from heaven, the Son of Man, who is in heaven. And as Moses lifted up the serpent in the wilderness, so must the Son of Man be lifted up, that whoever believes in him may have eternal life' (Jn 3:13 15).

This incident showed Jesus, that there was now no escape from the Cross, of which the bronze serpent is a type (Num 21:9); not only was the Council of Seventy determined to extinguish his ministry, but even the few men of good will within it were incapable of understanding his aims or of giving him any help at all. He was going to have a very hard time to find anyone to listen to him and to put their trust in him. He successfully overcame Satan in the wilderness; but finding men to work with him and willing to be formed by him was going to prove a far more arduous task. He was now on his own, with only his heavenly Father to support him. But he also knew that he had the strength of purpose and the fortitude to proceed along the path of sacrifice necessary for the attainment of his goal (Jn 3:34f).

For the next six months or so, Jesus, forced out of the Holy City, will be residing in the Judean countryside with his disciples, and waiting for a favourable moment to re-commence his mission (Jn 4:35). Jerusalem was the true heart of Israel and for his mission to succeed he must one day establish a firm foothold there, whatever the cost. An early return was now out of the question, for his life would be in danger. Meanwhile he must take all possible steps to broaden the basis of his support, and he accordingly set his disciples to continue the work of evangelisation in Judea while John the Baptist moved out of his way northwards to a place called Aenon in the territory of Herod Antipas. At one moment it had seemed possible that there might be a quarrel between the disciples of Jesus and those of John; but John relieved the tension by making it clear to both groups that Jesus is truly the Messiah and that he himself is merely the bridegroom's best man, so that 'He must increase and I must decrease' (Jn 3:30). John is confident that despite all the obstacles Jesus will succeed.

Summarizing the results of his first official visit to Jerusalem it would be no exaggeration to say that Jesus must have been bitterly disappointed and completely frustrated with the reception he received after having been so brilliantly heralded by John the Baptist. The long years of patient and silent preparation at Nazareth, the theophany at his baptism, his victory over Satan in the desert and the signs he had worked in the Holy City itself, had so far been in vain. From the purely human and pragmatic standpoint (and speaking from hindsight) one might argue that if only Jesus had stayed in Jerusalem at the time of his coming of age, he would have had friends among the ruling families, who would at least have allowed him a hearing. But of course, in that case he could never have endured to become part of that web of intrigue and self-interest, which the historian Josephus has so eloquently described in his history of *The Jewish War.*

How then did Jesus express his feelings when faced with this deadly hatred of all that he stood for? There are some verses at the end of the third chapter of John's Gospel which most scholars believe to be the meditation of the evangelist rather than words spoken by Jesus himself in the context of his exclusion from the corridors of power by the coldly calculating priesthood. However, these verses seem rather to mirror the working of the mind of Jesus and to articulate the sentiments he must have actually expressed in the presence of the custodians of the Temple, because they fit his predicament so exactly:

> He who comes from above is over all; he who is from the earth is from the earth, and from the earth he speaks. He who comes from above is above all. What he has beheld and heard, this he witnesses, and nobody accepts his witness. He who accepts the witness has attested that God is true. He therefore whom God has sent speaks the words of God, for God does not give the Spirit by measure. The Father loves the Son and has placed all things in his hand. He who believes in the Son has eternal life; he who does not obey the Son shall not see life; but the wrath of God remains upon him. (Jn 3:31-36)

From the first moment of his appearance in Jerusalem then, Jesus demanded faith in himself. Though sponsored by John the Baptist and commended by many signs, there he stood, a lone figure, with just his family and first disciples at his side, still visibly and truly a poor man, the carpenter from Nazareth, a man who had never had the specialist education to fit him to expound the Scriptures and to be a 'doctor in Israel', a man of the people with no political influence and no history of past achievement, an obscure man without property or connections, yet so clearly a man whom to know was to love. Deprived of the support of the very priests who should have been the first to welcome him, and unable therefore to minister in the Temple or in the Holy City, Jesus was forced to withdraw to the countryside of Judea where, as we have seen, he stayed for the remainder of that year. Even so he was not out of danger and towards the end of AD 28 he learnt that there was to be a fresh move against him as it became evident that he was attracting more disciples than the Baptist (Jn 4:1).

Furthermore, the news that John himself had been imprisoned by Herod Antipas in the grim castle of Machaerus on the eastern side of the Dead Sea, must have reinforced his decision to go back to his own native province where he hoped to be able to keep in contact with John in his prison. Galilee was a long way from Jerusalem, he would be less likely to be molested and he was assured of a friendly welcome from his native province. He would also be able to establish a base from which he could plan a return to Jerusalem when the moment seemed ripe. On this occasion he decided to pass through Samaria in order to avoid the tetrarchy of Herod Antipas.

8) The Samaritans welcome Jesus (Jn 4:5-42)

At this time there was very bad feeling between the Jews and the Samaritans. The Jews despised and disliked them as heretics and schismatics for refusing to worship at the Temple in Jerusalem and for setting up their own temple on Mt Gerizim, and for recognising only the Pentateuch among all the Old Testament books. The dislike was mutual and the two peoples would have nothing to do with each other. Furthermore there was also a cultural divide, for the Samaritans were of mixed blood, since in past centuries many of the Jewish inhabitants had been deported to Babylon, and pagan foreigners introduced in their place, and this had led to inter-marriage and the adulteration of the Jewish religion.

At Sychar, the ancient village of Shechem, some forty miles north of Jerusalem in Samaritan country, Jesus and his companions were resting on their way from Jerusalem to Galilee. Shechem nestles at the feet of two mountains held sacred by the Samaritans, Mt Ebal and Mt Gerizim, where at one time they had a rival temple. Within a mile of Shechem lies the piece of land which Jacob had given to Joseph more than a thousand years before; and where he had dug a deep well which is still functioning today, though now enclosed within a still unfinished church of the Greek rite. John is the evangelist who narrates the following story about Jesus' stay.

While the disciples had gone to Shechem to buy food, Jesus had remained alone seated by Jacob's well, for he was tired. While they were away a Samaritan woman from the village came up to draw water from the well. The time was midday, an unusual hour for a woman to come and draw water, but she would prove to be an unusual person anyway. Still more unusual was it for a Jewish rabbi to speak to any woman in public when alone; and to speak to a woman who was also a Samaritan was doubly shocking. Nevertheless Jesus at once opened up a conversation by requesting of her: 'Give me to drink'. She was quite taken aback and replied: 'Why do you, a Jew, ask me, a Samaritan woman, to give you a drink?' Jesus did not answer her question directly, because for him such distinctions as she mentioned were irrelevant, for he was entirely free of racial or social prejudice. As she offered him a drink from her bucket, he intrigued her by telling her that he can offer her Living Water in recompense. The uninhibited and even extravagant way in which he commends his own riches to her is quite amazing:

> If you had known the gift of God and who he is who is saying to you "Give me to drink", you would surely have asked him and he would have given you Living Water.

Already Jesus is initiating her into the mysteries of his grace by inviting her to ask for his bounty. She inquires:

> Sir, you've not got a bucket and the well is deep. Where then is this living water? Are you greater than our father Jacob, who gave us the well, and he himself drank from it and his sons and his cattle?

The woman is not only intelligent but greatly intrigued by his gracious advances and probes the meaning of his words as far as she can; if he can give her a stream of living water without any effort she would very much like to have it. So he draws her on by revealing that the water he is about to offer her has the quality of quenching all thirst and bestowing eternal life. Her reply is eager: 'Sir, give me this water, that I may not thirst nor keep coming here to draw'. She does not yet understand that he is talking in spiritual terms about supernatural grace; but she at once comments on the practical advantages of having a supply of water that would make it unnecessary for her ever to come back to the well!

Jesus has now got her really interested in what he has to

offer; but the conversation has gone on long enough for him to recall the recognised proprieties. So he abruptly changes the subject to her personal life by saying: 'Go and call your husband and come here', because this will give him the opportunity to let her know that her soul is an open book to him.

When she replied 'I have no husband', she was speaking the truth, but not the whole truth; and as the Good Shepherd he wants her to lay bare to him her present way of life to receive his healing grace. His next words reveal his full insight into her heart: 'You have well said: "I have no husband." For you have had five husbands, and the one you now have is not your husband. What you have said is true'. The woman takes this riposte without quailing. She certainly has a steady nerve! And instead of bursting out into protestations of one kind or another, she calmly swallows the accusation and uses it to confirm her opinion that Jesus is a true prophet, and swiftly decides to turn the conversation into another channel by asking a question then hotly disputed between the Jews and the Samaritans, in the hope that he can really settle it! She says: 'I perceive, Sir, that you are a prophet. Now our fathers worshipped on this mountain, and you say that in Jerusalem is the place where one must worship...'. Again he more than fulfils her expectation. He addresses her formally in his teaching capacity to inform her about the new spiritual era that will remove all barriers between Jews and Samaritans and between Jews and Gentiles. Salvation, he tells her, will come to all through the opening up of a revitalized Judaism to all nations:

> Believe me, O woman, that the hour is coming when neither on this mountain nor in Jerusalem will you worship the Father. You worship what you do not know, we worship what we know, because salvation is from the Jews. But an hour is coming, and now is, when the true worshippers will worship the Father in spirit and in truth; for indeed the Father seeks such people as his worshippers. God is Spirit, and those who worship him must worship in spirit and in truth.

Jesus has not minced his words; not only are the Samaritans ignorant and wrong and their worship divisive; but Jesus also

prophesies that the new development of Judaism will super-
sede even the Temple in Jerusalem. She realises that she is now
out of her depth, and sensibly replies: 'I know that the Messiah
is coming, and when he comes he will announce to us all things'.
The Samaritans, like the Jews, were waiting for the Messiah
to come and reveal all truth and straighten out all problems and
reunite all men under the one Lord God of Israel. The woman
for all her sinful ways, knows her Samaritan faith thoroughly,
and is content to wait on God's Providence for a final solution.
Nevertheless Jesus does her an extraordinary and indeed unique favour by now personally revealing to her that he himself is
the Messiah, seeing that she is ready to accept his word for it. So
he gently says to her: 'I am, he who is speaking to you'. The
woman must have been astounded, and she stood there silent
and transfixed by the implications of what she has just heard.
And then suddenly the silence was broken as the disciples of
Jesus came round the corner and saw him chatting with her.
The sight surprised and embarrassed them but they said nothing to him out of respect, though they wondered why he had
been speaking to her. Then the woman, leaving her water pot
behind, raced back to the village in order to announce to the
men in the market square that she had found the Messiah!

When the woman had gone and the disciples had recovered
from their embarrassment, they pressed him to eat something.
His reply mystified them: 'I have food to eat which you do not
know'. They were still very much in awe of him, and dared not
question him directly, and secretly wondered if the woman had
brought him anything to eat. After they had ruminated on his
statement and been unable to fathom it, he volunteered an explanation, which they never forgot:

> My food is to do the will of him who sent me, and to accomplish his
> work. Do you not say, "Yet four months and the harvest comes"? Lo,
> I say to you. Raise up your eyes and behold the fields, that they are
> white to the harvest. The harvester receives a wage and gathers up
> the produce for eternal life, so that both the sower and the harvester
> may rejoice together. For in this is the word true that there is the
> one who sows and the one who harvests. I have sent you to harvest

what you have not laboured for; others have laboured and you have entered into their labour.

These encouraging words fired the disciples with enthusiasm to begin their apostolic work, as Jesus was prophesying that despite the setback in Jerusalem and Judea there were countless millions in the Gentile world waiting eagerly to receive and to absorb his teaching. Moreover his disciples would one day enjoy the fruits of the labours of past heroes of ancient Israel, who had laboured in faith without seeing any apparent result. They would go out and reap the harvest that others before them had sown. And these heretical Samaritans, just now returning with the woman, represented, in fact, the first fruits of his ministry. The men of Shechem there and then begged him to remain with them, and he agreed to break his journey for two days in order to teach them. The effect on these citizens of Shechem was amazing; they remarked to the woman: 'No longer do we believe because of what you said about him; for we have heard him and we know that he is truly the Saviour of the world'. Later in his ministry Jesus was to recall sadly how much more receptive of his message were these despised Samaritans than his fellow countrymen. Their welcome had been a good augury for the future world-wide mission of his disciples, and it was to be hoped that the simple folk of Galilee would be equally welcoming.

6

The First Phase of the Galilean Ministry

1) The Healing of a Court Official's Son (Jn 4:43-54)

In returning to the district where he had lived ever since his childhood, Jesus was coming back to familiar territory and to people whom he knew well and who knew him well or who at least thought that they did. It seems that the Galileans had been greatly impressed by the many wonderful signs that he had worked during his appearance at the previous Passover in Jerusalem some eight months before. They also knew that the chief priests and the Sanhedrin had definitely refused to recognise his credentials to be the Messiah and that he had kept a rather low profile ever since. We find him first at Cana where his mother probably had some relatives and where he had previously worked his first miracle, the turning of the water into wine. Thus they were well disposed to receive him and were hoping for many more miracles.

News of his arrival soon reached Capharnaum some twenty kilometres away, and one of Herod Antipas' officials who lived there decided to rush up to Cana to beg Jesus to heal his son who was dying. It took him the greater part of a day to make the long ascent high up into the hill country. When he eventually arrived and appealed to Jesus, he met with what seemed an unexpected rebuff. Jesus disliked being thought of as a sort of magician or wonder-worker and said to the crowds in general:

'Unless you see signs and wonders you will not believe.' However the official refused to be put off by these words and continued to implore him to come down and heal his son. Jesus simply said to him: 'Go, your son lives'. The father believed that his son had been cured and stayed overnight in Cana. Next morning on his way back to Capharnaum his servants met him on the road and he learned about the cure and that it had taken place at the very moment that Jesus had spoken to him, namely at the seventh hour on the previous day. As a result the official and all his family at once converted to the Lord. This is the first recorded miracle that Jesus worked at a distance without seeing or knowing the recipient.

2) The first Visit to Nazareth (Lk 4:16f; cf. Mt 13:53f = Mk 6:1f)

Luke however informs us that, at an early stage in his first tour of Galilee, Jesus visited his home town of Nazareth; indeed the exegetes think that Luke has combined two separate visits into one. They surmise that early on there was a first visit to the town, followed by one somewhat later when its citizens got so angry with him that they tried to lynch him. Both visits deserve our attention.

The problem that Jesus had to face was how to introduce himself to his fellow-citizens who had only known him as a quiet and retiring member of the local community. Human nature being what it is, it was going to prove difficult for them to accept the new authority that his messianic role gave him. But out of a sense of loyalty to the town in which he had grown up he gave them the privilege of being the first Galileans to hear his message. So he went as usual to the synagogue on the Sabbath. During the service there were as a rule two readings; the first was prescribed according to the calendar, but the second was at the discretion of the invited speaker. His fame had gone before him and his miracles and his Cleansing-of-the-Temple episode were very much in the minds of the congregation. So they invited him to read the second lesson. When the attendant handed him the scroll of Isaiah, he chose the passage which aptly foretold and described the mission which he had already begun and which he was now about to bring to the notice of his fellow citizens of Nazareth. He unrolled the scroll until he came to these words:

> The Spirit of the Lord is upon me, because he has anointed me;
> to evangelize the poor he has sent me,
> to preach release to the captives
> and restoration of sight to the blind,
> to release those who have been crushed,
> to preach the acceptable year of the Lord. (Is 61:1-2)

And when he sat down to teach, the eyes of all in the synagogue were fixed upon him intently. And he said to them: 'Today this Scripture has been fulfilled in your ears'. For, by quoting this passage which is so clearly a reference to the Messiah, Jesus was identifying himself as that person. This was of course a great shock to the listeners, though their first reaction was to marvel at the words of grace with which he developed this theme of his messiahship. However, they could not reconcile this new role of his with the fact that he had hitherto been known only as the son of Joseph the carpenter. In the days and weeks that followed this sermon, opinion in the village changed; it simply could not be true that he was what he claimed to be; they knew him and his family too well. He might be either mad or an impostor. His next visit was to prove calamitous (see chapter 8.10 below).

3) Jesus at Capharnaum (Mt 4:13f = Mk 1:14f)

Nazareth, his native village, was thus no place to make his headquarters for his evangelical mission in Galilee. With his mother, friends and disciples he left Nazareth without delay and took up residence in Capharnaum, a fishing village in the midst of the plain of Gennesaret, on the north-western shore of the lake. Its location was suitable as a centre for his mission, as a glance at the map will show. Its road communications were good, for they ran north and south, and west to the furthest extremities of the province. The evangelist Matthew exults to tell us that by making this town the centre of his mission to Galilee Jesus was actually fulfilling another special prophecy of Isaiah:

Land of Zebulon and land of Naphthali, Way of the Sea, Across the Jordan, Galilee of the Gentiles. The people that sat in darkness saw a great light, and for those that sat in the region and shadow of death, for them a light rose up. (Is 9:1-2)

During this first phase in Galilee Jesus was not molested by his enemies in Jerusalem; and he was able to proclaim without friction or interruption his message: 'Repent, for the Kingdom of the heavens is at hand'. Within the space, it seems, of less than two months, 'his fame went out at once everywhere into the whole region of Galilee, so that', as Mark relates (1:45), 'he was no longer able to go openly into a town but he was outside in desert places'. Of this period, the evangelists record only a few incidents but they are most instructive ones.

4) An Unclean Spirit expelled (Lk 4:33f = Mk 1:23f)

Perhaps the first impact Jesus made on the citizens of Capharnaum was when he healed a demoniac in the synagogue on the Sabbath. This man had 'an unclean spirit' and called out to him: 'What have we to do with you, Jesus the Nazarene? Have you come to destroy us? I know you, who you are, the Holy One of God'. This demon was not only trying to disconcert him and spoil the effect of his teaching by rousing local jealousies, but was at the same time unwillingly confessing his Messiahship. But Jesus neither needed nor desired the witness of the demons whom he had come precisely to dispossess, and he rebuked this demon sharply, saying: 'Be silent and go out of him'. And the Devil went out of the man instantly in a great commotion. And all present in the synagogue were amazed at the power of his word and the authority with which he commanded the instant obedience of evil spirits.

5) Jesus at Simon's House (Lk 4:38f = Mk 1:29f)

Luke tells us that at the conclusion of the service Jesus went straight from the synagogue to the house of Simon and Andrew, with James and John. He had already met the first two a year before when they were disciples of John the Baptist, whilst the second pair were their business partners. They were now close friends of his, and they had no hesitation in asking him to cure Peter's mother-in-law who was in the house and seriously ill. At the touch of his hand the fever left her and she was able straightway to rise and take care of their needs. As it was the Sabbath on which these two healings had been done, Jesus now rested quietly in the house for the remainder of the day. But at sunset his peace and theirs was abruptly disturbed by the arrival at the door of all the local sick and those possessed by demons; indeed the whole town, excited by the healing of the demoniac, gathered outside, and Jesus going out laid his hand on each one of them and healed them all. And again the demons started to declare him to be the Son of God; but he immediately silenced them, for while they knew indeed that he was the Christ, they were from the other world and had made their choice against him before our world began. He had come to redeem this world and he wanted his own people and not the demons to recognize him.

That night Jesus slept in Peter's house;[18] and very early the next morning he rose before dawn and went out away from all habitation to pray to his heavenly Father. No sooner was his absence noticed than Simon Peter and those with him set out in pursuit and quickly tracked him down to tell him that the whole neighbourhood was looking for him. His reply revealed that he knew exactly what he was doing and what he had yet to do—namely, not to stay and enjoy his success, for his duty was to go and preach the Kingdom of God to the other towns of Galilee as well.

6) The Miraculous Catch of Fish (Lk 5:1-11)

Before Jesus set out on this first preaching tour of Galilee, he took another step towards setting up the new kingdom. Great crowds had converged on the little town of Capharnaum, and in order to be able to address them without upsetting either the townsfolk or the country-people by trampling over their land, he went down to the lake-shore. Seeing his friends Peter and

---

18 Archaeologists are now confident that they have discovered Peter's house between the synagogue and the sea-shore at Capharnaum.

Andrew, with James and John, getting their nets ready to go fishing, he asked Peter to launch the boat and anchor it a short distance off the shore so that he could speak to his audience from it. As soon as he had finished speaking, he said to Peter, 'Put out into the deep and lower your nets for a catch'. Peter was astonished at this request, because he and his partner Andrew had been out fishing all the previous night and had caught nothing. Both had had long experience of the lake and were sure that it would be useless to go out again that morning. Jesus knew it too when he gave the order, but it was for a special purpose. By this time Peter was coming to trust him and knew that he did not utter such a command without good reason. Nevertheless it still required a great act of faith in Jesus to stifle his doubts and obey the order, saying, 'Master, we toiled through the night and caught nothing; but at your word I will lower the nets'. And having done so, they at once enclosed a great quantity of fish, so great indeed that their nets were on the point of breaking. And they signalled to their partners James and John who had followed them out in the other boat to come and help them. And they came and filled both boats with so great a weight of fish that both boats were in danger of sinking as they brought them back to land. They were all amazed at the size of the catch, and Peter was so overwhelmed that he could do nothing but throw himself at the feet of Jesus, and mutter, 'Depart from me, O Lord, for I am a sinful man'. Jesus' reply, 'Come after me, and I will make you catchers of living men', changed the whole pattern of Peter's life and that of his partners. Without a moment's delay all four of them left their boats and followed him, Zebedee's sons leaving their father and the rest of his employees. We do not hear of the reaction of Zebedee at the loss of these two sons of his at the same time; but the miracle of the catch and the proceeds resulting from it must have sweetened the sacrifice that he had to make.

These four were the first to be invited to become his disciples and it is significant that they were all fishermen. During the time of their probation he will personally conduct their spiritual formation and teach them to forsake not only all earthly gain and prestige, but also to rely on God's providence to provide for them all the necessaries of life and everything required for the success of their apostolate. For Jesus himself was already setting them the example of relying entirely on God's providence for every human need; he himself had forsaken his home at Nazareth and his occupation as an engineer-carpenter in order to devote himself full time to the foundation of the Kingdom of God his Father. At a later stage of his ministry he will bring their number up to twelve and these will be the actual founders of his Church.

7) The Healing of a Jewish Leper (Mt 8:1f = Lk 5:12 = Mk 1:40f)

The Gospels note one further miracle that took place during this first missionary tour of Galilee, the cleansing of a Jewish leper (Mk 1:40-45). The fame of Jesus had grown so rapidly and so extensively that even the lepers, the outcasts of society, had by now heard of him. And one of them even dared to enter a town in which Jesus happened to be, and kneeling before him, begged him, saying, 'Lord, if you will, you can cleanse me'. The poor man was, it seems, a hideous sight; he was 'full of leprosy', and Jesus was moved with compassion for him and touched him with his hand, and instantly his leprosy was healed. For a Jew to touch a leper was to make himself at once ritually unclean for a whole week; but as the body of Jesus was holiness itself the touch of his hand, on the contrary, far from contaminating him, instantly healed the recipient and made him perfectly clean too. At the same time Jesus told the leper to obey the command of the Law to show himself to the priests of the Temple, whose duty it was to certify the cure of leprosy and to re-admit the person to the community. It is to be noted that Jesus insisted that the former leper should respect the authority of the priests and adhere strictly to protocol, because the Old Law had not yet been updated by the New Covenant that Jesus would soon seal in his own blood by his death and resurrection. He also told the man not to brag about his cure but to keep silent about it, for the simple reason that many of the people were coming to value his signs and wonders much more than his message. In addition the crowds were now becoming so great that his movements about the country were being seriously impeded, and he found himself forced to stay outside the towns in order not to inconvenience their inhabitants.

At the end of this first tour Jesus appears to have thought that the time was ripe for another visit to Jerusalem and for a further attempt to win acceptance for his mission from the chief priests and the Sanhedrin.

8) *Jesus at the Feast of Purim (Jn 5)*

Purim was a feast that commemorated the deliverance of the Jews from a plot to exterminate them during their exile in Babylon some six centuries earlier.[19] It took place on 14-15 Adar, that is, some time during February or March. Although the event it commemorates is graphically described in the Book of Esther, it was a secular occasion rather than a religious one. There was certainly no obligation to go up to Jerusalem for it, and it had no place in the list of official Jewish feasts. It was somewhat in the nature of the old-fashioned carnival, but this is no reason for assuming that Jesus did not take advantage of it to visit the Holy City again. Yet as the following story shows, the Temple authorities had no inkling that this was what he intended to do. The date of this feast—early spring—fits very well the order of events that we find in the Gospel of St John. Time was passing, indeed almost a year had gone by since the cleansing of the Temple that had so upset the high priesthood, and Jesus had made no progress at all towards winning over the key personnel in Jerusalem to his plan to establish the new kingdom. There can be no doubt that he was eager again to draw the attention of the Temple rulers to himself in order to insist on their submission to his authority. And this is how he ar-

---

19 Some scholars still hold that this feast was the Passover, in which case there would have been four Passovers in the course of the public life of Jesus. But the view taken here has more support. Also the year 29 was, it seems, the year in which an extra month was inter-calated, so that Purim was probably kept twice in 29 and Jesus' visit would then have been in Adar rather than Ve-Adar (the inter-calated month).

ranged the confrontation.

At that time there was a new district growing up on the rising land outside the city wall to the north of the Temple; it seems to have been called Bethzatha. On it there was a large rectangular man-made pool having five porticos, one on each of the four sides and one across the middle. It was the regular haunt of a large number of sick and crippled persons because of a popular belief that occasionally, and at unexpected moments, the waters of the pool would be disturbed by an angel of the Lord, and that the first person to jump into it after the moving of the water would be healed of his infirmity.

On his arrival at Jerusalem, Jesus quietly walked into the enclosure, which was packed with these pitiable sufferers waiting patiently for the moving of the water. No interest was taken in his arrival, for he was unknown to them since they had not been in the Temple during his great demonstration the year before. So far as we know he spoke to nobody except to a crippled man who had already suffered his infirmity for no less than thirty-eight years. Through his prophetic knowledge Jesus knew the whole history of this man, singling him out from among the mass of bruised humanity lying there, and saying to him, 'Do you wish to be made whole?'—Surely a curious question, given the man's long history of illness! Perhaps it was because the man had resigned himself to a profound despair and Jesus wanted him first to will his own cure. In any case his reply was matter-of-fact enough: 'Sir, I have no one, when the water is troubled, to throw me into the pool; for while I am coming another goes down before me'. Jesus laconically replied: 'Get up; take your pallet and walk'. And the man got up at once and walked off entirely cured.

Now it happened to be the Sabbath, and the rules for behaviour on the Sabbath had in course of time become extremely strict, and in the crowded city there were plenty of busybodies around who would take delight in reporting every infringement to the Temple authorities, with the pious intention of keeping the Holy City uncontaminated. The healed man, whose name is unknown to us, was quickly rounded up and questioned closely why he was breaking the Sabbath by carrying through the City the pallet on which he had been lying. His defence was quite simple. He said: 'The man who made me whole said to me, Take up your bed and walk'. The Mishnaic tract *Sabbath* (7:2; 10:5) has a list of 39 works forbidden to Jews on the Sabbath, and most of them were probably in force in Jesus' day. What is certain is that Jesus knew all about the existing regulations and for his own good reasons deliberately meant to make the paralytic infringe this scribal addition to the Law!

We must remember that the Law of Moses itself was only a provisional document despite its thousand years of history and the veneration of the Jews. It had been the chief means of preserving not only their national identity but also their loyalty to the God who had delivered them from their slavery in Egypt. Loyalty to the Law was fine, but now at last the Anointed Prince had come, their Messiah, who had the authority to update this Law and make definitive adjustments to it. Among other changes, he would now so modify its provisions that the Gentiles would find nothing to put them off from asking for admission into the Kingdom. And in the command given to this paralytic we see the Christ taking a small but decisive step in the fashioning of the new order. In the first place he is showing that works of mercy should always take precedence over man-made regulations. More importantly he is asserting that he himself is the Law-Giver. Moses received the Old Law from the hands of Almighty God, but here we have Jesus assuming the role of the divine re-moulder of the Law, by exactly determining what is the 'work' that can be done on the Sabbath. In the course of the exchange with the Jews that now followed Jesus revealed that, like his heavenly Father, he never ceased to work and thus proclaimed his equality with the Father, the Lord of the Sabbath.

In response to a further question from the rulers the man acknowledged that he did not know the identity of his healer, for Jesus had withdrawn as unobtrusively as he had entered. And if he was grateful to him for being cured, he did not show it, and indeed seems to have been on the point of resuming his former sinful habits. Nevertheless some time later Jesus found him in the Temple and gave him this warning: 'See, you have been made whole; sin no more lest a worse thing befall you'. Jesus did not reveal what his secret sin was, and the only visible reaction of the man was to go off and tell the Jews that it was Jesus who had cured him. They were very pleased at this news because it now gave them for the first time the opportunity to represent him as a law-breaker; and if he was a law-breaker, then, they argued, he could not possibly be the Messiah, for the Messiah, as God's plenipotentiary, was by definition sinless. And so we shall find that from this time onwards 'the Jews', that is to say, those responsible for the nation's religious policy, made a special point of attacking him for working cures on the Sabbath.

But this was not the end of the matter so far as Jesus was concerned; for this question of what was or was not to be classified as work on the Sabbath, the Lord's day of rest, gave him the chance to explain that the basis of his authority was his relationship with his heavenly Father. When the Jews taxed him with this violation, he replied: 'My Father is at work up to the present, and I too am at work'. Far from quailing at this accusation of breaking the Sabbath, Jesus responded by making it clear that the Lord God who established the Sabbath was also his Father and that he was working with him on a perfect equality. God is always at work and while keeping everything in existence and supporting all human activity, is yet entirely self-contained. It was therefore ridiculous to accuse him of breaking the Sabbath; they were only able to make this accusation because of their deliberate and total blindness to the nature of the person standing before them. The most brilliant minds in the Jewish world were concentrated in the law school of the Temple; and they rightly understood him to claim equality with God the Father. They also believed that for a man to arrogate divine sonship was technically a 'profanation of the Holy One' and a blasphemy. The Jesus of Nazareth who stood fearlessly before them, so courageous and so firm and yet so humble and meek, did not conform to their idea of the Messiah, even though he had had the backing of the saintly John the Baptist and the many extraordinary signs that he had wrought. The truth was that they were not ready for the coming of the Messiah and could not accept him because their lives were worldly and sinful.

Yet the Temple in which he stood and in which he confronted the leaders of the establishment' was actually his Father's House, and it was his destiny to explain his position and authority to them, whether they would ultimately be willing to accept it or not. It was his task to bear witness and to proclaim the message that had been given him by his heavenly Father until either he succeeded in convincing them or they succeeded in eliminating him, as they had now made up their minds to do. But he would use all his eloquence to help them see the truth of his position.

In addressing them now Jesus has to overcome the two great obstacles that the chief priests have about recognising him as the Messiah. First of all, the Lord God of Israel is totally invisible and not even Moses or Elijah could see him with the eyes of the flesh; and yet there is Jesus of Nazareth claiming equality with God! Secondly, they were tenacious and covetous of their wealth, power, and prestige, and the thought of handing the source of it all to this Galilean peasant was utterly repellent. He therefore sets out to explain to them why he is what he is, and why he cannot act otherwise than he is now doing. The reason for the union of the Father and the Son is the infinite love that they have for each other. This love is life-giving, and the Son gives this life to whomsoever he wills. And since the Son has now been sent down by the Father to the world and been given power to act in the Father's name, it is essential for all human beings to honour the Son in the same way as they have in the past honoured the Father. Hence failure to honour the Son will involve the loss of the eternal life that the Son is bringing. Because he and his Father are inseparable, though distinct persons, those who dishonour him equally dishonour his Father, the Lord God (Jn 5:19-23).

He then proceeds to stress the vital necessity of listening to him and of believing in him in order to possess eternal life, which cannot be obtained in any other way. The time will soon come when he, Jesus, will judge the living and the dead; and then he will lead those who believe in him into the resurrection of life, while the others will go into condemnation. They have no alternative but to accept what he says as the truth, because he has been sent by God himself (Jn 5:24-30).

In the next section of his discourse Jesus declares that there had been ample witness of his *bona fides,* although he did not need any human witness. All the same he has had the witness of his heavenly Father and the witness of John the Baptist—whom he has described as 'a shining light'. But the Jewish caucus had adroitly rejected all this witness 'because the love of God was not in them'. They were blind because they did not want either to see or to listen. They were also too blind to perceive that the sacred scriptures bore continuous witness to him. 'You refuse to come to me', he said, 'that you may have life'. In rejecting him they were rejecting life with him in glory (Jn 5:31-40).

In the final section of the discourse Jesus attacks the Jews for their stubborn rejection of him and his authority. They seek their own glory and not that of his Father. Moses himself, whose spiritual sons they claim to be, will accuse them for this crime. If they really believed Moses' words about him, they ought surely to believe in him. Jesus' peroration must be quoted in full because of its passionate depth of feeling:

> I do not receive glory from men, but I have known you that you have not the love of God in yourselves. I have come in the name of my Father, and you do not receive me; if another comes in his own name, him you will receive. How can you believe when you receive glory from one another, but the glory belonging to the only God you do not seek? Do not suppose that I shall accuse you to the Father; Moses is the one who accuses you, in whom you continue to hope. For if you believed Moses, you would surely believe me; for he wrote about me. For if you do not believe the writings of the latter, how will you believe my words? (Jn 5:41-47)

With this plain speaking Jesus tears aside the veil of hypocrisy which they have set up in order to justify their refusal to accept him. He is speaking within the precincts of his Father's House to inform them that he accepts none of their excuses. All the signs that Moses and the other prophets had predicted concerning him have been fulfilled, yet they continue to treat him as if he were a false messiah and a person of no significance. The only weapons the Messiah possesses are the utterance of the truth and a forthright appeal to all Jews of good will; he will never use force like former political messiahs. The men now in power in the Jewish priesthood, supported by the majority of the scribes, Pharisees and Sadducees, are not listening to him, because they are consumed with self-love, with the love of their own glory; so they hold on to their power in the only way they know, with lies aided by physical force. Although they hold the authority of God through their position as his priests, they are hypocrites. The historic moment to hand over their power to the Messiah has come, and they are too venal and too proud to do so. Despite the indications of the Scriptures, they are unwilling to acknowledge that God could approach his people so humbly as to send his Messiah in the guise of a theologically untutored citizen of Nazareth, a mere Galilean artisan. The moment for submission has come and gone, but even now it is not too late for them to acknowledge their sin of rejecting him and accept a chance to retrace their steps.

We may be sure that the passionate eloquence of Jesus must have moved the hearts of many of the theologians who listened to him on this occasion, but it had no effect on the stony-hearted inner circle who continued to maintain a brazen front against him. The fact that Jesus would never take 'No' for an answer may have been borne in on them at this time; for they will now take steps without delay to monitor his movements in his own native Galilee and to stir up trouble for him with Herod Antipas, the ruler of that region.

Thus his second attempt to secure recognition in the Holy City and in his own Temple has proved to be vain. The grip of the authorities on the daily life of the Jerusalem community is too great for him to overcome; he has no alternative but to return to Galilee where he has hitherto been free to preach without molestation.

9) Jesus' Mission faces Failure

This is a convenient place to stop for a moment in order to reflect on the progress of the mission of Jesus down to this point. In worldly terms it appeared very far from a success. In fact, he had achieved no part of his main aim, which was to receive from the hands of the Jewish high priesthood—still representing the authority of the Lord God—the full recognition of his spiritual authority over them and over the whole Temple complex. The failure of his visit to the Holy City at the feast of Purim clearly manifested their resolve not to accept him on any terms whatsoever. The blackness of this picture is of course a little relieved by the success of his first preaching in Galilee, and by his gaining a number of disciples from the locality. Unlike previous claimants to the messiahship, he had ruled out all use of force in the pursuit of his claim. He was no rabble-raiser, though if he had wanted to use force, he could by his eloquence have had the whole nation enthusiastically behind him; he was not going to be a political Warrior-Messiah, the only kind so far experienced by the chief priests and Pharisees. On the contrary, he was a man of peace, and when thwarted his policy was simply to appeal to reason and sound sense; and, if still ignored, to restate his case and issue a warning of the consequences of refusing him obedience. But while showing loving kindness to both friend and foe, he never withdrew one jot of his demand for their total submission to his authority. None could escape from the necessity of making a personal act of faith in him or rejecting him outright.

His first demonstration had been to proclaim his authority over the House of his Father by driving the buyers and sellers out of the Temple precincts, at the same time filling all the bystanders with awe at his majesty. When compelled by the threat of force to withdraw from Judea, after a short but unexpectedly successful visit to Samaria, he had re-entered Galilee, where he created sensation after sensation by his wonderful and beneficent signs—for he freed men from the degradation of possession by devils, cured illnesses and disabilities of every kind by his word and touch alone. In short, he went about doing nothing but good. Yet the Jerusalem authorities still remained totally opposed to him and refused to relent. And because they refused to give him any opening, he had to fashion his own opportunities for asserting the rightful position that they denied him.

Jesus knew better than anybody that the success of his mission ultimately depended on what happened in the Holy City; for Isaiah had prophesied that 'out of Zion shall go forth the Law, and the Word of the Lord from Jerusalem' (Is 2:3), and this prophecy had yet to be fulfilled. And this is why he brought himself to the attention of the Jews by deliberately healing a cripple on the Sabbath and by ordering the man to break one of the strict scribal regulations imposed on the people to help them to keep it better. The result was this head-on clash with scribes, Pharisees and priests, because he maintained his right and freedom to negate any of these regulations he thought fit. The immediate reaction of the Temple authorities—they are nearly always anonymous figures in the Gospels—was to set in motion a steady and relentless persecution. They realized that he was not going to let himself be suppressed or set aside; and so they will now proceed to follow him down to Galilee in order to circumscribe and, if possible, stultify his ministry there. Agents and spies were now to be sent down to dog his steps in town and country, and to monitor and to harass him whenever and wherever possible. They would try to denigrate him in various ways by accusing him of being lax over fasting, of associating with the detested tax collectors and of breaking the Sabbath rest and even of invoking Satan for his cures, matters which seem petty to us, but which in the eyes of the Pharisees were considered important. Nevertheless during the phase of his Galilean ministry, which we are now about to chronicle, Jesus refused to let his ministry of preaching and healing be either curtailed or intimidated. In fact he appeared almost to revel in the challenge which led him to disclose a further messianic power, as when in the healing of the paralytic he revealed and proved his authority to forgive sins.

7

The Second Phase of the Galilean Ministry

1) The Healing of a Paralytic (Mt 9:1f = Lk 5:17f = Mk 2:1f)

When Jesus re-entered Galilee after the feast of Purim, he soon had ocular proof that the Pharisees and the emissaries of the high priestly family were not taking his challenge lightly, but were in fact taking immediate steps to circumscribe his progress even in his own native province. For Mark relates that when 'after some days' he returned to Capharnaum and people learned that he had come home, Pharisees and law-teachers foregathered to listen to him not only from every village of Galilee but also from Judea and even from Jerusalem. It seems very probable that the critical and hostile element in his audience consisted of those who had come down from Jerusalem. Indeed during the remainder of his Galilean ministry he was never to be free from their surveillance and carping criticism. Mark and Luke now record a series of five clashes with these learned men who did their utmost to belittle and denigrate him in the eyes of his hearers, though with remarkably little success.

Mark reports that the house was crammed to the doors with a crowd from all over Galilee, including emissaries of the Sanhedrin from Jerusalem, who for very varied reasons had come to listen to his spiritual teaching. While he was still speaking the Word, there was a sound of thuds and scratching on the roof,

which consisted of dry turves laid on wooden beams. Fragments
of earth began to fall down onto the floor in the space in front of
him, and then the sky appeared above as someone started to
remove some of the beams laid loosely from wall to wall. And
then while all gazed thunderstruck a stretcher was seen in the
opening and a paralysed man was lowered to the ground at his
feet. Jesus waited patiently, and then seeing the faces of the
four bearers in the opening above and greatly moved by their
faith, which brooked no obstacle, said to the paralysed man: 'My
son, your sins are forgiven'. The text does not tell us whether
this paralytic or his bearers had sought out Jesus for the sake of
a physical healing or whether he himself was, in fact,
desperately seeking spiritual help. On the other hand he may
not have been particularly enthusiastic at being carted up on to
the roof and lowered down through it like a bundle of hay! Indeed our Gospel accounts imply that the man's sins were forgiven not on account of his own faith but on account of the faith
of his four persevering bearers.

Jesus' words of forgiveness shocked the scribes and Pharisees
in the audience; they could not believe their ears. Being trained
theologians they started to murmur among themselves that his
speech was blasphemous, since God alone can forgive sins. But
Jesus knew the inmost state of this poor sick man's conscience,
and seeing that the man himself also had some sorrow for his
sins, deliberately uttered those words in his profound understanding. His utterance was, of course, a challenge to his
enemies, for he was now about to give such a sign of his power as
no man of good will could either ignore or fail to acknowledge.

> Then Jesus, perceiving in his spirit that they were thus questioning
> in themselves, said to them, 'Why do you question these things in
> your hearts? Which is easier—to say to this man, "Your sins are for-
> given", or to say, "Get up, and take away your pallet and walk?" But
> that you may know that the Son of Man has authority to forgive sins
> upon earth (He says to the paralytic) I say to you, Get up, take away
> your pallet and go off into your own house. (Mk 2:8-12)

And the man did as he was told and at once got up and walked
out in front of them all. By this miracle Jesus publicly

demonstrated his power to forgive sins, a power that belongs to God alone and proved his unique relationship to the God of their Fathers. The crowd was amazed and the opposition was rendered speechless.

2) The Call of Levi [Matthew] (Mt 9:9f = Lk 5:27f = Mk 2:13f)

Jesus was still in process of inviting selected individuals to come and join his intimate circle and 'family' of disciples in Capharnaum, the centre of his operations in Galilee. One of the most important men there was Matthew (otherwise known as Levi), but he was ostracised by all strict Jews because he belonged to the hated class whose task it was to collect taxes and tolls on behalf of Herod Antipas, the much disliked ruler of Galilee. Jesus had decided that he wanted Matthew in the apostolic body he was going to create and had summed him up as one suitable to become his follower. By inviting Matthew to join him, Jesus caused a great sensation in the town because it emphasised his rejection of the Pharisaic distinction between unclean and clean occupations and showed that he was free from contemporary social and political prejudices. Matthew would have had plenty of time and opportunity in the preceding weeks to observe Jesus' demeanour, but in joining him he also realized that he was leaving behind all worldly security and by a blind act of faith entrusting himself and his future to a man, whose destiny was still obscure. However, Matthew had no doubt whatever of the rightness of his action, and joyfully celebrated it by inviting not only Jesus and his disciples but also his tax collector friends to a banquet. And because Matthew was a public figure, the Pharisees and their scribes were able to come in and chat with the guests; which they did with the intent of sowing dissension between Jesus and his disciples. They were murmuring to them: 'Why does your Master eat with tax collectors and sinners?' Jesus overheard their grumbling and sharply replied in the hearing of all: 'The healthy have no need of a healer but those who are ill. I have not come to call the just but sinners to repentance'. That is to say, his true followers were those who acknowledged their sinfulness and their need for forgiveness and who then relied on God for strength to leave their old ways.

3) A Question about Fasting (Mt 9:14f = Lk 5:33f = Mk 2:18f)

In another incident about that time the same group of critics, the Pharisees, openly remarked that his disciples neither fasted nor prayed to the same extent as those of John, thus implying that not merely were they slack by comparison but that the blame thereof rested with Jesus himself. His reply revealed that he not only approved of his disciples' behaviour but positively commended it. And his reason was striking. He was the Bridegroom and they were his 'best men' ('the sons of the bridechamber'). Since his time with them was going to be short, it had to be a time of intense rejoicing, and fasting would be quite inappropriate. But then he also made the prophecy, that he would be taken away from them and that then they 'would indeed fast in those days', which indicated he was fully conscious of his destiny and of the fact that he was soon going to be cruelly torn from them. Meanwhile they were to make the most of his presence among them. However it is clear that this oblique reference to his passion went entirely unnoticed at the time even by his disciples.

It was the contempt of the Pharisees for his disciples that stung Jesus into their defence. He told them that the current Jewish regime was played out, that it was too rigid and too decrepit to be able to meet his requirements. They were like old wine skins that were cracked and incapable of meeting new demands, and like old clothes not worth patching up. For the new kingdom he required new men capable of undertaking new tasks; they were to be like new wine skins, able to hold the strong ferment of a fresh vintage, and like new cloth made for hard wear that cannot be joined to old. And his new men were entitled to rejoice now because of their association with him and because he knew that they would be courageous enough to meet the exacting times that would follow his departure.

4) 'Working' on the Sabbath (Mt 12:1f = Lk 6:1f = Mk 2:23f)

However the resourcefulness of his antagonists was by no

means yet exhausted. Their very first charge had been to accuse him of sanctioning a violation of the Sabbath rest when he ordered the paralytic at the Pool of Bethzatha to pick up his mattress and carry it home. What they sought to do now was to smear his reputation by a ruse and thereby convince the multitude that he could not truly be the sinless paragon that the Messiah had to be. Despite their previous discomfiture they therefore made two further attempts to prove him a Sabbathbreaker.

The Israelites were enjoined to keep the Sabbath rest strictly even during harvest time (Ex 34:21), and by a process of casuistry the rabbis had come to frame a regulation that 'plucking' ears of wheat was also a form of harvesting, and was therefore proscribed! And this was precisely what the disciples of Jesus were doing on a peaceful Sabbath day as they walked along the narrow path that wended its way through a field of ripe corn. They were followed by some Pharisees who expressed horror as they saw them plucking the ears and rubbing them between their fingers to free the grain from the husks. There and then the Pharisees went up to Jesus and demanded: 'Why are they doing what it is not lawful to do on the Sabbath?' (Mt 12:1-7)

Of course in Palestine in those days, there were no proper roads in country districts, and the corn grew right up to and over the track itself, and it was a recognized and accepted practice that passers-by might break off ears without being accused of stealing. Since the disciples were hungry they broke off ears as they progressed and unconcernedly ate the grains to assuage their hunger-pangs. Jesus responded to the Pharisees' accusation by reminding them of an incident that happened when David was fleeing from Saul (1 Sam 21:1-6). David and his companions had been so harassed that they had long been without food and were starving. When he arrived secretly at the Sanctuary of Nob in the wilderness, the priest had nothing to offer him except the twelve holy loaves that were baked each week, placed beside the Ark of the Covenant and then consumed by the priests themselves. And so Jesus pronounced that if David and his followers might in these circumstances eat the holy loaves without infringing the Law, then his disciples could consider this a lawful precedent and could without blame pluck those ears of corn to assuage their hunger. Jesus reinforced his treatment of the Sabbath rest with the words: 'The Son of Man is the Lord of the Sabbath', thereby declaring himself equal to God who instituted the Sabbath (Gen 2:1-4). He concluded the colloquy thus:

> I say to you that a greater than the Temple is here. And if you had known the meaning of this: "I desire mercy and not sacrifice", you would not have condemned the guiltless. (Mt 12:7)

In a couple of sentences he had entirely demolished their casuistry.

5) The Man with the Withered Hand
(Mt 12:9f = Lk 6:6f = Mk 3:1f)

The climax of this series of petty persecutions was reached when the scribes and Pharisees, convinced that he had the power of working miracles, decided to find out if he would dare to work another miracle on the Sabbath. For, according to their line of reasoning, the exercise of the art of healing on the Sabbath was classified by the scribes as 'work', and so technically constituted an infringement of the Sabbath rest. They therefore contrived a plot to entrap Jesus by bringing into the synagogue on this particular Sabbath a man with a withered right hand. They placed the sufferer in a prominent place where Jesus, who was teaching, could not fail to see him, and then watched to see what he would do. St Luke tells us that Jesus already knew their thoughts. The wicked challenge of these sanctimonious men, who had deliberately set out to bait him in a holy place and time, aroused his righteous indignation. No doubt the man with the withered hand had been persuaded to come into the synagogue in the honest hope that Jesus would heal him, but had not been told the real reason why they had brought him there. Jesus was not going to dash the hope of the man they were using as a bait, and would of course treat him with the same respect that he bestowed on all who sought his help. However he first intended to discredit his persecutors by publicly exposing their infamous plan. He knew their thoughts and at the appropriate moment called out to the man with the withered hand: 'Get up and stand out in the middle'. And he did so. Jesus, turning to his persecutors whom he knew well by sight, took up their unspoken challenge by saying in the presence of all:

I will question you: Is it lawful on the Sabbath day to do good or to do evil, to save life or to destroy?

He paused and then as there was no answer he went on:

Will there be any man among you who will have a single sheep; and if on the Sabbath it falls into a pit, will you not take hold of it and lift it out? How much more then a man than a sheep. Thus it is lawful to do good on the Sabbath! (Mt 12:11-12).

Looking round on them with anger and being deeply pained at their hardness of heart, he said to the man: 'Extend your hand'. And he extended it, and his hand was at once restored. The sight of the restored hand sent a shock wave through the ranks of the bystanders and pandemonium broke out. The worshippers rushed up on all sides to congratulate the man made whole, but the scribes and the Pharisees with black scowls, and filled with madness, stormed out and straight away went and reported the matter to the courtiers of Herod Antipas, who was anxious to lay his hands on Jesus now that he had already got John the Baptist safely under lock and key. Thus the political authority in Galilee was lining itself up with the Jerusalem priesthood and its emissaries to plan his death. The 'writing on the wall' was clear; nothing less than the complete elimination of Jesus would satisfy his enemies. His destruction would be merely a matter of time, of choosing the right moment and the right pretext. Jesus was well aware of what was happening and withdrew to the Sea of Galilee.

Although Jesus had taken great care to keep his ministry totally non-political, he had in fact by his uprightness effectively antagonised the governments in both Judea and Galilee, the two regions where he should have had the most support. The threat in each region came not from the ordinary people but from the rulers, that is to say, the chief priests, who realised very clearly that their form of spiritual stewardship stood condemned by his own lofty moral standards. The initiative against him had been set in motion by the high priestly families who controlled the Sanhedrin, and they had now no difficulty in winning the support of the Herodians, for Herod Antipas likewise felt threatened by this man Jesus of Nazareth, who actually wished to make the faithful observance of the Decalogue the normal rule of life! This extraordinary person, Herod argued, seemed to have the power of a magician and at the same time to be capable of drawing immense crowds to himself. He was utterly fearless, and when confronted had always made his opponents look foolish. Although he had not taken any steps to back up his claim by force, as all previous messiahs had done, there was no doubt that he could do so if he wished and would then prove to be a most formidable antagonist.

6) Great Crowds come to Jesus (Mt 4:24f = Lk 6:17f = Mk 3:7f)

Jesus now knew that the time had come when he would have to act creatively if he wanted his mission to succeed. Since the high priesthood was not only corrupt but implacably hostile and unwilling to collaborate, he would have to rely entirely on his own efforts to make sure that his movement was not stifled and suppressed at its inception. For it to survive and develop, he would have to recruit an elite corps of followers and infuse them with his own spirit to carry on after he had been eliminated. This would require meticulous and time-consuming organization which in its turn could not be realized without attracting the attention of friend and foe alike. His enemies could not ignore that his growing fame had already made him powerful, for the report of his wonderful preaching and his extraordinary miracles was drawing thousands into Galilee from all quarters. The evangelist Matthew describes the situation as follows:

> And his fame went out into all Syria, and they brought him all that were ill from various diseases, and people suffering pains, and the demon-possessed, and lunatics and paralytic, and he healed them all. And large crowds followed him from Galilee and the Decapolis, and

from Jerusalem and Judea, and from across the Jordan (Mt 4:24-25).

Jesus viewed these crowds bringing their sick and their demon-possessed with a compassionate eye and said to his disciples with deep emotion:

The harvest is great indeed but the workers are few. Pray therefore the lord of the harvest to put forth workers into his harvest (Mt 9:36-37).

The gathering of this great crowd was to give him the opportunity to instruct them in the new spirit that he intended to infuse into the Law of Moses. But he also intended to make it the occasion of choosing the men who would form the nucleus of his new movement. To prepare himself for the momentous decisions he would be making the next day, he went up the mountain that evening to pray alone, and in the words of Luke 'spent the whole night in the prayer of God'. When it was day he came down from the mountain, and took his stand in the midst of the expectant multitude.

7) Jesus chooses the Twelve (Mt 10:2f = Lk 6:12f = Mk 3:13f)

For perhaps five or six months Jesus had been visiting the synagogues of Galilee preaching the good news of the Kingdom of God that he had come to inaugurate. During those months he had gathered a number of disciples whom he had personally invited to work closely with him in his ministry and he was now about to choose an intimate band of twelve from among them.

Now after long prayer and reflection he was going to take perhaps the most momentous step of his life, because as we have already noted, the time had come when he would have to set up his own organization if his message was to survive his own demise. As he descended the mountain and came to 'a level place', he saw the crowds assembled to meet him, his own disciples being in the forefront. He was going to take the first step to establish a new kind of society, one never heard of before, a living body of adherents for which there was no precedent. The ancient people of God had been founded on the natural family of the twelve sons of Jacob. By appointing twelve as his apostles, men prepared to forego family ties, Jesus was letting the world know that he was fulfilling his Father's plan to establish the new people of God, the new Israel of God, with himself as the link between the old and the new.

Jesus had ordered his disciples to be there that morning to receive his instructions, and they and the great crowd were to be the witnesses of this ceremony of induction which was to be followed by what has become known as the Great Sermon. 'He summoned those whom he himself wanted, and they came to him' (Mk 3:13), and so he selected the Twelve whom he had decided upon (including, as it happened, Judas the future traitor). These men were to form the College of the Apostles and be the foundation stones of the new Kingdom of God (or as Matthew calls it: 'The Kingdom of the heavens'). They were to live with him day and night so that later on they would be effective eye-witnesses of all that he had said and done during his mission on earth. Their ultimate vocation, after he had trained them and gone back to heaven, was to go forth in his name into the whole world 'to preach and to have authority to cast out the demons' (Mk 3:14-15). Jesus set the Twelve apart from the rest of his disciples and thenceforth they formed the inner circle to whom he entrusted his intimate thoughts and aspirations because they were to be his principal witnesses and the leaders of his Church. Later on Luke will tell us that he also appointed another seventy-two disciples 'whom he sent two by two into every village and place where he himself was about to come' (Lk 10:1); but the Twelve remained his special solicitude because of their future role. Their importance to the Church is attested by the fact that the Acts of the Apostles as well as all three Synoptic Gospels carefully list their names in a particular order, probably the order in which Jesus first called them. They are presented always in three groups of four, the same names appearing in each group.

Simon Bar-Jona heads the first group in all four lists. He is the one to whom Jesus at their first encounter had prophesied that he would be called 'Cephas', the Aramaic for 'Peter'. Next comes Andrew, who had the privilege of first discovering Jesus and then bringing his brother Simon to him. The other two in the first group are James (known as 'the Greater') and John, the sons of Zebedee, to whom Jesus gave the nickname 'Boanerges', signifying 'Sons of Thunder' because of their impetuosity. Together with Simon and Andrew they had formed a fishing-partnership on the Lake of Galilee.

The second group of four contains the names of Philip and Bartholomew, the latter of whom tradition identifies with the Nathanael of the first chapter of the Gospel of John. The other pair are Matthew (also known as Levi) the tax collector and evangelist, and Thomas, best remembered for his obstinate doubting followed by his confession of faith in Jesus (Jn 20:25).

The third group consists of three who were probably kinsmen of Jesus: James of Alphaeus (also known as James 'the Less'), Simon 'the Zealot', and Thaddeus, also known as Jude of James (either the son or the relative of James), together with Judas Iscariot (the man of Kerioth in Judea), the only non-Galilean, the man who betrayed him.

The significance of this action of Jesus in setting up his own organization to make sure that his message of salvation would not be lost—whatever might first happen to himself—dawned on at least some of his entourage. Mark refers to them as 'those with him' (Mk 3:21); but exactly who they were remains uncertain—probably not his own immediate family, but nevertheless close enough to have had ready access to him, people who thought they had a right to save him from himself. For it signified a challenge to the policy of the chief priests—the government of the country—and accordingly spelt danger to him and to his friends and family. Mark is the only evangelist to record that those well-wishers attempted to seize him, saying that he was 'beside himself'. They did not succeed in doing so, but the mere fact that they tried to do so revealed anxiety for their own safety as well as his on account of his intransigent attitude to the Jerusalem authorities.

8) Introduction to the Great Sermon

There are two versions of the Great Sermon, Matthew's and

Luke's. Matthew's is much longer and more complete; but Luke's is shorter and is thought by many to be a more primitive version. However, the two versions are in close parallel and in both cases immediately follow the calling of the Twelve.

When Matthew wrote, the Church, in my opinion, had not yet expanded significantly beyond the border of Israel, and Paul had not yet begun his first missionary journey (AD 46-48).[20] Matthew's aim was to provide the first Christians with a reminder of the foundational work of Jesus and a proper understanding of their Christian calling in the light of the severe persecutions they had had to endure after his death and resurrection in AD 30. Matthew therefore made a selection, based no doubt principally on his own memories and those of his fellow Apostles, of the words and deeds of Jesus that he knew to be appropriate for the circumstances of the Jerusalem Church. It is quite obvious that he took special pains to please his readers by recasting his memories in the five contemporary literary forms—the *chreia* (or brief story), the *apomnemoneuma* or longer reminiscence, the maxim, the parable, and the narrative—and above all in six long discourses which form the core of Jesus' teaching. Furthermore it is evident that in the selection of his material Matthew consciously limited himself to the length of a standard commercial scroll.

The Sermon on the Mount takes no more than about fifteen minutes to recite and is clearly only a summary of what Jesus had actually delivered to the people. Nor does it necessarily follow that he spoke these words all on that one occasion in exactly this order. In fact, the Great Sermon, as well as the other discourses, all appear to be Matthew's literary constructs carefully compiled from Jesus' words on various occasions during his ministry. There can be no doubt however that the words which the evangelist specifically attributed to Jesus are indeed his very own, because the Holy Spirit of God, the Spirit of Truth, is equally the author along with the Apostle.

---

20 For justification of this chronology, see my *Order of the Synoptics*, pt. III, pp. 246-250.

The Catholic Church teaches that the Twelve Apostles handed on without error to the Jerusalem Church all that Jesus had taught them. In particular the text of Matthew as we now have it represents exactly what the Holy Spirit wanted Matthew to record in writing of what Jesus had said some ten years before. But the Jerusalem readers of Matthew's Gospel, and all subsequent readers, formed a very different audience from the original one. Hence the Holy Spirit in union with Matthew refashioned what Jesus had then said, but also in such a way as to provide us with Jesus' true original mind without falsifying or diminishing in the slightest the content he wished to be expressed. That is to say, the actuality and the power of the Word of Jesus come to us not in their exact original context (because that is past and done with, although fully effective in the minds of the hearers at the time, and so in Matthew's mind too!), but through the power imparted to the words of the Gospel through Matthew, a free agent, acting in union with the Holy Spirit who wishes them to be equally valid for the generations to come. The conclusion therefore is that because the words of the Gospel are the inspired words of the living Spirit of Jesus, they do in fact accurately evoke for us what the Lord wants us to know now about that original Sermon.

Luke, when writing his Gospel some twenty years later, must have been aware that Matthew had adequately related all that needed to be said on this point, and therefore keeps his own account as brief as possible.

9) The Great Sermon (Mt 5-7 = Lk 6:20-49)

Out of a much larger following Jesus had thus chosen his twelve 'Apostles'—the special title he gave them, the word 'apostle' meaning 'one who has been sent'. Behind them stood the great crowd of spectators who had been drawn by the fame of his miracles and preaching. One and all gazed expectantly on the Master as he went to take his seat on some outcrop of rock facing the lake. His message for them was simple but striking: he had not come to undo either the Law of Moses or the Writings or message of the ancient Prophets; 'until the heaven and the earth pass away, not one iota or one pen-stroke of the Law will pass away until all things be done'. On the contrary, he had come to fulfil them by imbuing them with his own spirit, the spirit of the love of God and one's neighbour. Outward conformity with the Law was no longer sufficient; there must be an inward adoration of God leading to an inward obedience coming from the bottom of one's heart as well as from one's own free will. His aim was to free the religion of his people from a certain legalism into which it had degenerated on the part of the majority.

Jesus begins by authoritatively describing the sort of person the true Jew ought to be and his proper relationship to God his Father, the God of Abraham, Isaac and Jacob; and he does so by means of a series of maxims. These are the eight Beatitudes, which are all summed up in the first: 'Blessed are the poor in spirit, for theirs is the Kingdom of heaven', which is to be the possession of those who totally rely on the grace of God who has called them through no merit of their own and who respond to his call in faith. By recognizing that everything they possess is God's gift they will be enabled to practise the virtues of detachment from riches, of eagerness to fulfil the Commandments of God, purity of conscience, love of peace; and they will also be given the strength patiently to endure even calumny and persecution for the sake of Christ, their Lord and Master. Looking in particular at the Twelve he insists that they are to be 'the salt of the earth' and 'the light of the world'. Furthermore, 'their light must so shine before men that all will see their good works and in consequence give glory to their Father in heaven (Mt 5:15-16). Thus high then is the standard that he is going to demand from his followers!

Jesus aims to quiet the fears of those who thought he might be wanting to change the Law of Moses. He asserts on the contrary that he has come to give a far deeper and more radical expression to its interiority. Moses understood very well that the Lord God required his people not only to fear him but to love him and serve him with all their heart and soul (Dt 10:12).

Jesus has come to spell it all out and to demand fulfilment not just in the letter but truly in the spirit. He has come to make plain to all that the Lord God looks always at the heart of a man, not just at his outward appearance. Even to look on a woman in order to lust after her is a grave sin. Hence to attempt to offer a sacrifice in the Temple while the heart is still filled with the desire to hurt one's neighbour, or with adulterous thoughts or with the desire to retaliate for an injury received, or while still living a hypocritical life, will be regarded by the Lord as a sacrilege and will be most displeasing to him. The golden rule in human society is 'whatever you want men to do to you, you should also do to them' (Mt 7:12). Jesus then goes even further; he orders his followers to love their enemies, to bless those who curse them and to do good to those who hate them (Mt 5:44). In fine, 'they must be perfect as their heavenly Father is perfect' (Mt 5:48). This perfection is to be sought in three ways: by almsgiving, by prayer and by fasting; and these practices must be performed as secretly as possible in order to avoid the snare of being praised for doing what one ought to do in any case.

This interiority of worship of the Lord God of Israel, of the One who is our heavenly Father, is to be practised in everything; that is to say, all charitable help to one's neighbour should be given secretly, so that 'the left hand does not know what the right hand is doing' (Mt 6:3). Whatever ascetical practices one adopts, including fasting, they should be done without revealing them to the outside world; and one's private prayers should as far as possible be made in the privacy of one's own room and not made visible to others in order to be praised.

All private prayer should be directed in the first place to praise and honour God our Father and to ask for strength to accomplish his divine will. We do not need to pray specifically for our material wants because he knows all about them, and will supply us with all our essential needs if only we trust him, just as the birds of the air do. If we seek the Kingdom of God and his justice, all these things will be added unto us.

Most important of all is to remember that the Lord will not

forgive us our own sins unless, before we start to pray, we first forgive our neighbour his sins against us; otherwise we shall not be heard. And the best way to succeed in this matter is never to condemn others, for 'with what judgement you judge, you in your turn will be judged, and in the measure you measure out to others it will be measured to you' (Mt 7:2).

The true Christian is the one who will try to adopt the values and motivations that Jesus lays down and who will endeavour to please him by only seeking 'treasures in heaven', for 'where your treasure is there too will be your heart' (6:21). No one can successfully serve two masters, 'you cannot serve God and Mammon' (6:24).

Above all the Christian needs clear spiritual insight and a profound trust in God his Father. For the gate that leads to eternal life is narrow and the route is hedged in. Siren voices and false prophets will not be lacking on the way; 'not every one who says to me "Lord, Lord" will enter into the Kingdom of heaven, but he who does the will of my Father who is in heaven' (Mt 7:21). Those who act in this way will be like the wise man who built his house upon the rock which the autumn torrents could not wash away but left intact.

There was nothing essentially new in this teaching of Jesus; it was but the reaffirmation of the Ten Commandments. In one way it was simply inspired common sense, but none the less the thorough application of these astonishingly piercing insights into human behaviour would one day transform the world. Matthew relates that when Jesus had finished speaking, the crowds were in admiration at his teaching, because he taught them 'as one having authority and not as their scribes'.

8

The Training of the Twelve

1) The Service of the Women Followers (Lk 8:1-3)

After this wonderful discourse the first care of Jesus was to give an intensive course of training to these twelve new followers of his. They had much to learn and his time was short, probably not more than a year. He was going to set out with them to crisscross purposefully the whole of Galilee. During their long journeying their regime would be spartan and physically exacting. He was in his physical prime and so were his disciples, and since they had mostly experienced tough manual labour, the physical strain accompanying their mission could not possibly deter them. In order to ensure that his companions were properly fed and neatly clad and to provide for all those chores that traditionally no oriental man would ever undertake, Jesus sanctioned 'some women who had been healed of evil spirits and infirmities' to accompany them, including Mary, known as the Magdalene (probably because she came from the pagan city of Magdala recently founded on the western shore of the Lake). With her was Joanna the wife of Chuza, king Herod's estate manager, Susanna and some others (Lk 8:1-3). These women undertook their service of Jesus and the Twelve as an expression of their gratitude to the Lord for having liberated them from lives of sin, devil-possession or other infirmities. They seem to have been educated women of some wealth, which would have given them a certain independence. Joanna's presence indicated that the influence of Jesus must have extended into the very heart of the dissolute court of Herod Antipas himself. The service of these women meant that Jesus and the Twelve were free from having to worry about their material needs and were able to concentrate fully on their apostolic mission. If we include these women there must have been twenty or more persons in the caravan that accompanied him from this time onwards.

2) The Cost of Following Jesus (Mt 8:18f = Lk 9:57f)

When recording Jesus' first departure from Capharnaum the evangelist Matthew takes the trouble to point out to his readers what was involved in 'following' him. Jesus was not a rabbi as then understood although he responded when addressed as 'rabbi', which simply means 'my teacher'. Matthew wishes to emphasise that 'following Jesus' was a radical act of self-sacrifice involving a lifetime of service in the cause of the Master and not just a matter of studying his teaching and learning from him. He provides two illustrations of what this 'following' meant, and Luke adds a third. Jesus required those, whom he called to have a direct share in his apostolate, to assume a special solidarity with him by forsaking their homes like 'the Son of Man who had nowhere to lay his head' (Mt 8:18-20), and unlike the foxes and the birds who each have their own holes or nests.

Nor was this all; for the sake of the Kingdom of God they are to relinquish even normal family ties because 'he who prefers father and mother to me is not worthy of me' (Mt 10:37). The evangelists give two further illustrations. Matthew and Luke note that the follower of Jesus must even be prepared to forego the sacred family duty of burying a dead relative when called on to do so (Mt 8:21-22, Lk 9:59-60). Luke further records that the Lord's invitation is so urgent that there is no time for the one called to go home and 'take leave of those in his house' (Lk 9:61-62). In fact, the call of God to discipleship is so exigent that it may even cause division in a man's household since he must always prefer God's call to the wishes of his family (Mt 10:34-35; Lk 12:49-53).

3) The Teaching by Parables (Mt 13:1f= Lk 8:4f= Mk 4:1f)

Matthew and Mark relate that at the beginning of his Galilean ministry Jesus began to preach that 'the Kingdom of God is at hand' (Mt 4:17 = Mk 1:14) and to outline the precise nature of this kingdom.

Jesus inherited the kingship of Israel by right of royal descent. However, he had not come to reinstate the glories of the old terrestrial kingdom of David and Solomon; his kingdom was to be over the hearts of men and women. He alone, of all ever born and still to be born of women, from the beginning of the world to its end, had been endowed by God Almighty with the vision, the power and the authority to found the institution promised by God to his people from ages past. The ancient pillars on which Israel rested, i.e. the Law, the Code, the Covenant, the Priesthood of Aaron, had merely been foreshadowings, proto-types of what Jesus would empower his Apostles to establish. Now by the will of God the Father, Jesus is the last prophet to be sent; for he is the Son of the Father, the King of the Kingdom of God, the sole Priest of the New Covenant between God and his people. He is to be their champion and the supreme example of what his heavenly Father wanted every Israelite to be.

God's design for the new kingdom had hitherto been shrouded behind the veil of prophetic generalities, which essentially promised that God would in due time cause all nations to 'flow towards the mountain of Sion', and that his people of Israel would in some way be made responsible for fulfilling this mission. But explanations of how this was to come about, explanations which everyone could understand quite easily, had not yet been forthcoming. While waiting impatiently for further revelation the Jews started to look in the wrong direction which led them to expect a new kingdom of military and terrestrial splendour like that achieved under king Solomon, one to rival Rome.

Until then the only kind of supra-national institution known to men had been the 'empire', such as that of the Persians or the Romans. Jesus was the first to outline a new concept and to explain the novel extension of God's Kingdom over the earth, its territory here being the hearts of its adherents of all nations, climes and times. It was his plan that after his ascension the Twelve Apostles were to go out into the world and build the structure of this kingdom under the direction of the Holy Spirit. So in order to provide them with a sort of 'blue-print' for this new institution, Jesus used the then much loved literary form of parables to teach the people. Furthermore, his parables have ever since continued to provide bishops and theologians with fresh insights into the true nature of God's Church. Jesus knew that it would be difficult if not impossible for his apostles to understand straightaway the hidden meanings of what at first sight appeared to be nothing more than beautiful stories well told. And this was why he had taken great care to select the right men for the job, men who one day, when reviewing how things had taken shape under their eyes, would remember what he had taught them, and under the influence of his Holy Spirit consider it their privilege faithfully to implement the new insights they were to discover in his original instructions.

The parables of Jesus embody the following messages: The sole purpose of his coming into the world was to bring about its salvation by the implanting of the Word of God. The new kingdom was to be the main instrument of its diffusion. Hence it was like a pearl of great price that a merchant would beggar himself to buy (Mt 13:45f). It was also like a treasure hidden in a field, which a man on discovering would give all he possessed to acquire (Mt 13:44). It was to start in a very small way, like the mustard seed, but was to grow into an enormous institution, just as the mustard seed eventually becomes a great shrub in which the birds are able to build their nests (Mt 13:31f). And like that shrub, God's Kingdom is to be a living organism capable of meeting all needs and of adapting itself to diverse cultures, climates and soils. At the same time its process of growth would be as quiet, peaceful and silent as the action of leaven or yeast in a basin of flour (Mt 13:33). Though in its constitution this kingdom would be perfect, its countless subjects would form a complete spectrum of good and bad, like the field in the parable in which wheat and weed grow to maturity side by side until the time of harvest (Mt 13:36-43). Then the reapers on the instructions of the owner are to come and burn the weeds and garner the good wheat into his barns. Furthermore, the sphere of action of the Kingdom is as wide as the sea, and it is like a net which gathers into itself anything that crosses its path; when it is finally hauled ashore the good fish are saved and the uneatable are thrown out (Mt 13:47f). In several parables he insists that one day, at an unspecified date, the time of in-gathering will be completed, and then the owner, i.e. the lord, will return to receive the profits made by his servants and to settle all outstanding accounts. All nations will be summoned to this final assize from which there will result either 'a great grinding and gnashing of teeth' or a glorious and everlasting feast (Mt 25:31-46).

In addition to the parables dealing explicitly with the structure of the Kingdom, there are some other very important ones regarding the actual communication of the Word of God. The parable of the Sower is one of these (Mt 13:3-9). It teaches that the efficacy of the Word, despite its immanent power, depends on the quality of the soil on which it falls. Just as the sower faithfully sows the seed on every type of soil, so the apostle must preach the Word prodigally in order to give all an equal chance of profiting from it. Nevertheless he must realize that he will not be at fault if the response in places is poor or negative, provided he has done his part fully and properly. In fact the power of the seed is immense and it has the in-built faculty of self-development without the sower having to worry about how it grows and reaches maturity (cf. Mk 4:26-29).

4) The Healing of a Centurion's Slave (Mt 8:5-13; Lk 7:1-10)

When Jesus returned to Capharnaum, a centurion, who had heard about his miraculous cures, decided to contact him on behalf of a good slave of his. The centurion was a wealthy pagan officer in the pay of Herod Antipas and had been so taken with the Jewish religion that he had even built the local synagogue.

He was a so-called 'God-fearer', a believer but uncommitted, a modest and humble man, one who felt himself unworthy in person to approach Jesus, since he was known to be ministering only to his fellow-Jews. At the same time the centurion was desperate to secure help to save the life of his slave and therefore asked some of the elders of the synagogue to appeal in his name to Jesus. So the elders came and begged Jesus to do this favour to their centurion friend, saying: 'He is worthy that you should grant this favour to him'. Rather surprisingly in the circumstances because he had previously announced that his mission was only to 'the lost sheep of the House of Israel', Jesus replied: 'Yes, I will come and heal him'.

The news that Jesus would come personally to his house was swiftly relayed to the centurion while Jesus was on the way. The officer was overwhelmed by this display of condescension and being filled with confusion at the thought of his unworthiness to entertain this holy prophet, asked his friends to convey the following message:

> Lord, do not trouble, for I am not worthy that you should enter under my roof. For this reason I did not consider myself worthy to come to you. But only say a word and my boy will be cured. For I too am a man set under authority, having under me soldiers. And I say to this one: Go, and he goes; and to another: Come, and he comes; and to my slave: Do this, and he does it.

When Jesus received this message he was overjoyed and exclaimed to the apostles and the crowd following him: 'Amen I say to you, with no one in Israel have I found such faith'. He at once sent the messengers back, saying: 'Go back, and tell him: It is done to you as you have believed'. When they returned to the centurion's house they found the slave had been healed at the very moment Jesus spoke.

St Matthew attaches an epilogue to this story which reveals Jesus' disappointment at the lukewarm faith of his own people towards him; for he relates that Jesus was forced to admit that the pagan centurion's faith was greater than that of any Israelite he had yet come across. Jesus indeed was filled with foreboding for the future when he added: 'And I say to you, that

many will come from east and west and will recline with
Abraham and Isaac and Jacob in the Kingdom of the heavens;
but the sons of the Kingdom will be cast out into the exterior
darkness'. That is to say, he now foresaw with prophetic insight
that the pagan nations would eagerly enter into his Kingdom,
while the 'sons of the kingdom', the leaders of his own people,
would for the most part choose to walk out into the exterior
darkness of unbelief.

5) The Raising of a Widow's Son at Na'in (Lk 7:11-17)

Nevertheless Jesus continued spontaneously and compas-
sionately to heal and bring joy to his own nation wherever he
found hearts ready to accept him, as we can see from another
miracle in this period of his ministry. For about that time he
went with his disciples to Na'in, a village some five miles south-
east of Nazareth. As they drew near to its gates, a mournful
sight greeted them. It was a funeral procession going forth to
bury a young man, the only son of his mother, who was herself
a widow. The little family was much loved and respected, and so
the whole village had turned out to show its sympathy. Jesus of
course knew in his own spirit all about her and her pitiful situation. Seeing her crying, the Lord spontaneously said to her: 'Do
not weep'. Walking up to the bier on which the young man lay
wrapped in the burial sheet, he touched it, and its bearers stood
still. Before anybody realized what was happening Jesus said to
the figure on the bier: 'Young man, I say to you—rise up'. At
these words the dead man sat up and began to speak, and Jesus
'gave him to his mother'. This brief encounter on the road and
the astounding miracle performed without any fuss awed all
present into momentary silence. But then they all burst out
with: 'A great prophet has risen among us, and God has visited
his people'. Perhaps the most remarkable thing about this anecdote is the gratuitous and unsought intervention of Jesus which
revealed the depth of his sympathy with the human predicament. Suddenly confronted with this widow's desolation, he expressed his compassion by instantly raising her son to life and
turning her sorrow into joy.

6) The Stilling of the Storm (Mt 8:23f = Lk 8:22f = Mk 4:36f)

It would seem that his first preaching about the Kingdom through parables had taken place down by the sea-shore from a boat moored near the water's edge (Mk 4:1). When he had finished, he asked his disciples to take him to the other side of the Lake 'just as he was' (Mk 4:35-36), for he felt very tired and wanted to escape the crowds for a while. In fact he was so exhausted that no sooner had they sailed off than he fell asleep on the cushion in the stern of Peter's boat. Then something extraordinary happened. A freak storm suddenly hit their boat in mid-lake and threatened to swamp it and drown them all. The danger was very real and they panicked. Jesus however was still sleeping peacefully though the boat was being tossed about and rapidly filling with water. In their alarm they roused him, calling to him above the howling of the gale: 'Master, master, save us, we are drowning! Are you not concerned?' Jesus woke up and rising to his full height, stretching out his hand over the waters he commanded the wind and the sea: 'Be silent and stop!'. At once the wind stopped and the waves went down. Then there came a great calm. Jesus turned to them and scolded them: 'Why are you afraid, you men of little faith?' The miraculous calm of the Lake filled the Apostles with awe. When they at last found their speech all they could say was: 'Who is this man, for the winds and the sea obey him?'

7) The Possessed at Gadara (Mt 8:28f = Lk 8:26f = Mk 5:1f)

Jesus then directed them to land on the south-eastern shore of the Lake in the area under the jurisdiction of the pagan city of Gerasa which lay some distance inland. It was an isolated spot and had but few inhabitants. Those who lived there had been intimidated by two men possessed by evil spirits, who haunted some nearby tombs. These two rushed up to the party as they landed, and said: 'What have we to do with You, Jesus, Son of God the Most High? Do not torture us.' For the devils in the possessed men immediately recognised his divine sonship and were terrified as to what would happen to them. One man in particular had been very badly treated; he had been bound with chains and put in prison because of his violent behaviour, but the demonic strength in him was such that he had burst his fetters and escaped into this desert place, where he had been left to fend for himself. Jesus questioned him: 'What is your name?' The reply came: 'My name is Legion, for we are many'. The devils infesting the poor man then pressed Jesus not to send them out of that region, and noting the swine grazing on the nearby hillside pleaded: 'If you send us out, please send us into those swine over there!' Jesus assented and said: 'O unclean spirits, go out of the men'. And they went out and instantly entered into the swine which were peacefully grazing. The whole herd then suddenly turned and panicked, rushed down the hillside, across the slope that borders the lake at that point, and were drowned in the water. It was a catastrophic sight, because the herd numbered about two thousand.

Then with local help Jesus and the Twelve managed to clean up the poor man (Luke and Mark speak only of one, while Matthew speaks of two men) and found him some clothes for he had been quite naked. Meanwhile the herdsmen had rushed back to the town and informed their masters of what had happened. As a result the whole town came out to see Jesus to discover exactly what had happened, since they were naturally worried and upset at this heavy loss. On arrival they marvelled to see the man, formerly possessed by the demons and well known to the whole neighbourhood for his savage behaviour, sitting at the feet of Jesus fully clothed and in his right mind. However, being pagans they were also afraid that this divine visitation might in some way be a punishment, and to ward off any further disaster they begged him to depart from their territory. Jesus meekly agreed to do so. As he was getting into the boat, the man who had been healed begged to be taken with him; but he refused, saying: 'Go back into your own house to your own people, and report to them the things that the Lord has done for you and how he pitied you'. So the man went back as commanded and started preaching about Jesus to all the cities in the Decapolis, thus preparing the way for a visit of the apostles after the resurrection.

8) The Raising of Jairus' Daughter
(Mt 9:18f = Lk 8:40f = Mk 5:21f)

When Jesus returned to Capharnaum the crowds were eagerly waiting to receive him, because the news of these miracles had been noised around very quickly. On his way into town he was approached by Jairus, one of the rulers of the synagogue, whose twelve-year old daughter, his only child, was dying. Falling at Jesus' feet he begged: 'My little daughter is at the point of death; will you please come and lay your hand upon her that she may live?' Jesus agreed with alacrity and so they set off for his house followed by the disciples and a large crowd.

They had not gone very far when Jesus suddenly stopped and turning round enquired from the crowds: 'Who has touched my garments?' There was a moment's silence before Peter and several of his disciples objected : 'Why do you say, "Who touched me?", when the crowds are thronging all round you?' Jesus replied: 'Someone touched me, for I know that power has gone out from me', and he looked around to see who the culprit was. Finally a woman who had been standing near came forward in fear and trembling, knelt before him and told him her story. She declared that for the past twelve years she had been enduring a menstrual flow that would not stop and had spent her whole fortune on doctors in search of a cure but to no avail; indeed she had got steadily worse. So hearing about Jesus, she decided to come up quietly behind him and just touch his garments without attracting attention. This was a daring and risky thing to do as by Jewish law a menstruating woman was ritually unclean; and for her to touch a holy man while in this condition would bring down upon her the wrath of scribes and Pharisees. Nevertheless she had said to herself, 'If I can just touch his clothes I am sure I shall be healed'. And she did so, and at once she realized that she was now cured by his power and wholeness. Jesus then sent her away with the words: 'Take heart, O daughter, your faith has saved you; go home in peace'.

After this Jesus turned and walked on towards the house of Jairus. But before he got there he was stopped again, this time by a messenger from the house to tell Jairus that his daughter had just died and therefore he need not trouble the teacher any further. Jesus overheard the conversation and simply said: 'Fear not; only go on believing and she will be saved'. And he forbade anyone to come any further with him except Peter, James and John. When they got to the house, the customary mourning had already begun among the women of the house and their friends, uttering loud cries and moans. Jesus went in ahead of his disciples and called the mourners to order, saying: 'Why are you all wailing away like this? The girl is not dead; she is only sleeping'. At this remark they all burst out in sarcastic shrieks of laughter, because they knew for sure that she was dead. Without more ado Jesus ejected them all from the room where the child was lying dead, himself staying behind with only the father and mother and the three Apostles, whom he had specially selected to be the witnesses of the most important events of his public ministry. He then went over to the bed and grasping the child's hand said to her: '*Talitha koum*' (which means in his native Aramaic: 'Maiden, arise'), and to everyone's astonishment the little girl stood up at once and started to walk about. As she had been too ill to eat anything for a long time Jesus told them to give her some food. Before letting everybody go, he sternly ordered them not to divulge what had happened, for the crowds of wonder-seekers were now proving an embarrassment to the progress of his mission, because they were merely hungry for miracles and never stopped to think why he performed them. All the same it was impossible to restrain either the Apostles or the overjoyed parents of the child from telling everyone what he had done by raising their dead daughter to life.

There was a further reason why Jesus now wanted to keep people from exploiting his miracles, important though they were as signs of his messianic authority. As mentioned earlier, the image that the Jews had of the Messiah was of a fearless and all-conquering warrior who 'would restore the kingdom to Israel' by force of arms. Even the Apostles seem to have remained uncertain about the real nature of the Kingdom until after the resurrection. Though his ministry was entirely spiritual and non-political, the greater and the more marvellous his works, the greater the danger that he would be considered a national saviour from foreign oppression. Hence from now on he tried to keep his miracles out of the public eye because he did not want to risk either himself or his disciples being cast in the role of 'political agitators'.[21]

9) The Healing of Two Blind Men (Mt 9:27-31)

The healing of two blind men whom Jesus met while on circuit in Galilee is a typical example of the kind of miracle that roused the enthusiasm of the crowds to fever-pitch. They were healed because they had faith in him and believed from all they had heard that he was indeed the 'Son of David'—a Messianic title. In response to their act of faith Jesus restored their sight by the touch of his hands. Here again he vehemently forbade them to tell anyone about their cure, but they on the contrary joyfully proceeded to 'make him known in all that land'. From what we can gather, the whole situation seemed to be getting out of hand; the Messiah was finding it impossible to control the enthusiasm of the crowds who lacked understanding of the true nature of his mission. Jesus accepted the fact that this had to be so for the time being and that in order to dampen the patriotic ardour of the crowds his teaching about the Kingdom had to be delivered in parables. It would be the privilege of the Apostles after the resurrection to explain to all the 'mystery of the Kingdom', a fact which Mark especially noted (Mk 4:11).

10) The Second Visit to Nazareth (Mt 13:53-58; cf. Lk 4:23f)

When Jesus came to Nazareth again, he found that the jealousy and incredulity of the inhabitants had got the better of their

---

21 The so-called 'Messianic Secret' is a term attributed to the German exegete W. Wrede (c. 1900), which he used to describe the anxiety of Jesus in the Gospel of Mark to restrict the knowledge of his messiahship to the disciples in order to avoid political complications.

earlier welcome; and Luke indicates that they had also acquired a grievance against him in that he had not worked the same miracles for them as already in Capharnaum. He warned them however that in their own sacred history the Lord did not regard himself bound to restrict his favours to Israel, but had freely chosen for example to single out the pagan widow of Zarephath and to cure the heathen Naaman of his leprosy. And when he upbraided them for their lack of faith in him and reminded them that 'a prophet is not without honour save in his own home town and in his own house', they got so furious that they ran him out of the synagogue and attempted to lynch him by throwing him down from a height in order to stone him to death. But because his 'hour' had not yet come, he mysteriously passed through their ranks and went on his way. Matthew, probably writing less than ten years later, is silent about their crime, seemingly from a desire to spare the feelings of the Christians of Nazareth, and contents himself with observing that 'he did not there work many signs because of their unbelief'. The tragic thing now was that Jesus had not only been rejected by the chief priests in the Holy City, but had also become an outcast from his own home town. He who was not only entirely innocent of any transgression, and who had done nothing but unobtrusive good to others throughout his whole life, was already condemned and outlawed for simply stating the truth about himself. Thus the outlook for his future ministry was inauspicious in the extreme.

By now the Twelve Apostles were becoming aware that associating with Jesus meant being involved in a struggle of cosmic dimension with the powers of evil, a struggle that would test their courage and endurance to the uttermost. However, at this stage they were unable to imagine that his power and majesty could ever be thwarted by his enemies, and the notion of his final success only coming through the sacrifice of his life did not enter their ken. But after his resurrection their eyes would at last be opened to the reality of the deadly battle in which he had been single-handedly engaged, a victory that was to be won only at the price of his life (cf. Jn 10:1-21).

11) Blasphemy against the Spirit
(Mt 9:32f = Mt 12:22f = Lk 11:14f)

Meanwhile the devil, the father of lies, was fomenting further opposition against Jesus. The chief instruments of his enemies were lies and calumnies, and the scribes who had come down from Jerusalem made full use of them. They were saying about him: 'He has Beelzebul, and by the prince of the devils he is casting out the devils' (Mk 3:22). When he heard this slander, Jesus summoned the scribes and publicly contradicted them in front of his disciples showing how false was their logic:

> How can Satan cast out Satan? A kingdom divided against itself cannot stand. And likewise a house divided against itself cannot stand. And so if Satan has risen up against himself he cannot stand, but has an end. (Mk 3:23-26)

The scribes were deliberately accusing him of calling on Satan to work his miracles of healing. Jesus however argued that this could not possibly be true, for if it were, then Satan would only be hurting himself. In fact the scribes were intentionally contradicting the known truth; they were calling 'white' black, and to speak thus was to speak against the Holy Spirit. Jesus warned them that every sin against him, the Son of Man, was capable of being forgiven because he was also a man. But he then concluded that whoever speaks against the Holy Spirit, the Third Person of the Blessed Trinity, will not be forgiven either in this age or in the one to come, because he is attacking the very well-spring of truth, his mind being fixed on falsehood, and so against God himself.

And to make his own position clearer still, Jesus likened himself to the warrior who in order to regain his patrimony had first to overcome the mighty usurper of his splendid palace, namely Satan, who claimed ownership of the world. That meant that the first task of Jesus was to chain up Satan and take over his domain. Once having succeeded in this, he would then be able to rescue those living under Satan's domination. In this way Jesus used the scribes' calumny to teach his Apostles something about the scope of his epic struggle for the souls of men. For later on in their turn they would suffer in the same way, since the servant is not greater than his master (Mt 10:24).

There are two more anecdotes to relate regarding this period of Jesus' ministry which illustrate the way in which he wished his Apostles to behave towards people. One concerns members of his own family, and the other his attitude towards a notorious sinner.

12) The Mother and Brothers of Jesus
(Mt 12:46f = Lk 8:19f = Mk 3:31f)

Jesus was one day addressing a group of people in a house when his mother and some relatives came to see him, but could not get through the dense crowd sitting in a circle around him. So they relayed this message to him: 'Your mother and your brothers and sisters are standing outside seeking you'. His reply was unexpected: 'Who is my mother, and who are my brothers?' And looking on those around him, and with a sweeping gesture of his arm over them all, he told them: 'See my mother and my brothers. For whoever does the will of my Father in heaven, he is my brother and sister and mother.' By these words he wished to teach them that now that he had left his maternal home to dedicate himself to the service of God and his neighbour, the rest of the world was just as dear to him as his own mother and family and had the same right of access to him. The corollary was that his own blood relations from now on had no more call upon his time or service than anyone else. Of course, his love for them had not diminished, it was as great as ever; but he now treats all the world with the same concern. This was indeed a new and radical doctrine in a society in which people had grown up to have no particular interest in anyone outside their own family blood-relationship. Any other mother might have been hurt by what sounded like a rebuff; but we may assume that Mary already understood that he was continuing to prepare her for her future role as Mother of all the Redeemed; and in any case we can be sure that she had full confidence and trust in his wisdom. The Apostles however had yet to learn that their mission would be to go to all peoples of all nations and of all classes without discrimination.

13) Jesus anointed by a Woman (Lk 7:36-50)

The other story concerns his encounter with a prostitute when he was dining at the house of a wealthy Pharisee. This Pharisee, by name Simon, had received Jesus with scant courtesy by failing to show him the usual marks of respect, such as washing his feet on his arrival, anointing his head with oil, and giving him the kiss of peace. However in the course of the dinner a well-known courtesan entered. Without saying a word she knelt at his feet as he lay reclining in the fashion of the time at the dining table. Heedless of the other guests—all men of course in keeping with oriental custom—she shed silent tears over his feet, still dusty from the road, wiping them with her luxuriant hair, kissing them and anointing them with precious perfume from an alabaster flask she had brought with her. None of the guests at table said a word, waiting for their host to intervene, but Simon felt too embarrassed to do so. Yet he did not seem in the least worried at his own lack of courtesy, and was merely wondering how a prophet like Jesus could seemingly fail to realize the woman's profession and not shrink from her ritually unclean touch. Eventually the conversation came to a standstill, and all turned to look at Jesus, who had been watching her with compassion. At last he broke the silence by saying: 'Simon, I have something to tell you'. And the Pharisee replied, perhaps a little flippantly: 'Teacher, tell me'.—'There were two debtors of a certain creditor; the one owed five hundred denarii, and the other fifty. Neither having the means to pay him back, he forgave both. Which of them therefore will love him more?' Simon answered: 'I suppose the one to whom he forgave more'. Jesus said to him: 'You have judged correctly'. The rest of the episode is best told in the words of the Gospel:

> Then turning to the woman, he said to Simon: 'Do you see this woman? I entered into your house. Water for my feet you did not give me; but she has washed my feet with her tears and wiped them with her hair. You gave me no kiss, but she from the time I entered

in has not stopped kissing my feet. You did not anoint my head with oil, but she has anointed my feet with precious perfume. Thanks to this, I say to you, her sins are forgiven, because she has loved much. For he loves little, to whom little is forgiven.' And he said to her: 'Your sins are forgiven. Your faith has saved you. Go in peace'.

At these words the fellow-guests of Jesus looked surprised and thought within themselves, 'May not this man after all be the prophet, since he claims the authority of God himself?'

The evangelist fails to give us any hint of how Simon was feeling; but he must have wanted the earth to open up and swallow him! In all the Gospels there was never so crushing a rebuke delivered so gently and yet so devastatingly. He knew he was in the wrong and his humiliation was made even greater by being rebuked in front of all his guests and this strangely fascinating but notorious woman. Now his rudeness and its consequences would make him the laughing-stock of the whole city. Jesus had analysed the situation to perfection. Simon had always thought of himself as a very devout Jew, as one who perfectly fulfilled all the minutiae of Pharisaic observance, beyond reproach in all essentials, and no ordinary mortal. And now he realised what a colossal pride he had, and that his sin was far greater than that of the woman who had not hesitated to acknowledge her sinfulness to this prophet and express her sorrow to God through him. Christian tradition does not tell us if Simon truly repented, but he may have been 'Simon the Leper' who was the host at the banquet prepared for Jesus by his friends at Bethany at the beginning of the last week of his life. If so, he had indeed converted to the Lord as the result of this rebuke.

There are several other intriguing questions begging for an answer that we may rightly ask before we pass on. What was it that led this woman to repent of her former way of life? What led her to make a parade of herself in public before all Simon's guests? Why didn't she wait for a less public occasion to profess her repentance and her determination to change her way of life?

In the first place her compunction may have been generated by some word or sign that Jesus had given on an earlier oc-

casion, something that touched her heart so profoundly that it
'turned her over' completely and persuaded her, there and then
to renounce her past life, which was to remain a secret between
him and her.

But why did she feel it necessary to make such a public
demonstration of her conversion? Had some of the diners been
her former clients? Did she consider it essential to let them all
know without delay that that phase of her life was over? However, she must surely have heard the words of Jesus, his call to
'Repent for the Kingdom of God is at hand', and his presence in
the town may have brought them forcibly to her mind, and she
had the urgent desire to fling herself at his feet. But why such
lavish signs of her love? Perhaps because her emotional life had
been stirred to its depths by his goodness. Her feminine in-
stincts made her see clearly enough that he represented God in
a unique way, and her gratitude to him for her conversion was
so great that she could brook no delay in expressing it personally to him. Oriental custom ruled out any close contact between
Jesus the rabbi and women. And therefore she might well have
calculated that only in public—and on this one unique occasion—would she have the freedom to show her love for him,
and so be able to lavish on him the purest caresses to replace
those impure ones she had so often in the past squandered on
her former clients. For she now clearly realised that only from
the touch of his all-holy and all-pure body could she obtain the
grace and strength to enable her to lead a new life of perfect
chastity and purity.

And finally, who was she? The Gospels do not permit us to
come to a firm conclusion. The exegetes for the most part refuse
to identify her either with Mary Magdalene or with Mary the
sister of Martha and Lazarus. The liturgies of the Churches of
East and West have sometimes identified her with the one and
sometimes with the other, but are not agreed. Let her therefore
remain anonymous.

9

The First Mission of the Twelve

1) Instructions for the Twelve[22] *(Mt 10:1f = Lk 9:1f = Mk 6:8f)*

Jesus had now completed the first stage of the training of the twelve Apostles and felt that the time was ripe for sending them out on their own to give them some first-hand experience of what would later become their lifework. For some months they had had the privilege of his example and his way of life to inspire them. They were aware of the people's need for spiritual guidance, and Jesus had told them that he wanted 'to take pity on the crowds, for they were distressed and dejected like sheep without a shepherd', and had added, 'The harvest is great indeed but the harvesters few; so pray the Lord of the harvest to send workers into his harvest' (Mt 9:36-37). Thus the Twelve must have swelled with justifiable pride that the Lord Jesus now thought them worthy to start co-operating with him in active work for the Kingdom.

22 It is extremely difficult to establish the exact sequence of events in the Galilean ministry. However, my Synopsis reveals that there are four places where the respective accounts of Matthew, Luke, and Mark come together in parallel: namely at Mt 10:1, 11:1, 14:1 and 19:1; and these form the framework for placing the other events in a measure of chronological order. They mark respectively the instructions Jesus gave the Twelve before he sent them out, the mission itself, their return to Jesus, and the date of his final departure from Galilee. Jesus seems to have moved into Galilee early in the month of December AD 28, and the mission probably took place in the following spring (about the middle of March according to our modern reckoning).

And so some weeks after his Purim visit to Jerusalem, but
before the Passover of AD 29, Jesus considered that the time had
come to test the Apostles' capacity to represent him, by sending
them out to preach in his Name. So he called them together and
solemnly gave them power to cast out 'unclean spirits... and all
the demons, and also to heal every sickness and malady'. Furthermore he gave them explicit instructions as to how they
were to behave and act as his ambassadors by commanding
them as follows:

> Do not go into the territory of the Gentiles, and do not enter any city
> of the Samaritans. But go only to the lost sheep of the House of
> Israel. And as you go, preach saying: "The Kingdom of the heavens
> has come". Heal the sick, raise the dead, cleanse the lepers, cast out
> demons. Freely you have received, freely give. Do not accept gold or
> silver, or copper for your purses; do not take a begging-bag for the
> road, nor two coats, nor sandals, nor a staff. For the workman is
> worthy of his hire. Whenever you enter a town or a village, find out
> who in it is worthy, and stay there until you depart. And as you
> enter the house, greet it. And if indeed the house be worthy, let your
> peace come upon it. But if it is not worthy, let your peace come back
> to you. And whoever does not receive you and does not listen to your
> words, going forth outside that house or city shake its dust off your
> feet. Amen I say to you, it will be more tolerable for the land of
> Sodom and Gomorrah in the day of judgement than for that city.
> (Mt 10: 5-15)

The above is the core of the guidance given by Jesus to the
Twelve at this their first sending. According to Luke (10:1f)
Jesus a little later gave similar instructions to seventy-two
other disciples. Just as the twelve Apostles corresponded in the
mind of Jesus to the twelve tribes of Israel, the plenitude of the
People of God, so it may be assumed that the seventy-two were
meant by him to correspond to the seventy-two whom Moses
was advised to institute in order to help him 'bear the burden of
the people' (Num 11:16f). It is perhaps not fanciful to see these
seventy-two as future assistants and counsellors of the twelve
Apostles in the early days of the Church in Judea.

All the instructions were extremely practical and covered the
eventualities the Apostles would have to face in Galilee at that

time. The evangelist Matthew also recorded additional directives that Jesus delivered on later occasions to prepare them for
future trials on their journeys abroad (Mt 10:16-42). These
directives are particularly interesting because they represent
the code of practice that Jesus himself observed while he was
'on the road' in Galilee. He was always aware that what he did
had already been foreshadowed in word and action in the Old
Testament. However it was not that he was acting in accordance with the Old Testament prophecies, but his heavenly
Father had framed the whole of the Old Testament to
foreshadow the future actions of the Messiah: *Novum testamentum in antiquo latet; antiquum testamentum in novo patet* (The
New Testament lies hidden in the Old; the Old is made manifest
in the New).

The Messiah had been promised to the Jews. Therefore the
instructions that Jesus had received from his heavenly Father,
when he had been commissioned at his baptism, restricted him
to the evangelization of his own fellow-Jews in the region that
we call the Holy Land. It was not until after his resurrection
that the Holy Spirit would inspire the members of the newly
formed Body of the Risen Christ, the Church, to commence the
work of the evangelization of the nations and to bring them all
under his benign sway and influence. The Apostles were to reap
a harvest they did not sow; Jesus was to labour and they were to
enter into his labour (Jn 4:38). At this stage of the formation of
the structure of God's Kingdom the disciples were warned to
avoid communities of Gentiles (i.e. of pagans); and that is perhaps why we find for example no mention of the city of Tiberias
in our Gospels, for it was an entirely pagan colony founded by
Herod only a few years earlier. On the other hand there was
nothing to stop the inhabitants of pagan Magdala from going
out to meet Jesus. Indeed it is possible that Jesus did visit that
city if Simon the Pharisee lived there; and this would explain
how Mary of Magdala came to see Jesus at Simon's house.

The Apostles were similarly told not to go into Samaritan vil-
lages, since their evangelization would come later (see Ac 8:14ff).

In fact, Jesus expressly directed the Twelve to concentrate on inducing the 'lost sheep of the House of Israel' to return to the Lord. Jesus himself adhered strictly to this rule all through his ministry (see Mt 15:24); he only made exceptions when he found among pagans a faith equal to or excelling that of the Jews, which permitted him to treat them as if they were already Jews and therefore members of his family. The message of the disciples was to be the same as that of their Master, that the Kingdom of the Heavens (i.e. the Kingdom of God), had already arrived in his person. 'The lost sheep', to whom their message of salvation was to be addressed, were therefore circumcised Jews and their families, who had lapsed from the practice of their faith and had been unable for one reason or other to find their way back to it.

What did the Twelve have to say about Jesus himself at this early stage of their preparation for ministry? It is all contained in the sentence: 'As you go, preach saying, The Kingdom of the Heavens has come' (Mt 10:7). This of course means that they must preach about Jesus himself. And so as they set out two by two to instruct the people of Galilee they must have proclaimed something like this:

> At one time we were disciples of John the Baptist who taught us all how to prepare for the coming of the Kingdom of God, by confessing our sins and being baptised by him in the Jordan. John, as you know, pointed out Jesus of Nazareth to us and to the crowds as 'he who is to come',—the prophet and law-giver whom Moses foretold would complete his work. Jesus has called each of us personally to leave our families and everything to follow him out of love, and he now sends us to you to invite you in your turn to become members of his Kingdom. For he is truly Son of God.
>
> We want here and now to testify to you that the Spirit of the Lord God of our fathers is upon him and that he is the Messiah, the Anointed One, prophesied by Isaiah, to bring salvation not only to our own race but also to the whole world. He is the perfect fulfilment of our Holy Scriptures and has already given us many proofs of his power to destroy Satan and all his devils, to raise the dead and to cure leprosy and every disease.
>
> You also know that when he entered the Temple not long ago to claim his inheritance the chief priests and the scribes refused out of

envy and love of riches to receive him and are even now trying to thwart him. But you may take it as certain that he will succeed in establishing his Kingdom, for it is not of this world. For while he was on his way back to Galilee after his rejection, even the Samaritans, as he passed through, proclaimed him to be the Saviour of the World. He has a great role for you in his Kingdom, if only you will keep the Law of Moses in the spirit he will teach you. He has made us new men, and we ask you to open your doors and hearts to him when he comes.

The message the Apostles brought was to obey the Law of God as already made known in the Ten Commandments and the other prescriptions of the Law of Moses, subject only to the modifications that Jesus himself decreed. He endowed the Apostles with the charisms of 'healing the sick, raising the dead, cleansing the lepers, casting out the demons', the most important power being that of driving out the devils and terminating the rule of Satan over the souls of men. Since these powers were a free gift from God, they were to exercise them always without accepting any payment whatever. To accept money in payment for the exercise of their ministry would therefore have been a grave sin (later called the sin of simony). In this respect, namely, in always giving their spiritual services gratuitously, they were to be in contrast with the pagan ministers and healers plying their trade within the Roman empire and usually insisting on payment in advance. Jesus then specified in detail what their attitude towards money should be. They were not to carry any money at all with them on their mission tours, nor even a begging-bag for soliciting alms from passers-by. Neither were they allowed to take any spare clothing with them, nor a staff to use as a weapon to ward off 'muggers'.

The teaching the Apostles were to impart was truly life-giving, and they were to trust the Lord to inspire those listening to their preaching to provide them with all they needed, since 'the workman is worthy of his hire'. They were however to behave prudently. When they first entered a town where there had been no previous evangelization, they were first to find out some household well-disposed towards them, and stay there as long as they remained in that town, bringing their peace upon that house. The 'peace' that they brought with them was the special favour of the Lord God of the universe, and the greatest possible honour to the people of that house. Should the householder knowingly and deliberately reject the offer of 'peace' from God's representative, the missioner was to make sure that its occupants realized the enormity of the insult they had inflicted on Almighty God, and was then after due warnings to withdraw. Citizens who rejected the plenipotentiary of God would suffer a spiritual fate worse than that of the twin cities of Sodom and Gomorrah which had been wiped out by fire and brimstone, and whose very sites had been overwhelmed by the bitter waters of the Dead Sea (Gen 19:24). Inspired by the example of Jesus and armed with these explicit instructions, the Twelve were sent out two by two on a short missionary tour of Galilee. He would later augment these instructions after they had successfully completed their initial training. Mark says that they preached repentance and that 'they cast out many demons and anointed many sick and healed them' (Mk 6:12f).

2) *The Baptist's Disciples visit Jesus (Mt 11:2f = Lk 7:18f)*

It may be recalled that Jesus partly for reasons of personal safety had moved from Judea into Galilee when he heard that the Baptist had been unjustly imprisoned by Herod Antipas in the fortress of Machaerus on the eastern side of the Dead Sea. From the dungeons of that grim palace John had been closely following the progress of Jesus by means of reports from his own disciples who continued to have access to him and were able to bring him regular news. Whilst he was free, he had done his best to make known the Messiah and establish his credentials, and he was aware of the kind of opposition that Jesus was enduring and the frustrations to which he was subject. But now his voice was silenced and there was nothing he could directly do to further the cause of Jesus.

After their briefing the Twelve set out two by two on their first independent mission in Galilee, while Jesus went his own way preaching and healing (Mt 11:1). And then John the Baptist had an inspiration that would enable him even while in prison to promote the cause of the Messiah. He therefore sent two of his own disciples to ask Jesus publicly if he was 'the One Who was to come' prophesied by Malachi; and he sent them not for his own sake (because he knew Jesus to be the Messiah), but in order to give Jesus himself a further opportunity to demonstrate that he was indeed the One to come, and that he was neither anti-Roman nor pro-Nationalist, but had come solely to restore spiritual health of mind and body to 'those who were sick' (Mt 9:12). Jesus responded to John's question with alacrity in the way that John expected, namely not merely by words but by the miracles of healing that only the Messiah would perform. And so in that very hour Jesus healed many from diseases and evil spirits and restored sight to the blind. He then said to John's messengers:

> Go and report to John what you have seen and heard: the blind see again, the lame walk, lepers are cleansed, and the deaf hear, the dead are raised, the poor are evangelised. And blessed is he who has not been scandalised over me.

John's disciples therefore saw with their own eyes how Jesus was fulfilling Isaiah's prophecy of the Messiah:

> Behold your God... will come and save you. Then the eyes of the blind shall be opened and the ears of the dumb unstopped; then shall the lame man leap like a hart, and the tongues of the dumb sing for joy (Is 35:4-6).

And he then sent John's disciples back with the following panegyric of their master ringing in their ears:

> Amen, I say to you, there has not arisen among those born of women a greater prophet than John... and if you wish to receive it, he is the Elijah who is to come (Mt 11:11-14).

With these words Jesus offered comfort to John in prison in the last days before his execution in macabre circumstances (Mk 6:14-29). And in this way he was able to reassure John that he had successfully accomplished his mission and that as a result Jesus' own ministry was now bearing its intended fruit.

3) Herod Antipas seeks to apprehend Jesus
(Mt 14:1f = Lk 9:7f = Mk 6:14f)

At this time a further complication entered into the ministry of Jesus. Herod Antipas, one of the sons of Herod the Great, a dissolute old man, began to get very apprehensive and wanted to lay hands on him. The evangelists indeed give us the following brief glimpse of the alarm raised in Herod's mind by the ceaseless activity of Jesus and his disciples in the province of Galilee.

Soon after John's disciples had relayed Jesus' comforting message, Herod had had John the Baptist put to death (see Josephus, *Antiquities* XVIII 116-119). Yet his worry was not ended, because his spies and frequent visitors to his court were now bringing him tales of the wonders being performed by Jesus, and how these wonders were being multiplied manifold by the little parties of his Apostles purposefully visiting two-by-two every corner of the province. Jesus was becoming a real vexation to this evil and adulterous ruler, who was quite incapable of rising to the spiritual level on which Jesus was operating. However, he still had strong guilt feelings about the murder of John the Baptist during his birthday dinner party. The thought was haunting him that the God of Israel, whom John had worshipped, had perhaps raised him up from the dead just to remind him of the retribution that might come upon him in due course. To his horror the reports reaching him confirmed that Jesus was working signs exceeding those of all the ancients prophets and that some were saying he was John the Baptist risen from the dead. Herod reckoned that the wisest course would be to entice Jesus to come and see him voluntarily, since he was superstitious enough to realize that force against him— at least at this stage—would be most unpopular and might well bring down divine retribution with overwhelming suddenness. He hoped that, once he had Jesus trapped inside his palace, he could easily find means to spirit him away without any fuss. Jesus was well aware of the type of man he had to deal with, once referring to him as 'that fox' and had his plan ready to avoid capture, which he would put into operation as soon as the

Apostles returned from their mission. The Twelve had been given a definite date by which to return to Capharnaum and in the interval Jesus wisely kept on the move.

4) The Feeding of the Five Thousand
(Mt 14:13f= Lk 9:10f = Mk 6:32f = Jn 6:1f)

The Apostles returned just before the Passover (about the beginning of our April), elated with their successes. Everything had turned out as their Master had said and now they were tired but happy. However, the ceaseless coming and going around the headquarters in Capharnaum was very wearisome, so much so that they did not have time even to eat, and he suggested to them: 'Let us go away to some unfrequented place and rest a little together'. So they took ship across the lake to some point well to the south of the fishing village of Bethsaida. On landing however they found that the crowds had guessed their destination and were there to greet them, so that their longed for peace and quiet were out of the question. Jesus resigned himself to the situation and decided to humour them, although they were attracted to him not so much by his gracious words as by the hope of obtaining miraculous cures for their sick and seeing further wonders. So he ascended an eminence with his disciples in order to address them; and after healing their sick he sat down and spoke to them at length about the Kingdom of God. In many ways the scene was reminiscent of the occasion of the Sermon on the Mount delivered some weeks before. Indeed it may have been the very same mountain.

The time passed all too quickly and by late afternoon the disciples became restive as they were getting hungry and thought that the crowds must also be feeling the same. So some of the Apostles approached Jesus and suggested that it was getting near sunset and time to let the people go as they were a long way from any place where they might obtain food for themselves or the crowd. Jesus, however, knew what he was going to do, and to prepare the way for it, he said provokingly to Philip: 'Where can we buy enough food to feed all this crowd?' Philip sharply reminded him that even two hundred denarii would not be sufficient to provide a modicum for everyone there. Jesus retorted: 'You yourselves give them to eat'. Philip and the others countered: 'Do you mean that we should go off and buy two hundred denarii' worth of bread to feed them with?' He answered: 'There is no need to go; you give them to eat'. And he added: 'How many loaves have you? Go and see.' Then Andrew, the brother of Peter, informed him: 'There is a young lad here, who has five barley loaves and two salted fish. But what is this among so many?'. For there were at a rough estimate about five thousand men present, besides women and children. Without more ado Jesus gave the order: 'Get them all to sit down in groups of fifty or a hundred and leave an aisle between the groups.' The disciples swiftly marshalled the compliant crowd, telling them that the Master was arranging a meal for them. The following seems to be the scene that the evangelists depict.

Jesus then took the five loaves and the two fishes and raising his eyes to heaven and giving thanks to his Father, blessed and broke the loaves and fishes and distributed them to the disciples who queued up to receive them from him and then hurried down the gangways distributing as they went. How the food lasted out they did not know, but they did not have to go back to Jesus for more, and soon all the hundred or so groups were served and the Apostles too. Everyone had as much as they wanted, the portions of fish serving as a condiment to make the bread palatable and providing a nourishing meal. When all had finished and were satisfied, the Lord directed the Twelve: 'Go now and gather up the left-overs, so that nothing may be lost'. And they did so and filled no less than twelve large baskets, one for each of the Twelve.

The multiplication had taken place so quietly and mysteriously that none perceived it while it was happening; but even before the meal was over the crowd as well as the Apostles realized that Jesus had worked a sign that could only have been performed by the prophet of whom Moses had spoken (Dt 18:15). The bolder spirits among the diners at once saw that Jesus had both the power and the authority to change the future of their nation at a single stroke, and when some one shouted out, 'Let us make Jesus our King', the cry was taken up enthusiastically. But he had already anticipated this reaction on the part of the crowd. Swiftly summoning the Twelve, he ordered them to go down at once to the boat and sail off back to the other side without waiting for him. Turning to the crowd he insisted that his mission was one of peace and not of rebellion and that he had still greater benefits to offer them if only they would come and listen to him on the morrow in Capharnaum. With these words he persuaded them to depart quietly. Then he thankfully turned his steps up the mountainside as night fell and spent some hours alone in prayer and communion with his heavenly Father.

5) Jesus walks on the Water
(Mt 14:22-23 = Mk 6:45-52 = Jn 6:16-21)

While he was praying on the mountain the Twelve were having a hard struggle during the night on the waters of the lake. The wind was contrary, the water was rough and they were making little or no headway towards Capharnaum, where they expected Jesus to rendezvous with them sometime the following day. In the darkness before the dawn they suddenly descried him walking on the sea and apparently about to pass them by. They could not believe their eyes at the sight of this luminous figure looming up out of the darkness, and shouted out for fear, 'It is a ghost'. But the voice of Jesus, as he came close, at once calmed them: 'Don't be afraid; I am I—it's me take heart'. And Peter, fascinated by the sight and eager to get to him, said: 'Lord, if it is you, command me to come to you on the waters'.— 'Come', said Jesus. And Peter without hesitation stepped out of the boat onto the water, despite the gusting wind lashing the waves, and started to walk towards him. He had hardly taken a step when he realized what a rash thing he was doing, and the force of the wind and the waters moving under his feet made him panic. Terrified, he felt himself sinking and cried in alarm, 'Lord, save me'. Jesus stretched out his hand and grasped him firmly, saying: 'O man of little faith, why did you waver?' As they got into the boat together, the wind stopped instantly. The other Apostles were dumbfounded at this miracle and the sudden calm that followed. It was now beginning to dawn on them that he was indeed the Son of God, and Peter was shortly to voice their belief. And though they did not yet understand the meaning of the multiplication of the loaves and fishes they felt it fitting all the same to give him divine honours there and then by worshipping him.

6) The Discourse on the Bread of Life (Jn 6:16f)

Living with Jesus was indeed a most exciting business, and there was never a dull moment. For no sooner had they landed on the western shore at the plain of Gennesaret than a thrill of excitement went through all the inhabitants of the district. The crowds had last seen him going up the mountain on the other side of the Lake in the dark of the previous evening and were now amazed to find him back at Capharnaum with his disciples. They could not understand how he had got back unobserved, because they knew that he had stayed behind that evening and no other boat had been able to cross. Overjoyed at seeing him again, they brought their sick from all directions and laid them out in the roads and in the market squares, wherever they thought he might pass, and he healed them all. Even those who touched just the hem of his cloak were completely cured (Mk 6:53-56).

When the crowd questioned him as to how he got back, he did not enlighten them, but rebuked them for being interested in the free meal he had given them rather than in the spiritual meaning of the miracle of the loaves and fishes. He admonished them: 'Do not work for the food that perishes, but work for the food that remains for eternal life, which the Son of Man will give you. For God the Father has set his seal upon him'.

Jesus then set about explaining to them the nature of this heavenly food, nourishment so wonderful as to be incomprehensible to earth-bound people, and which even the Apostles had to take on faith. This food would be different from the manna that God had given the Israelites when Moses was leading them through the desert and which indeed had been a special and miraculous gift. The function of that food had only been to nourish the body and not the spirit of a man. The new food that Christ would give his faithful followers would nourish the soul and confer eternal life.

St John considered this revelation so important that he took the trouble to name the place in which Jesus now chose to make it, namely the synagogue at Capharnaum (Jn 6:59). Here on the next day, the Sabbath, the people were eagerly waiting to question him. 'What should we do to work the works of God?', they asked, always thinking in terms of physical activities. His answer was a startling challenge to them: 'This is the Work of God, that you simply believe in the One whom he has sent'. That is to say, they are to trust him here and now, accept what he says and do what he tells them! They are to believe in him just as the Twelve Apostles have done. They were just to ask for the gift of faith in him! There he was, standing tranquilly before them, dressed in the common attire of a labourer, with no outward sign or badge of authority, such as distinguished the scribes and Pharisees and the priests of the Temple. Once before he had made the same demand for credence and trust to the Temple authorities after the healing of the paralytic at the Probatic Pool, but vainly. Would he now be more successful here in his native Galilee, especially after the miracle of the feeding of the five thousand? How would this audience react?

Their next question was: 'What sign then do you do, that we may see and believe you? What do you work? Our fathers ate the manna in the desert, just as it is written: He gave them bread from heaven to eat' (Jn 6:30-31). By this remark they were inferring that the feeding of the five thousand was no greater sign of God's presence than the manna had been and were now asking him for a still greater sign, before they would be prepared to believe him and accept his authority. Lack of belief is already appearing. Jesus replied:

> Amen, amen I say to you, Moses did not give you the bread from heaven, but my Father gives you the true bread from heaven. For

the bread of God is that which comes down from heaven and gives life to the world. (Jn 6:32-33)

He was telling them that whilst the manna came down all those years ago like dew on the grass, it did not have the quality of being 'heavenly', i.e. food for the spirit. But he on the contrary is now promising bread of an altogether higher order, life-giving nourishment from the heaven where God dwells. Even then they did not really understand, but they had grasped enough to realize that he was offering them something most desirable, so they answered: 'Lord, give us always this bread' (Jn 6:34).

This request provided Jesus with an opportunity to enlighten them as to the true content of this 'new heavenly bread': 'I myself am the Bread of Life. He that comes to me will not be hungry, and he that believes in me will not thirst any more' (Jn 6:35).

With these words he offered them the further challenge that they must believe that he was going to feed them from the very substance of his own Being. Yet he was fully aware that many among his hearers would not be able to make such an act of faith, but only those persons given to him by his Father, indicating those he would raise up at the Last Day. Here we have a further concept, that of the Last Day when the dead who belong to him will be raised by him personally to enjoy eternal life (Jn 6:36-40). This marvellous promise was contingent on those who heard him believing in him. The audience however concentrated their attention on his statement that he was the Bread that had come down from heaven, and they compared it with the known fact that he was Jesus, the son of Joseph, whose father and mother they knew. How could what he was saying be true? It seemed absurd and impossible! And yet...? He turned on the murmurers and doubters and refused to modify the claim he had just made. On the contrary, he repeated it with still greater vehemence and added that he had not only come down from heaven but that he alone had actually seen the Father, that he himself is the Bread of Life, which gives eternal life, and he then concluded with the bombshell that this Bread would be his own flesh.

In their amazement the Jews burst out with: 'Is he not the son of Joseph whose father and mother we know? How says he now: I have come down from heaven?' Jesus retorted in words whose meaning could not be misunderstood but which still required an act of faith to accept:

Amen, amen I say to you, he who believes in me has eternal life. I am the Bread of Life. Your fathers ate the manna in the desert and died. This is the bread that comes down from heaven, so that if anyone eats of it indeed he will not die. I am the living bread that comes down from heaven; if anyone eats of this bread he will live for ever. And indeed the bread which I will give is my flesh for the life of the world. (Jn 6:47-51)

The full depth of the mystery has now been set forth by Jesus in the simplest possible terms. He touches on the mystery of predestination when he refers to those the Father will give him as those who have been taught by God (Jn 6:45). God the Father teaches all mankind but not all respond because of the misuse of their free will. However, we learn that the life-giving flesh of Jesus will be communicated through this bread, because he is going to offer his flesh, his body, as a sacrifice for the life of the world. The programme of events is now becoming clear. His body will become the food of men as the result of the sacrifice of his life. As we shall see, the Jews understood his words quite literally in the sense that he was proposing to cannibalize himself for their good. He does not directly contradict such a crude understanding of his words, but he will later in the dialogue explain that this eating is real but also spiritual—'the flesh profiting nothing'. And he endorses without hesitation that it is a matter of a real eating of his body and a real drinking his blood. Far from withdrawing from the position he has taken up, he now clarifies and reinforces it in the most solemn manner:

Amen, amen I say to you, unless you eat the flesh of the Son of Man and drink his blood, you will not have life in yourselves. He who consumes my body and drinks my blood has eternal life and I will raise him up on the Last Day. For my flesh is veritable food and my blood is veritable drink. He who consumes my flesh and drinks my blood remains in me and I in him. Just as the Living Father has sent me and I live because of the Father, so also he who consumes me he also will live because of me. This is the Bread that has come down from heaven—not just as your fathers ate the manna and died—he who consumes this Bread will live for ever. (Jn 6:53-58)

Jesus is now doing so much more than merely passing on sound Old Testament teaching. He is proclaiming himself to be the healing medicine and balm that the world needs; he alone can impart the gift of eternal life and free all mankind from death. Furthermore, actual contact with his person, with his body will be necessary for every single human being whom his Father will inspire to come to him. They are all expected to eat his flesh and drink his blood if they want to enter into eternal life at the Last Day when he is going to 'raise them up'. Yet the whole notion of eating his flesh sounded disgusting to the Jews for whom cannibalism was abhorrent. And this thought was passing through their minds; can Jesus really be in his right mind? Indeed, he is in deadly earnest and in no way withdraws or modifies anything in spite of close questioning. But no one can as yet perceive how he could possibly make himself available in the way he said. Men of good will who believe in his integrity must take it on trust that he is able to do what he has consistently maintained throughout the long dialogue. Everyone must take it or leave it; which is what happened. But before letting the disbelievers go, Jesus makes a final effort to persuade them to an act of faith in him.

Many of his listeners continued to remain sceptical, saying 'This word is hard; who can accept it?'. And to give them a hint of what the real but spiritual eating of his flesh really meant, he explained that it was related to his return to heaven, 'It is the Spirit that gives life, the flesh is of no avail' (Jn 6:63). Nevertheless Jesus now saw clearly that he had to resign himself to the fact that many would not believe in him (including the one who was later to betray him). For belief in him is a gift from his heavenly Father; and many would deliberately turn back from following him through rejection of the Father's gift.

We have now come to the real watershed in the Galilean ministry, the moment when his whole mission trembled in the balance. Would Peter and the Eleven also walk away from him and desert him? It was a distinct possibility. The poignant moment has arrived when Jesus, seeing so many leaving him in unbelief, turns to the Twelve and asks: 'Do you too wish to go away?' To which question Peter, speaking for the Twelve, made the immediate and decisive answer: 'Lord, to whom shall we go? You have the words of eternal life. And we have believed and have realised that you are the Holy One of God.' This reply gave Jesus the answer he had hoped for, because at least it supplied the minimum amount of support to carry on and upon which to build the visible Church, the nucleus of his future Kingdom. So Jesus now knew that the Twelve as a group would give him their whole-hearted trust, despite the human frailty they would continue to display. But his gratification was tempered by the knowledge (which he openly voiced) that even one of these Twelve—Judas Iscariot— would become the Devil's minion and before long would walk away and betray him. 'Did I not chose you Twelve', he said, 'and one of you is a devil?' For Jesus saw into the heart of Judas that he had other plans and ambitions and no longer trusted him. To sum up, it had now become apparent to him that after a year and more of ministry he had few active friends apart from the Twelve and a group of holy women.

10

A Detour North and East of Galilee

From the time of the Passover (normally early in April AD 29) until the Feast of Tabernacles (September/October) Jesus spent the time partly in Galilee and partly in the pagan regions that fringed it to the north and east; and we shall be following his movements as they are found in the Synoptic Gospels.

1) The Tradition of the Elders (Mt 15:1-20 = Mk 7:1-23)

The next recorded incident is again connected with the messianic authority that Jesus was exercising quite independently of the rules for proper religious behaviour laid down by the scribes and Pharisees. They had created a web of precepts covering every aspect of daily life, referred to as 'the tradition of the elders', and on account of their number and intricacy they could be properly observed only by Pharisees and the well-to-do. The system had grown out of all proportion and had got out of hand. The question at issue arose in the following way.

The chief priests had decided to monitor the activities of Jesus in Galilee and had sent down some observers who now took exception to the behaviour of his disciples for not washing their hands ritually before eating bread. In fact, by implication they were accusing him personally of not making sure that his disciples kept every one of a host of minor scribal regulations originally prescribed to promote the faithful observance of the

Law in letter and in spirit. In his indifference to these legal niceties they saw a challenge to their authority to interpret the Law, and quite rightly so. In virtue of his supreme authority as Messiah to update the observances of the Law, he had already sanctioned the present behaviour of his disciples, and therefore had no case to answer and could rightly ignore the accusation. So he responded by counter-attacking, charging them with failing to observe the Law itself, the Torah, on a serious moral issue while insisting on inessential trifles.

Why do you also transgress the commandment of God for the sake of your tradition? For you negate the commandment of God in order to observe your tradition. For Moses said: Honour your father and mother, and: He who curses father and mother shall die the death. But you say: If a man says to father and mother: Anything of mine through which you might be benefited is Korban, a sacred gift, you no longer allow him to do anything for father or mother, annulling the Word of God by your tradition, which you have handed on. (Mt 15:1-6 = Mk 7:9-13)

It is evident here that Jesus was condemning a practice whereby a son could evade his obligation to support his needy parents by dedicating to the Temple the amount that he should have set aside for them, but in such a way that he could still have the use of it for himself. The duty of sons to take care of and support their old parents in case of need was of course strongly affirmed in the Law of Moses. It is likely that Jesus brought up this matter in this context because there may have been some recent case in the Jerusalem courts that ended in a judgement that scandalised the public. Jesus knew himself to be justified in reprimanding them, and his revelation of their hypocrisy destroyed any shred of value in their charge against his disciples over their failure to wash their hands ritually before eating. Jesus gave his own judgement on the matter in the following words: 'They teach the commandments of men as if they were doctrines', i.e. as if they were divine precepts (Mt 15:9); and his questioners were shamed into silence.

2) 'The Things that defile a Man' (Mt 15:10f = Mk 7:14f)

At this point Matthew added another pertinent anecdote that underlined the duplicity of his enemies and at the same time revealed Jesus as the supreme legislator with sovereign power either to modify or to cancel or to enlarge the scope of the Law of Moses. Matthew and Mark recorded that:

> Summoning the crowd he said to them: "Hear and take it in. Nothing that enters into the mouth defiles a man; but what comes out of the mouth defiles a man".

By this juxtaposition of anecdotes Matthew indicated that to be exceedingly scrupulous about the food laws of Leviticus 11 and at the same time to speak or act wrongly was a blatant hypocrisy yet one which did not seem to trouble the Pharisees' conscience. Jesus was not advocating the breaking of the Law of Leviticus; he was making the point that it was useless and thoroughly hypocritical to keep these dietary laws about what one puts into one's mouth, if one was in the habit of allowing any words displeasing to God and harmful to one's neighbour to issue from it. According to the mind of Jesus these prohibitions against eating certain kinds of food, designated as 'unclean' and 'an abomination' to the person who ate them, had not been imposed because of any intrinsic evil in such action or in the food itself, but only to train the nation in obedience and in habits of healthy living.

Hitherto it had, of course, been sinful for any Jew to break these laws because doing so constituted a disobedience to the Law of God. The Pharisees were good theologians and knew that God could change his own laws at any time if he wanted to. They also knew that if the Messiah, when he came, were to change these or any other laws, the old laws would no longer be binding under sin. But they had blinded themselves to the fact that God's prophet had now come among them in the person of the Christ Jesus. And so when he learnt from his disciples that the Pharisees were scandalised at his words, he simply condemned them as 'blind leaders of the blind; and if a blind man should lead another blind man then they will both fall into the ditch'(Mt 15:14). Jesus did not think it prudent to attempt to explain the finer points of theology to the Pharisees or the crowd, but when his disciples returned to the house, Peter and the others questioned him closely. Jesus then opened his mind fully to them:

> Are you also without understanding? Do you not know that everything that enters into the mouth removes into the stomach and is cast out into the drain? But the things that come out of the mouth come out of the heart, and these things defile a man. For from the heart come forth evil schemings, murders, adulteries, sexual sins, thefts, perjuries, blasphemies. These are the things that defile a man; but to eat with unwashed hands does not defile a man (Mt 15:16-20).

It is worth noting here that if the early Church Fathers are right in affirming, as they unanimously do, that the Gospel of Mark is the accurate text of discourses that Peter had delivered before a Roman audience some twenty years after Matthew had written and with Matthew's text before him, then Mark has preserved here Peter's own words adding magisterially in a brief parenthesis 'making all foods clean'(Mk 7:19), thus revealing Jesus' intention to abrogate the food laws in due course.

Matthew may have provided this anecdote to furnish the Christian Jews of Jerusalem with the support they needed to tolerate the fellowship of the many Gentile converts who began to trickle into the Church in Antioch and elsewhere soon after Pentecost (Ac 11:22). Of course Jesus was not ordering his followers to give up the habits of a lifetime, and the Apostles certainly did not interpret his words as if they were at once to forsake the existing dietary laws. Indeed we know that they adhered to them as tenaciously as any Pharisee, from the words Peter uttered when he was bidden by the heavenly voice to eat of unclean animals: 'No, Lord, I have never eaten anything common or unclean'(Ac 10:14). But after the resurrection the pressure of the Gentiles desiring to enter the Church would bring the Lord's words back to mind, and the Apostles, devout Jews though they were, would realize that belief in Jesus and the acceptance of baptism into his Church were after all the sole requirements that could be demanded of the pagan converts. The Christian way of life was morally speaking the same as the ancient Torah, the way of life of the Jews; but Christ had come to give it a new spirit, for he himself was the new Torah, 'the Way and the Truth and the Life' for all men of all races (Jn 14:6). For the Pharisees however this teaching of Jesus, and its momentous implications, constituted a blasphemous breach of the Law of Moses.

3) The Leaven of the Pharisees (Mt 16:5-12 = Mk 8:14-21)

From this time onwards Jesus started to warn his disciples more and more insistently to beware of the 'leaven', i.e. the teaching of the Pharisees. For he foresaw the pressure they would exert against his Church as soon as his own death had removed him from the scene. This pressure to conform to the old Judaism would be extremely subtle and persuasive, and unless the Apostles were to take the greatest care it would enter into the Church like the leaven or yeast into the flour (Mt 16:6ff). The recall of these words of Jesus would help the persecuted Church of Jerusalem to survive the onslaughts made on it during the forty years leading up to the destruction of the Holy City and its Temple and, in its train, the eclipse of the Pharisees.

4) The Demand for a Sign from Heaven (Mt 16:1-4 = Mk 8:11-13)

Before Jesus and his disciples left Galilee to escape the attentions of Herod Antipas by going north into what was pagan territory, the Pharisees and Sadducees made a further attempt to harass him by slyly coming up and asking him to show them a sign from heaven. Of course they had already had an abundance of signs from the Baptist and from Jesus himself sufficient to convince all men of good will. His reply revealed still more clearly the depth of the gulf between him and them. He pointed out to them that while they were able to forecast the weather correctly, they were unable to grasp the meaning of his presence among them. Consequently 'an evil and adulterous generation seeks a sign, and a sign shall not be given it, except the sign of Jonah'. The sign of Jonah is of course the sign of his resurrection from the dead, a prophecy of which none of them as yet understood the import. Jesus condemned his adversaries for their stubborn and wilful refusal to accept the proofs of his messiahship; and he prophesied that no further proofs will be offered them except this sign.

5) The Syrophoenician Woman (Mt 15:21-28 = Mk 7:24-30)

Jesus and the Twelve then travelled some fifty miles to the north into the beautiful and mountainous region of the Lebanon, the hinterland of the proverbially wicked cities of Tyre and Sidon, into which however he did not enter. His fame had preceded him and Mark reports that 'entering into a house he wanted no one to know and he could not be hidden'. The house in question may have been the house of some Jew, on whose friendship he could rely, someone who could also accommodate his twelve disciples at the same time. As he drew near to the house, the Apostles could not save him from being tiresomely accosted and pursued by a local pagan woman who would not go away and persistently followed him, whining: 'Lord, Son of David, my daughter is evilly possessed by a demon.' The Apostles got very annoyed with her and asked Jesus to shoo her off. But he did no more than firmly say to her: 'I have not been sent except to the lost sheep of the House of Israel.' Despite this rebuff, she followed him to the house and eventually forced her way in and knelt at his feet, saying: 'Lord, help me.' He then gave the first sign of relenting when he answered: 'Let the children first be fed; for it is not good to take the bread of the children and throw it to the puppy-dogs.' And then in a flash she saw her way to his heart: 'Yes, Lord, but even the puppies under the table eat of the crumbs of the children.' Jesus' heart melted and he said: 'O woman, great is your faith. For this saying, go away; the demon has gone out of your daughter.' And going home she found her daughter entirely cured.

6) The Healing of a Deaf-Mute (Mk 7:31-37)

Jesus did not remain long in the hinterland of Tyre and Sidon, one reason perhaps being that he was now being followed by a crowd of many thousands that must have caused considerable embarrassment and disturbance to the local inhabitants wherever he went. Anyhow, he came back southwards to the eastern side of the Sea of Galilee into the mainly pagan region of the Decapolis. According to Matthew and Mark he came by the mountain of the Great Sermon, and, going up onto it again, worked countless cures; for 'the crowd marvelled that they were seeing the dumb speaking, the maimed whole, and the lame walking, and the blind seeing, and they glorified God' (Mt 15:31). Mark records a remarkable cure not mentioned by the other evangelists:

> And they bring him one dumb and impeded in speech and they beg him to lay his hand upon him. And taking him away apart from the crowd he thrust his fingers into his ears and spitting he touched his tongue. And looking up to heaven he sighed and says to him: *"Eph-phatha"*, which means, Be opened. And at once his hearing was restored and at once the binding of his tongue was set free, and he began to speak properly. And he charged them not to tell anyone, but the more he charged them, the more effusively they proclaimed it. And they were exceedingly amazed, saying: "He has done all things well; he causes both the deaf to hear and the dumb to speak".

The above little anecdote is a story of Peter's, his memory being prompted by Matthew's note that Jesus worked a great many miraculous healings on that occasion (Mt 15:30).

7) The Feeding of the Four Thousand (Mt 15:32-39 = Mk 8:1-10)

It was also characteristic of Jesus that as the crowd had been following him for three days without having anything to eat he now took it into his own hands to feed them as he had done before, possibly on the very same mountain.[23] The feeding of the four thousand followed the same pattern as the feeding of the five thousand. When the disciples queried the possibility of feeding them in a sparsely inhabited countryside, Jesus told

23 Many scholars think it unlikely that Jesus repeated the miracle of the loaves and fishes, and that it is still more unlikely that he did so on the same hill-top. But Matthew and Mark are both clear that there were indeed two miraculous feedings, and such generosity is entirely in keeping with his attitude to his followers throughout (cf. Mt 16:9-10 = Mk 8:18-20).

them to collect whatever food the crowd had, which proved to be only seven loaves and a few little fishes. Having ordered them all to sit down, he thanked Almighty God, blessed the loaves and fishes, broke them and apportioned them to his disciples who in turn distributed them to the crowd. This time the disciples collected a mere seven hampers of left-overs, and when all was cleared up he dismissed the crowd and then took ship with the Twelve 'to the parts of Dalmanutha' near the southeastern shore of the lake.

Despite careful comparison of the Synoptic Gospels, it is not possible to follow the exact itinerary of his swift and urgent passage around the Sea of Galilee. We are told of continued harassment by the Pharisees but no places are mentioned. Mark next records another rather unusual miracle outside the fishing village of Bethsaida which again involved physical contact, and more than one touching, in order to effect a perfect cure. It is worth recording in full as it is again peculiar to the Gospel of Mark:

> And they come into Bethsaida. And they bring him a blind man and beg him to touch him. And grasping the hand of the blind man he led him out of the village. And spitting into his eyes, laying hands upon him he questioned him: "Do you see anything?" And looking he said: "I see men, because I behold as it were trees walking." Then again he laid hands on his eyes, and he looked steadily and was restored, and he saw everything clearly. And he sent him to his house saying: "Do not enter into the village". (Mk 8:22-26)

There are here two stages in the cure and this may be a way of Jesus' indicating that God can and often does cure by stages rather than instantly. In telling the man not to enter into the village, the original home of Peter and Andrew, Jesus is hoping to avoid the attribute of 'miracle-worker' that so often hindered and obscured peoples' attention to his teaching.

In order to provide his future Kingdom with its proper foundation on earth, Jesus had been devoting and would continue to devote the greater part of his time to the character training of the twelve men whom he had destined to be its foundation stones. His task was twofold, firstly to develop the individual talents of each and secondly to teach them how to overcome their particular faults of character in order to make them fit instruments for making him known to the world. To know him was to love him, and the better they knew him the more they would love him, and the greater would be their efforts to obey his ascetical teaching and conform their own personal lives to his. The time was now drawing near for him to unfold to them the central mystery of his person, for they had now been living with him intimately night and day for many months. It was in fact as they were striding again north into territory only sparsely inhabited by Jews, in the neighbourhood of Caesarea Philippi, that he judged that the moment had arrived when he could both fully reveal his identity and also reward their recognition of it, as we shall see in the next chapter.

11

The Conclusion of the
Galilean Ministry

1) Peter's Confession of Faith (Mt 16:13f = Lk 9:18f = Mk 8:27f)

Some time during a rest period in the course of their journey, Jesus stopped and gave himself up to private prayer alone, although his disciples were not far away. He needed to elicit their true opinion about himself, so that he could take the next step in their training. Rising from his prayer he rejoined them, and, to get their minds working properly first, he asked them to tell him who the populace thought him to be. The disciples were able to repeat the various opinions current; some people were saying that he was John the Baptist risen from the dead, others that he was Elijah or Jeremiah or one of the ancient prophets. They of course knew that all these identifications were false and Jesus did not bother to refute them. Instead he turned to them and put the direct question: 'And you, who do you say that I am?' It was Simon Peter who answered on behalf of the Twelve as their spokesman: 'You are the Christ, the Son of the Living God'.[24] The meaning of this confession of Peter has to be under-

24 There is here a literary and critical problem, about which there is as yet no final agreement among exegetes. For Luke has 'the Christ of God', i.e. God's Messiah, and Mark has simply 'The Christ', while both omit Mt 16:17-19, the promise to Peter, although they both retain with Matthew the final sentence of the section (*pericope*). Having decided on literary grounds that Matthew is the original Gospel composed before Luke and Mark, I argue that Luke and Mark omitted these verses for their own good reasons, and perhaps because Jesus made this promise on another occasion. Nevertheless, while these considerations do not establish that Jesus made Peter this promise at this moment on the road to Caesarea Philippi, they do establish that they were part of Matthew's text when he published his Gospel not later that AD 44 (cf. note 52 below).

stood in the light of the reply of Jesus:

> And Jesus answering said to him: "Blessed are you Simon Bar-Jona because flesh and blood has not revealed it to you, but my Father who is in the heavens". (Mt 16:17)

Because of the warlike, nationalistic and patriotic association of the term 'Messiah' Jesus would not use it of himself in public nor allow it to be used about him, as we have already seen. However, Peter's addition of 'the Son of the Living God' to the title of the Christ, not only threw new light on the person of the Messiah as the Jews had so far understood the term, but acknowledged the unique relationship of Jesus to Yahweh, the Lord God of Israel. In no way could Peter have arrived at this knowledge by his own effort or genius. As Jesus himself said, it required a revelation from his own heavenly Father to enlighten Peter and enable him to make this confession. The divinity of Jesus and his equality with the Father is the central mystery of the incarnation. Now that Peter has got the basic fact firmly fixed in his heart and mind, Jesus is in a position to take the next step in the formation of his Kingdom, namely to make Peter the rock on which it is to be built and its leader and key-person.

Jesus continued:

> And I say to you, that you are Peter, and upon this rock I will build my Church, and the Gates of Hades will not prevail against it. And I will give to you the keys of the Kingdom of the Heavens, and whatever you bind upon earth will be bound in the heavens, and whatever you loose upon earth will be loosed in the heavens. (Mt 16:18-19)

Whilst Jesus is the King to whom the Kingdom rightfully belongs, Peter is to be its steward, the person to whom are entrusted the keys of the Kingdom, having full authority over its activities and undertakings. His pre-eminence was to be given still further clarification when at the Last Supper Jesus prayed that his faith would never fail (Lk 22:31-32), and that when it was confirmed he in his turn was to confirm his brethren (Jn 21).

Since Christ himself is the Lord of all and he gives Peter the promise that he is to be his plenipotentiary on earth, the latter already glimpses that his authority is to be co-extensive with the span of the world, though always under Christ himself. The other Apostles do not take easily to this exaltation of one of their number, and after the third passion prediction made a few weeks later on the way up to Jerusalem, the envy of James and John becomes apparent when they persuaded their mother to ask for them to be given the two places of highest honour, on his right hand and on his left (Mt 20:20-28). Jesus then replied that it was not in his power to grant their request but that they would, however, be permitted to drink with him the chalice of martyrdom. The place of Peter as the steward on earth of the Kingdom has been assured by the will of his heavenly Father (Mt 24:45f = Lk 12:41), and these two places are likewise in the gift of the Father himself for those for whom he has destined them. Peter's own over-confident reaction to the exalted position to which the Lord has destined him will become clear in a moment.

2) The First Passion Prediction (Mt 16:21f = Lk 9:22 = Mk 8:31f)

The promise made by Jesus to Peter has made the Twelve realize that they are to be full partners in the establishment of his Kingdom on earth, and that their authority is to be as real as his. Jesus therefore loses no time in explaining that his Kingdom cannot come into operation except through his passion, death and resurrection. And so immediately after affirming Peter's place in the Kingdom, he reveals to them that after much suffering he is going to die in Jerusalem at the hands of the Sanhedrin, and that he is going to be raised up after three days. In a second prediction a few days later he will add that he will be betrayed (for in no other way could he be taken). Later still on the road up to Jerusalem, he was to add that he would be handed over to the Romans and scourged and crucified, the death reserved for slaves and criminals. But they were very slow to comprehend the vastness of his plan, being as yet unable to understand that the scale of values in his Kingdom was to be the reverse of those of the kingdoms of this world, and that success for him, its

Founder, was only to come through his sacrificial death and resurrection—in fact through the most disgraceful death it was possible to imagine.

But when Jesus made this horrendous and seemingly incredible announcement of his future death, Peter was in such an exalted mood that he was revolted by the very notion and foolishly thought that his power and his counsel could save Jesus from this fate. For how could he, the rightful Messiah and the king of the Jews, ever suffer such a shameful death at the hands of the Jewish spiritual authorities? 'May God be merciful to you, Lord', said Peter, 'by no means shall this happen to you!'—thus taking on himself the role of protector of Jesus from the cruel death that he had prophesied for himself. Peter was still far from being the spiritual man of later years, and he had no idea as yet of the depth and complexity of God's plan for his Messiah. However, if Peter were to have had his way, the divine plan would have been blocked. Unwittingly Peter was attempting to dissuade Jesus from the path of suffering that he had willingly undertaken to follow for the sake of the salvation of the world.

The reaction of Jesus was swift, uncompromising and forceful. 'Get behind me, Satan', he said, 'because you do not perceive the things of God but the things of men'. For by attempting to deter him from following the path that would lead to the sacrifice of his life, Peter was doing the work of Satan, whose dominion over fallen mankind could only be abolished by the victory of the Cross.

3) The Cross and Self- Denial (Mt 16:24f = Lk 9:23f = Mk 8:34f)

Jesus now perceived the urgency of reinforcing his teaching on the royal way of the Cross. Ever since the fall of Adam and Eve the path of righteousness leading to eternal life had been closed to mankind. Jesus was going to reopen it and make it possible for all to walk along it by following him, the pioneer of our salvation. Christianity is no easy option. The more faithful the Christian, the stonier and rougher his path, because the path of Jesus himself was roughest of all. Mark tells us that he now specially summoned the crowd as well as his disciples and expounded to them the harsh realities of the way to God:

> If anyone wants to come after me, let him deny himself and take up his cross and follow me. For whoever wishes to save his soul will lose it; and he who would lose his soul for my sake will find it. Therefore what will a man be benefited if he should gain the whole world but forfeit his soul? Or what will a man give as an exchange for his soul? (Mk 8:34-37)

In these words Jesus first of all disclaims the role of a political Messiah. Not only has he no intention of restoring the ancient military glories of the Maccabees or of king David and king Solomon, but to follow him means the rejection of all the commonly held worldly values of men. The battle into which he is leading his followers is into warfare over the dark desires in the human soul, and over the pride that rejects the commandments of God in favour of the love of self. To win external glory as the commander of a victorious army, even if he subdues the whole world to his sway, is of no benefit to the commander if at the same time he loses his own soul by acting in a manner contrary to the will of God and of his Christ. Every human being has received all he possesses as a gift from Almighty God, and especially his own body and soul which is given to enable him by the exercise of his free will to co-operate with God and so attain his ultimate destiny. If he corrupts his soul for the sake of power or lust or pride, he has nothing to offer the Son of Man when he comes in the glory of his Father.

The Christian is one who has to live out the words of Christ that 'he who humbles himself will be exalted, and he who exalts himself will be humbled' (Mt 23:12). The only reasonable and prudent course for someone who wishes to avoid the shame of being rejected by Christ is to humble himself in order to overcome his own personal moral weaknesses and so come to perceive 'the things of God'. The spur for action ought to be the certain knowledge that Jesus Christ, at that moment present in the world in his role as the Suffering Servant, will come again at the end of time in the glory of his Father with the holy angels to judge the deeds of all mankind according to the standards he has laid down. As he forthrightly added: 'Whoever is ashamed of me and of my words in this adulterous and sinful generation, the Son of Man too will be ashamed of him when he comes in the glory of his Father with the holy angels' (Mk 8:38).

For the rest of his time on earth Jesus is going to devote himself to making sure that his Apostles have fully understood firstly, who he is, namely truly God and truly Man, secondly, the nature of the Kingdom of God that he is in process of founding (and which he is co-opting them to run on his behalf), and thirdly, the fundamental principles of the spiritual life of which he himself is the perfect exemplar. Little by little he is now going to reveal to them the full details of his Father's plan and his own part in its fulfilment. In future the Christian who is ashamed of Christ's words and deeds will not escape punishment, because the Lord is not only going to rise from the dead but is going to return one day in the glory of his Father with the holy angels to judge the world.

4) The Transfiguration (Mt 17:1-13 = Lk 9:28-36 = Mk 9:2-13)

To prove to the disciples that this was no empty boast, a week later he took with him the innermost three, Peter, James and John, up on to a high mountain to pray and there and then revealed to them a tiny fraction of his true glory. The purpose of this vision was to deepen their understanding of the revelation that he is 'the Son of the Living God' and to give them an awareness of the 'glory' that lay hidden under his outward appearance. The special selection of these three was a foreshowing of the key positions that they were later to hold in the Apostolic Church. The other nine Apostles were left at the foot of the mountain and meanwhile had the humiliating experience of failing to cast the devil out of a possessed boy.

From the accounts of the evangelists it seems probable that the vision took place during the hours of darkness, because the drowsiness of the Apostles suggests that they had climbed the mountain at the end of the day. While the three settled down to sleep, Jesus continued to pray. But they were awakened by a great light and in front of their very eyes they saw that his appearance had been suddenly and totally transformed. His garments were dazzlingly white with an unearthly brightness and his face was transformed so that 'it shone like the sun'. And then they saw two men standing beside him and talking with him. By their clothing and demeanour they were able to identify them as Moses and Elijah, who of course represented the Law and the Prophets. They were near enough to gather from their conversation with Jesus that they were discussing his 'departure' from this life which he was about to accomplish in Jerusalem. The Apostles were transfixed with amazement and spellbound until, as Moses and Elijah were taking their leave, Peter blurted out: 'Lord, it is good for us to be here; let us make three tents, one for you, one for Moses, and one for Elijah'. But he had no sooner finished speaking than a cloud overshadowed them and hid them from their sight, and a voice came from the cloud saying: 'This is my Son, the Beloved One, in whom I am well pleased; hear him'. At the sound of the voice the Apostles fell flat on their faces in fear, and when at last they raised their eyes there was no one in sight but Jesus. He came up and touched them, saying: 'Get up and have no fear; do not tell the vision to anyone until the Son of Man be risen from the dead'.

The evangelist Mark tells us that though they were forbidden to speak to others about this vision, yet among themselves they debated the meaning of the phrase 'to rise from the dead'. The purpose of the vision was to prepare them for the shock of his crucifixion by revealing that his death and resurrection had been foretold in the Scriptures and were well known to the Blessed in heaven, represented by Moses the Law-giver and Elijah the Prophet. Moreover, it was intended to make them conscious of the reality and nearness of heaven, which is not the abode of the dead but of the living. In fact, the glory of heaven and the glory of Christ are ever-present, though invisible and imperceptible to those living on earth.

The appearance of Elijah alongside Jesus raised a question in the minds of the three (Mt 17:10-13), and they sought an immediate answer. Only a week earlier he had openly spoken of his coming in glory and had added that some of them would not die 'until they had seen his Kingdom come in power' (Mk 9:1). And now they had just witnessed his glorious transfiguration in the presence of Elijah whose coming before 'the great and terrible day of the Lord' had been foretold in the prophecy of Malachi (4:5). Since there was already a true sense in which the Son of Man had already come, the three were confused about these various comings of the Lord and enquired whether the scribes were right in asserting with Malachi that Elijah had yet to come as the precursor of the Day of Judgement. Jesus replied that Elijah had indeed yet to come in his own person and set things up for the Final Coming of the Christ. The Baptist, however, had already suffered a martyr's death for his witness to the first coming of the Christ, who himself is now about to suffer a similar fate; in this way Jesus was repeating and reinforcing his recent prediction of his passion. Finally, it is worth noting that there is a tradition that the 'two witnesses' of Apoc 11:3 are Elijah and Enoch, who will return and suffer martyrdom in the End Time after heralding the final coming of Christ in Glory.

Yet in spite of all these warnings it is clear from their later behaviour that during the lifetime of Jesus none of the Apostles could reconcile themselves to the notion that he was going to die a cruel and shameful death, nor could they envisage his resurrection from the dead. All the same this vision burnt itself into their consciousness, and after his resurrection its full meaning became clear to them and especially to Peter who referred to it some thirty years later in his Second Letter (2 Pet 1:16-18).[25]

5) The Healing of a Possessed Boy
(Mt 17:14-21 = Lk 9:37-43 = Mk 9:14-29)

During the absence of Jesus and his three disciples on the mountain, the remaining nine had been having an uncomfortable time. A distraught father had brought his devil-possessed son to them and in front of a large crowd, among whom were

---

25 A number of scholars deny Petrine authorship to 2 Peter, but the lack of external evidence before AD 180 does not invalidate the strong internal evidence and the Church tradition.

some scribes with whom they were now debating, they had signally failed to cast out the devil. But as soon as the crowd saw Jesus coming down they made for him, and he asked the nine what they were discussing with the scribes. There was an awkward silence and then the man who had brought his son explained his disappointment at the disciples' failure. Jesus' reply showed his distress at the lack of trust and faith shewn by the disciples: 'O unbelieving and perverse generation! How long shall I be with you? How long shall I put up with you? Bring him to me.'

When they brought him the poor boy, the evil spirit became frantic at the presence of Jesus and convulsed the boy, throwing him foaming and writhing to the ground. Jesus turned to the father and questioned him: 'How long has he been like this?'—'From infancy. he replied, 'And often it has thrown him now into fire and now into water in order to destroy him. But if you can, help us and take pity on us'.—'If you can...', queried Jesus, 'all things are possible to him who believes'.—'I believe', exclaimed the father, 'please help my unbelief!'. The tension had now become unbearable, and Jesus swiftly spoke: 'Dumb and deaf spirit, I command you. Go out of him and never return into him'. And with a loud shriek the devil went out of the boy leaving him looking as if he was dead. But Jesus took him by the hand and raised him up. The boy stood up, and Jesus handed him back to his father fully cured. In the words of Luke, 'all were amazed at the majesty of God'.

The nine Apostles were really crestfallen at their failure; and as soon as they got back to the house at Capharnaum, they begged him to tell them why they had been unable to cast out this devil, despite the powers that he had given them. His response was revealing:

> Because of your little faith. Amen, I say to you, if you have faith like a grain of mustard seed you shall say to this mountain, "Remove from here to there", and it will be removed; and nothing will be impossible to you. But this kind does not go forth except by prayer and fasting.[26]

26 The sentence 'This kind never comes out except by prayer and fasting' (Mt 17:21) was omitted by an older generation of text critics, but the textual evidence in its favour fully justifies its inclusion.

Their faith in him was still woefully weak. They had called on the Name of Jesus to cast out the demon, but the evil spirit had not gone forth as they were not yet confident enough in the face of this daunting devil. Moreover they had also failed to grasp that they had not as yet the right dispositions for the power of Jesus to work through them; they did not yet share the perfect self-control that can only be obtained through prayer and fasting. Their imitation of Jesus was still a long way from perfection.

6) The Second Passion Prediction
(Mt 17:22-23 = Lk 9:43-45 = Mk 9:30-32)

As they continued their journey, still digesting his reproof of their lack of faith, he repeated his prophecy that he was going to die and rise again, adding that he would, in fact, be betrayed to his enemies. The inability of the Twelve to grasp the significance of what he was trying to hammer into their heads is very surprising, and the evangelist Luke, writing some thirty years after the event, offered two suggestions in explanation. He suggested firstly that they may have been afraid to question him from fear that if they were to do so their whole world would fall apart, for they could not face the thought of having to go on without him. But their lack of courage does not seem to be a sufficient explanation of their lack of understanding, and Luke perceived that there must be a more profound reason, namely, that 'they did not understand this saying [about his shameful death], because it had been veiled from them that they should not perceive it' (Lk 9:45). In other words, the Spirit of God allowed them to have such confidence in the power that he radiated that they were altogether oblivious to his vulnerability to dying. Only after the resurrection would they recall and understand that their blind confidence had not in fact been misplaced.

We are now nearly at the end of the accounts of the Galilean period of Jesus' Ministry furnished us by the Synoptic Gospels. There are just three items left that call for comment. The first concerns another special favour that Jesus showed to Peter: the payment of the Temple tax, a story related only by Matthew.

7) The Payment of the Temple Tax (Mt 17:24-27)

Every male Jew over the age of nineteen was expected to contribute annually a half-shekel (the Greek *didrachmon*) for the upkeep of the Temple. When Jesus and his disciples returned to Capharnaum the collectors of the tax accosted Peter in the street and asked him rather truculently: 'Does not your teacher pay the tax?' The collectors would certainly have known about his Master's claim to be the Son of God and Lord of the Temple but were nevertheless testing Peter to find out why Jesus had not paid the tax. It is to be remembered that he no longer had any income since he had given up his livelihood at Nazareth and depended solely on the charitable support offered by his followers and the women who accompanied them. Peter had felt in honour bound, though wrongly, to say 'Yes', but he had no sooner entered the house, than Jesus, knowing in himself exactly what Peter had said, forestalled him with the question: 'Simon, what do you think? Do the kings of the earth levy tax or tribute from their sons or from the others?' To which Simon replied: 'From the others of course'.—'In that case', said Jesus, 'the sons are exempt. But lest we should scandalise them, go to the sea, cast a hook and take the first fish coming up. Open its mouth and you will find a shekel. Take it, and give it to them for me and you.' The evangelist did not bother to chronicle the foregone conclusion that Peter did exactly as Jesus told him, and collected the coin of the tax from the fish's mouth and paid it on behalf of Jesus and himself.

Many modern commentators are inclined to regard this story as an invention of the Church of Jerusalem to justify its members paying the Temple tax, by claiming that Jesus himself had indeed paid it. Certainly this was one reason why Matthew included it, writing as he did within ten years or so of the resurrection for the edification of the persecuted Christians of the Holy City; but there are fully adequate grounds for believing that this story is as factually true as the other miracles of Jesus. At the same time this intimate association of Peter with Jesus would not be lost on Matthew's readers, as it enhanced his importance and counterbalanced the sharp reproof he had just received.

8) Who is the Greatest? (Mt 18:1-6 = Lk 9:46-48 = Mk 9:33-37)

Before concluding their account of the Galilean Ministry the evangelists give us two further illustrations of his method of training the Apostles. The first concerns their rivalry and jealousy among themselves.

When the Apostles returned to the house in Capharnaum, they were taken aback when Jesus suddenly said to them: 'What were you debating on the way?' A guilty silence ensued because there had been a somewhat unedifying altercation as to who among them was the greatest. Jesus decided that immediate action was required and sitting down in their common-room (the mention of his sitting down was the sign that he was going to give them some formal teaching), he summoned the Twelve and announced: 'If anyone wants to be first he shall be last of all and servant of all'. And suiting the action to the word he took up one of the many young children who seem to have had the free run of the house at all times; and standing this child—it was a little boy—in the midst of the gathering and hugging him, said solemnly:

> Amen I say to you, unless you change and become as little children you may by no means enter into the Kingdom of Heaven. Whoever therefore humbles himself like this little child, he is the greatest in the Kingdom of Heaven. And whoever receives one such little child in my name receives me; and whoever receives me receives not me but him who sent me. And whoever should scandalise one of these little ones who believe in me, it is better for him for an ass's millstone to be suspended about his neck and to be drowned in the depth of the sea. (Mt 18:3-6)

This was indeed a crushing rebuke and a sharp lesson for the Twelve. It taught them that such wrangling over questions of precedence was trivial, wrong, demeaning, and unworthy of any true follower of his. These were the values of the political and social world from which he had extracted them. The values that were to rule in his Kingdom and in their lives were the exact contrary; every kind of self-assertiveness was wrong; there was no need to assert any claim to superiority over one's fellows. This little boy exemplified the virtues he wished them to acquire, namely humility, simplicity, openness to all, acceptance of oneself and of others without demur, no wish to dominate or to be thought superior; such were the qualities necessary to find acceptance with his heavenly Father. His Kingdom is to operate on principles entirely different from those of the world they had hitherto known.

9) The unauthorised Exorcist (Lk 9:49-50 = Mk 9:38-41)

The final anecdote concerns a Jewish exorcist, who was not a recognised follower of Jesus, but a man of good will who had noticed the power of Jesus to cast out demons, and who was successfully invoking his Name for the same purpose with conspicuous success. John had observed him with displeasure and chagrin. Despite their recent severe telling off, the morale of the Twelve remained exceedingly high; and John thought that he knew how to interpret the mind of Jesus when he found someone, not a follower, successfully using his Name to expel demons, though seemingly not authorised to do so. He succeeded in stopping him and triumphantly reported the incident to Jesus, whose answer surprised him:

> Do not prevent him, for there is no one who will work a mighty deed in my Name and will be able quickly to speak evil of me. For he who is not against us is for us.

Jesus did not deny that his Apostles had received from him power over the demons; but he made it clear to them that he did not channel his power exclusively through them, but was sovereignly free to work through anyone he chose. He also implied that if he allowed this exorcist to utilise his Name for a good reason, that person must already have a profound respect for him, or else the Lord would not be acting through him. It follows from this incident that he knew the mind of all people at all times and not just the minds of his chosen followers.

The concluding aphorism in Mk: 'He who is not against us is for us' (in Lk 9:50: 'He who is not against you is for you') needs to be kept in mind today by all those involved in ecumenical dialogue. The evangelists Luke and Mark, in the light of thirty years' experience of the obstacles that had impeded the spread of the Gospel, recalled this saying of Jesus, to remind its preachers not to antagonise such people as this exorcist who, while not knowingly supporting the Church of Jesus Christ, at least were not hindering it, and even promoting it by advancing his Kingdom along parallel lines.

10) Jesus' final Departure from Galilee
(Mt 19:1-2 = Lk 9:51 = Mk 10:1)

All three Synoptic Gospels suggest that Jesus departed from Galilee during the autumn of AD 29. Large crowds were still following him everywhere, but several reasons determined his departure. There was the danger of being apprehended by Herod Antipas' soldiers and of being imprisoned, as John had been, in the fortress palace of Machaerus; there was the magnetic attraction to return again to Jerusalem to his Father's House; and finally, 'the days of his assumption [returning to his heavenly Father] were drawing near and he set his face to go to Jerusalem' (Lk 9:51 = Mk 10:1).

It has often been noted that the literary method of Matthew required him to combine and place all the activities of Jesus at Jerusalem into the last eight chapters of his Gospel rather than in strict chronological order. But John, writing some years later, has corrected the picture and has related three important visits omitted by the Synoptic Gospels between the Passover of AD 28 (The Cleansing of the Temple episode) and the triumphal entry described by all four evangelists on the eve of the passion (Jn 5:1 f; 7:12-10:21; 10:22f). Jerusalem and its Temple courts were the seat of power and of religious authority, and the hostile opposition to the recognition of his credentials was precisely located there; whereas in Galilee, his native province, the people as a whole were very friendly and willing to accept him. These considerations largely explain the great difference in content, method and style between his speeches in Galilee and those in Jerusalem.

The third visit to Jerusalem took place during the later part of the Galilean period, and the fourth between leaving Galilee and the final journey up to Jerusalem, and it will be appropriate to take them together in the next chapter.

12

The Third and Fourth Visit
to Jerusalem

1) Further Confrontation with Scribes and Pharisees (Jn 7:1-8:59)
The third visit to Jerusalem confirmed all Jesus' anticipations
of the enmity in which he was held by the chief priests and their
supporters in Jerusalem. He foresaw that the revelations he
would have to make about himself would give them further excuse for putting him to death for blasphemy. But he had to
await the hour appointed by his Father when he would allow
himself to be delivered into their hands in order to make an entirely free sacrifice of his life for the redemption of the world. He
was delighted to fulfil the will of his Father and take over the
leadership of his own people for the sake of the human race. As
the author of the Letter to the Hebrews was later to declare,
Jesus was 'the pioneer of our salvation' (Heb 2:10), but his claim
to leadership had now to be spelled out in the clearest terms in
order to challenge those in charge of the destiny of the Jews to a
public decision whether or not to accept it. So he guided the
dialogue to get them to ask the vital questions: 1) Who was his
Father, whose authority he claimed for their obedience to his
teaching? 2) Who was he himself? His replies proclaimed his
full equality and unity with the Lord God of Israel, and
demanded a categorical acceptance of, and a total submission
to, his messiahship, thereby recognising in him the real
presence of God, his Father and theirs.

Between the feast of Purim (Jn 5:1-47) and the feast of Tents

(Jn 7 & 8), a period of a little more than six months, Jesus had continued his mission in Galilee, because it was dangerous for him to venture into Judea or to go up to Jerusalem, where he had already been unofficially condemned as a blasphemer, and the friends of the chief priests would have had no hesitation about arresting him at sight. As we have seen, he had used the time to evangelise Galilee and to train his twelve disciples for their future mission. However, the spiritual as well as the economic and political centre of the nation was the Holy City and his first duty was to leave no stone unturned to win the co-operation of the authorities in Jerusalem. His family, with whom he continued to remain in touch, fully supported his plan of going to Jerusalem since they realised his potential as an out-standing leader of men and were urging him to try his luck again in the hope that they too would be able to share in his success if he came to power. But they failed to grasp that his mission was not a worldly but a spiritual one and that it was solely for spiritual reasons that he had to go to Jerusalem and so incidentally fulfil the prophecy of Isaiah about the Messianic age:

> It shall come to pass in the latter days
> that the mountain of the House of the Lord
> shall be established as the highest of the mountains
> and shall be raised above the hills;
> and all the nations shall flow to it,
> and many peoples shall come and say:
> Come, let us go up to the mountain of the Lord,
> to the House of the God of Jacob;
> that he may teach us his ways
> and that we may walk in his paths.
> For out of Sion shall go forth the Law,
> and the Word of the Lord from Jerusalem'. (Is 2:2-3)

Time was passing and he could not delay a further confrontation with the high priesthood and the Sanhedrin, although he was aware that his chances of a successful outcome were minimal, because the hatred that his message and person had already engendered was implacable.

In the struggle that was about to ensue Jesus did not want his family to be involved, and so he waited behind after they had gone up until the feast was half over before quietly following all by himself (Jn 7:1-10). On arrival in the Holy City he found that there was a great deal of furtive talk about him both for and against, but nobody dared to take his side openly as the chief priests were known to be ready to punish savagely anyone suspected of supporting him. He would therefore have to face alone the all-powerful Sanhedrin and its numerous allies with no one to stand by him. His two previous visits had been undertaken to test their willingness to accept him and he had had no opportunity to sit down and teach alongside the other rabbis in the Temple porticos; but this time he was determined to take up a teaching position in the Temple colonnade and to pour out the message of his heavenly Father to all passers-by who were willing to listen.

His enemies rallied round straightaway, and their first question was to query why he was aligning himself with the rabbis sitting in the porticos, since he had never qualified as a teacher by serving an apprenticeship with a recognised rabbi. He explained that his teaching was not his own but that of his Father who had sent him, that he was not seeking fame or honour for himself but the glory of his Father who had given the Law to Moses, the Law that they were no longer observing. Proof that they were failing to keep it lay in the fact that some of them were now thinking of killing him. He was addressing in particular the vocal section of his audience, partisans of the high priests, who had been eager to stone him for his alleged blasphemy at the feast of Purim, when he had claimed that he and his Father were sovereignly free to work on the Sabbath.

The mob of partisans from the chief priests and the Pharisees were very annoyed at the way Jesus now dealt with their objection, and accused him of being a pretender because he was a Galilean and a citizen of Nazareth. They had evidently taken no steps to find out (or were ignoring the fact) that he fulfilled the prophecy that the Messiah would be born in Bethlehem. An attempt was then made to seize him (Jn 7:30), but they were unable to touch him. At the same time some bystanders had sent an urgent message to the authorities to order his arrest, an action which in fact they postponed attempting until the final day of the feast just before the pilgrims went back home.

Meanwhile Jesus had his own plans for giving the pilgrims something by which to remember him on their return journey. So on 'the last, the great day of the feast', he made a spontaneous announcement, an extraordinary prophecy of the future outpouring of the Holy Spirit: 'If anyone is thirsty, let him come to me and drink; he that believes in me, from his side will flow rivers of water' (Jn 7:37), meaning that in times to come the true Christian will be a channel of Christ's grace for all his neighbours.

When the Temple police arrived they were held spellbound by his preaching, and returned to report to the chief priests and the Pharisees that they were unable to arrest him because 'no man had ever spoken before like this man' (Jn 7:46). The police were severely reprimanded by the priests and accused of being his supporters. Now it happened that Nicodemus, a Pharisee and a member of the Sanhedrin, who had earlier come to Jesus under cover of night, was present when the police received their rebuke, and ventured to question their attack on Jesus: 'Surely our Law does not condemn a man before it has heard him and knows what crime he is accused of'. But all he got in reply was abuse and ridicule to the effect that he too must be a 'Galilean'. Jesus was now manifestly the great threat to their way of life, and for the first time they have openly attempted to silence him by force.

Nevertheless Jesus, unruffled and undismayed, continued to teach and resumed his practice of uttering maxims that not only provoked careful thought but which helped to illustrate his mission as saviour, incidentally giving further scope for the accusation of blasphemy. This time he announced: 'I am the Light of the World; he who follows me will not be walking in darkness, but will have the light of life'. Such a statement was guaranteed to stir his critical audience to instant objection, for only someone with the powers of the Creator could rationally speak in such terms. The Pharisees returned to their former objection that such assertions were baseless unless supported by some credible witness. Jesus granted that the Law of Moses required such a witness, but added that in fact he did not need any witness at all because he was from God and knew himself to be from God; moreover he also had the witness of his Father. They enquired: 'Where then is your Father?' A good question, as Jesus was there alone. They failed to understand his response: 'If you knew me, you would know my Father. But in fact you know neither of us'. The explanation is of course that God is spirit, and it is uniquely his Son who has appeared in the flesh; and they were unwilling to learn from him that 'where the Son is there also is the Father'.

Jesus still stayed teaching near the treasury, and continued to make tantalising statements that mystified his antagonistic hearers. 'I am going', he said, 'where you cannot come'. He meant of course that he was shortly going back to heaven, but they could not think of anywhere they would not be able to pursue him and reach him with the aid of the funds supplied by the chief priests. Could he possibly be planning to take his own life and in disgrace go down to Hades? Hardly. Jesus helped them by going on to say: 'I am from above, you are from below; you are of this world, I am not of this world', and warned them: 'If you do not believe that I am, you will die in your sins'. This direct accusation of their spiritual peril provoked them to ask him: 'Who are you?' To which he responded: 'I am exactly what I am telling you'. He reiterated that what his Father had prompted him to say was true, but he would not judge their obstinacy now. Their ignorance, culpable or otherwise, of the nature of his person, would be replaced only when he had been 'lifted up' - a recognised euphemism for crucifixion. Then they would learn something of the intimacy of the relationship that exists between him and his Father. The Father is with him always and he always does what pleases the Father.

Some of the Jews appeared to be impressed, so he set them thinking with another aphorism: 'If you remain in my word, you are truly my disciples; and you will know the truth and the truth will make you free'. But his critics bridled at his presumption that they were not free. Despite the Roman army of occupation, they liked to imagine themselves free men and to assert they were not subjects of anyone and never had been, because they were the people of God and heirs of the promise to Abraham. But Jesus was not concerned with political freedom and reminded them that anyone who commits sin is a slave of sin. They were now of course by then in a state of sin because they were intending to kill him for blasphemy and therefore could not be true spiritual sons of Abraham. If Abraham was truly their Father, they would love him, Jesus, because he had come forth from God. But by denying his God-given credentials they have proved that their spiritual father is the devil who has been a liar and murderer from the beginning. They have alienated themselves from the God of Abraham, whereas Jesus obeys him and does the truth, and they ought to admit in their hearts that there is no wrong-doing whatsoever in him.

At this juncture his enemies again fall back on abuse and declare that he must have a demon (the only explanation possible, if they refuse to admit that he is from God). Jesus answers: 'I do not have a demon, but I honour my Father and you are dishonouring me (Jn 8:49). And he then utters a further truth that they must deny since the devil is their father: 'Amen amen I say to you, if anyone will keep my word he will live for ever'. With these words his opponents are quick to perceive his renewed claim to impart divine life, and they retort: 'We are certain now that you must have a demon', and they challenge him with the question: 'Are you greater than our father Abraham? Who do you make yourself out to be?' That is to say, is he claiming the Godhead itself? The way in which Jesus replies to this question indicates that it embarrasses him to proclaim his own glory and that he would prefer to leave to his Father the plain revelation of his equality with him. But as he cannot evade an answer and cannot deny the truth that his Father has always been with him, he now resolves obliquely to declare his own dignity by saying: 'Abraham your father rejoiced to see my day; he saw it and rejoiced'. The Jews pounce on these words at once and demand a clarification: 'You are not yet fifty years old and you have beheld Abraham?' And his answer justifies them—in their own eyes—in picking up stones to stone him, for he said: 'Before Abraham came to be, I AM' (Jn 8:58), thus applying to himself the sacred name of the Lord God Yahweh, which had been revealed to Moses at the Burning Bush (Ex 3:14). But Jesus' Hour had not yet come, and as the evangelist writes 'he hid himself and went out of the Temple' (Jn 8:59).

2) The Healing of the Man Born Blind (Jn 9:1-41)

The next incident was introduced by the evangelist John to illustrate the contrast between the wilful blindness of the sophisticated and highly educated chief priests and Pharisees in regard to Jesus and the insight of a theologically uneducated beggar, a representative of the despised 'people of the land'. While the former stubbornly refuse to believe in the person and mission of Jesus, the latter is ready to fall down and adore him in simple faith as soon as he learns the identity of his healer.

As Jesus left the Temple at the end of his exhausting debate with the Pharisees he passed a young man blind from birth, who was soliciting alms from the passers-by. The disciples thought this was a good occasion to ask Jesus about a problem that had long been troubling them, namely the popular belief that such a disability as blindness from birth must be the consequence of some grave sin on the part either of the sufferer or of his parents. Would Jesus please explain? He told them that this notion was wrong and that the man's blindness had been permitted for the sake of revealing God's glory. Their casual question gave him the opportunity to prove to them that he was indeed what he had proclaimed himself to be, the Light of the World. He would not be passing that way again in this life because his time was short; and he therefore at once used the occasion to restore the man's sight in order to impress on his disciples his power to give light to the world. The whole discussion had taken place in front of the expectant beggar, and Jesus set about the work of healing him in an unusual way. Spitting on the ground he made some mud with the dust of the earth and used it to anoint the blind man's eyes and then ordered him to go and wash in the pool of Siloam. The beggar went down with his friends and having duly washed returned home with his sight restored. The man's neighbours were baffled at his recovery, and so they decided to take him to the Pharisees to verify his cure.

On hearing his story the Pharisees astutely pointed out that as it was the Sabbath there must have been an infringement of the Sabbath rest and therefore the man who had worked the cure could not be from God! Other Pharisees retorted that no sinner could perform such a sign. An argument started up, while the man himself looked on in amazement. Thus divided among themselves the Pharisees turned to the man and asked his opinion about Jesus. He answered without hesitation: 'He is a prophet', a reply that infuriated them. To gain time they sent for the man's parents, simple people, who were terrified at this summons because they had heard that anyone confessing that Jesus was the Christ would be outlawed from the synagogue, which in practice meant losing one's civil rights. Under inter-rogation, all his parents were prepared to admit was that he was indeed their son and that he had been blind from birth until that very day; but they refused to venture any opinion as to how he had regained his sight. They added that in any case he was grown up and could now answer for himself.

Having drawn a blank here, the restless persecutors of Jesus turned back again to the man to get him to incriminate Jesus in some other way, or at least to persuade him to deny the cure. They threatened him: 'At least admit the truth, that this man must be a sinner because he has broken the Sabbath'. But the young man was honest and refused to be browbeaten into telling a lie and replied: 'I don't know if he is a sinner; all I know is that I was blind and that due to his intervention, I can now see' (Jn 9:25).

Being at their wits' end to break him down, they asked him to repeat what Jesus had done to restore his sight. The young man was by now getting somewhat irritated by this persistent questioning and retorted: 'I have told you already and you obviously did not listen. Why do you want to hear it again? Do you actually want to become his disciples?' This remark annoyed them beyond measure, and their tempers flared up. 'All right', they declared, 'You be a disciple of this man, but we are certainly disciples of Moses. For we know that God has spoken through Moses. But whence this man is we do not know'. The lad at once saw the fallacy in their argument. 'Is not this a marvellous thing', he rejoined, 'that you do not know whence he is, and he has opened my eyes? We know that God does not hear sinners, but if anyone be God-fearing and does his will, he hears him. Moreover from before time began it has never been heard that anyone opened the eyes of one born blind. If this man were not from God, he could not have done this thing'. His logic was unquestionable, for in all the miracles of the Old Testament there is no record of a healing of anyone born blind. These learned rabbis, now utterly defeated in argument by an unlettered young lad, had no answer but to bluster and curse him: 'How dare you try to teach us, you who were totally born in sin as is proved by your blindness'. And without more ado, they expelled him from the synagogue.

But this was not quite the end of the incident, for Jesus, hearing that they had excommunicated the man he had healed, sought him out and asked him: 'Do you believe in the Son of Man?' To which he replied: 'Who is he, Lord, that I may believe in him?' And Jesus revealed himself to him just as he had done to the woman at the well, saying: 'Indeed you have both seen him, and he it is who is now speaking to you'. And falling down on his knees, the lad said: 'I believe, Lord'. And Jesus proclaimed: 'For judgement have I come into the world, that those who do not see may see and those who see become blind'.

Some Pharisees overheard this remark and asked him: 'Surely we are not blind too?'. The reply of Jesus was perhaps the most devastating remark he ever made: 'If you were blind you would not have sin; but now you say, "We see". Your sin remains' (Jn 9:41).

In the foregoing story we have the clearest revelation of the lengths to which the Jews, by which the evangelist meant the leading members of the ruling faction in the Sanhedrin, were prepared to go in order to deny the messiahship of Jesus. They were very shortly to try again to stone him. Yet Jesus fearlessly stayed on teaching in the Holy City to give them the benefit of a further insight into the sanctuary of his own person. He had completed the theme of himself as the Light of the World and the One who comes to give sight and light to those who are spiritually blind and in darkness. Though at the time his proclamation of himself as the Light of the World fell on deaf ears, yet it made a profound impression upon the evangelist John who would later record it. Jesus was indeed the Light of the World, firstly, because he was the only human being who could dispel the darkness of human error and illumine human minds with the light of God's grace; and secondly, because he alone possessed the power to break the bonds of evil customs, habits and cultures that enslaved the human race to the power of the devil.

3) Jesus the Good Shepherd (Jn 10:1-21)

In the presence of virtually the same audience Jesus now describes his mission to the world by means of a new metaphor, that of the Good Shepherd, who is prepared to give his life rather than allow the flock entrusted to him by his Father to be scattered and destroyed. Thus he now attributes to himself the role of Yahweh's Good Shepherd pictured by the prophet Ezekiel (Ezek 34:11-24). He begins with a parable about a sheep-fold that is surrounded by a fence with a gate and a gate-keeper. Bandits and thieves have sought to enter by climbing the fence, and, by gaining unauthorised entrance, have scared the sheep, who do not recognise the voices of these strangers. But the real shepherd, the one who guards the flock always enters by the gate, calls his sheep by name and leads them out to pleasant pastures; and the sheep follow him because they know his voice and his presence gives them assurance. The listeners of Jesus however cannot fathom his meaning and so he has to spell it out for them.

He explains to them that he himself is both the gate through which all the sheep must enter, and that as the Messiah he is also the one and only true shepherd; those who have claimed the title of Messiah in the past have been false shepherds and no better than thieves and murderers. The false shepherds will in every crisis abandon their sheep and leave them to their fate when the robbers get in, simply because they are just paid staff and the sheep not theirs. Jesus includes of course the chief priests and their colleagues, who are no more than hirelings who have failed to give the proper leadership and who have deserted their duties as soon as the spiritual life of the nation is threatened by evil forces and internal corruption. The true shepherd and leader will however never desert his own people, because they belong to him, and he is prepared to lay down his life for them. Jesus reiterates that his knowledge and love of his flock is so great as to be in fact the equal of the knowledge and love that exists between himself and his Father in heaven.

He completes this discourse with two further affirmations, still using the language of the parable: firstly he has other sheep beside those in the fold of Israel with whom they will one day form a single flock under his guidance, and this seems to be a reference to the future call of the Gentiles; secondly, his enemies have no power to take his life at their own good pleasure. On the contrary, it is at his Father's command that he will lay it down by his own power and authority and will take it up again in the same way.

These utterances of Jesus caused a further division among the throng in the Temple courts. While the majority declared him to be devil-possessed or crazy, a certain number felt obliged to assert that the others must be mistaken since 'no demon could or would open the eyes of a man born blind'.

After many days of gruelling confrontation with 'the Jews', that is, with the chief priests and the scribes and Pharisees who sided with them, Jesus had failed to win enough support to enable him to assume his rightful inheritance, the Temple. Some indeed now believed in him but they were neither numerous nor influential enough to overcome those determined to take violent action against him. It was impossible for him to stay there any longer and so he decided to return to Galilee, but for a short time only, since he considered that he had already evangelised it as far as circumstances and the soldiery of Herod Antipas would allow. Jerusalem however continued to beckon him, because as he himself said it was impossible for a prophet to die outside the Holy City (Lk 13:33). He would have to return once more to make a last effort to convert the authorities and, if he failed, to suffer death at their hands.

4) *The Feast of the Dedication (Jn 10:22-39)*

And so at the end of AD 29 Jesus paid one more special visit, this time at the feast of the Dedication, also known as the feast of Lights, which had been established by Judas Maccabeus in 165 B.C. to commemorate the purification of the Temple after its desecration by the Syrians. As soon as he returned to the Portico of Solomon where he had previously taught, he was surrounded by the same hostile swarm of Jews demanding that he tell them openly if he was or was not the Messiah, the Christ. Their question was not put with any intention of worshipping him if he answered affirmatively, but simply to provide them with the pretext for stoning him as a blasphemer. Jesus gave them a spirited reply that at once defied them to do their worst and at the same time gave them the answer they wanted. He reminded them that he had already plainly told them about his equality with his Father and about his divine mission, but that his affirmation was of no consequence to them as they did not belong to the flock that his Father had given him. However, they could not steal that flock from him, because it belonged to God his Father and they were to know that in any case he and his Father were of one and the same nature (Jn 10:30). This was the signal they had been waiting for and they took up stones there and then to stone him to death. But Jesus made them pause by demanding to know what his crime was. He proceeded to make things as difficult as possible for them in order to stave off and deter their violence and so to preserve them, if possible, from a grave sin. For when they alleged that his crime was blasphemy, 'because you are making yourself God', he argued in rabbinic fashion that as the Psalmist David referred to men as 'gods' and 'sons of God' (Ps 81 [82]), he above all was fully justified in calling himself 'the Son of God'. And if they could not believe his word, they ought at least to admit the relevance of his deeds, which manifested that God was his Father and that the Father was in him. Nevertheless, they remained totally impervious to any argument and once more tried to arrest him, but again failed to do so as his Hour had not yet come.

Jesus again walked away untouched and unscathed, and since he had already ceased to reside in Galilee, he went eastwards down to the Jordan and crossed over into a territory where they would not want to pursue him. Nevertheless his fourth attempt to reason with the Temple authorities had again ended in complete deadlock; they remained adamant in their opposition and firmly entrenched, while he continued to be barred from the exercise of his messianic power in the Holy City.

13

*Some Events on the Final
Journey to Jerusalem*

It seems impossible to discover from the Gospels the exact route
that Jesus followed as he set himself to go to Jerusalem to meet
the fate that he knew was in store for him there. All that we can
really be sure of is that he had left Galilee never more to return
to it on a journey that ultimately brought him to Jerusalem. But
many months were to pass and many adventures were yet to
befall him, before he arrived there for the last Passover of his
life. Our evangelists are now especially at pains to show Jesus
as intensifying the training of the Twelve to become the ambassadors of his Gospel. He expects them to adopt a celibate way of
life similar to his own (Mt 19:10-12),[27] to embrace a life of poverty (Mt 19:16-29), and to be willing to follow their Master, if he so
desires, even to a painful and shameful death (Mt 19:28). Little
by little he is initiating them into, and getting them used to, the
notion that their life also is to be one of continuous self-sacrifice,
thus following quite literally in his footsteps.

1) 'What God has joined together...' (Mt 19:3-10 = Mk 10:2-12)

One of the favourite stratagems of his opponents was to try to

---

27 It is controverted whether the apostles later on took wives round with them or
not (*adelphen gunaika,* cf. 1 Cor 9:5). The latest and best research seems to
suggest that if the apostles and the early bishops had wives they lived with them
in celibate fashion (cf. Roman Cholij, *Clerical Celibacy in East and West,* Fowler
Wright 1989; J. McRory, *The Epistles to the Corinthians,* 1935, on 1 Cor 9:5).

trap him into saying something that could be construed as an attack on the Law of Moses in order to have a colourable excuse for accusing him of blasphemy. Now there were at that time two schools of rabbinical thought about the grounds required for a man lawfully to divorce his wife. The Book of Deuteronomy (Dt 24:1-4) states that Moses permitted male Israelites to divorce their wives 'for some indecency'; the dispute turned upon the interpretation of these words. What sort of sexual irregularity did it mean, if any? The School of Shammai on the one hand permitted divorce only for adultery; but the School of Hillel permitted it for much slighter, even trivial, reasons. And though a male Israelite could divorce his wife, the Law of Moses did not grant her the right to institute divorce proceedings against him. Roman Law however, as we shall see, did allow a wife to divorce her husband.

Now the Pharisees had heard that Jesus was opposed to divorce, and they were anxious to get him to commit himself to contradicting the permission Moses had granted. So they framed a special question and put it to him in the form: 'Is it lawful for a man to divorce his wife for any reason at all?' His magisterial reply avoided the trap they had set him, and at the same time restored the ancient Law to the form intended by God: 'Have you not read that the Creator from the beginning made them male and female?', quoting the Book of Genesis (1:27) as setting forth God's original plan for monogamy. Jesus then proceeded to lay down with clarity and simplicity the true meaning of the words of Genesis: 'For this reason a man will leave his father and mother and will be joined to his wife and the two shall be in one flesh; and so they are no longer two but one flesh. For what God has yoked together, let man not separate' (Mt 19:6).

The Pharisees could not deny that Jesus had correctly interpreted the mind of the author of Genesis, but they at once countered with the question: 'Why then did Moses command to give a deed of repudiation and to divorce?' Jesus retorted: 'It was because of your hardness of heart that Moses permitted you to divorce your wives. But from the beginning it was not so'. They could not deny that Moses had only extracted from the Lord God the concession of this relaxation of the marriage bond because of their frailty (Dt 24:1-4). The final pronouncement of Jesus in his teaching capacity as the Messiah and Law Giver, superior to Moses, was couched in clear and uncompromising terms:

> Amen I say to you, that whoever divorces his wife, except for incest, and marries another, commits adultery; and he who marries her who has been divorced commits adultery.

Since Roman Law also permitted a woman to divorce her husband, Peter (whose discourses, delivered in Rome long after Mt, came to be known as our Gospel of Mark as the early Church Fathers assure us), commenting on these words of Jesus, added the following clarification: 'And if she, having divorced her husband marries another, she too commits adultery' (Mk 10:12). The Gospels do not tell us the effect of this 'hard saying' on the Pharisees who had asked the original question, but it had a shattering effect on the Twelve Apostles. Despite Jesus' saving clause—'except for incest'—they rightly understood that he was restoring marriage to its pristine state of indissolubility, and felt that he was asking too much of weak human nature. The Greek word translated here as 'incest', namely *porneia* (Hebrew: *zenuth*) until recently has been rendered as 'fornication' or 'unchastity', but modern research has now proved that in this context *porneia* means 'marriage within the forbidden degrees'.[28] What Jesus is in effect saying is that marriages contracted according to God's law cannot be dissolved by the laws of men, and the widely held view that Jesus was allowing adultery or fornication as a sufficient justification for a divorce is ruled out. So Jesus has again used his supreme messianic authority, this time to restore the permanence of the fundamental institution of the human race. The effect of his decree was in principle to re-

---

28 Modern research has proved that it is incorrect to render *porneia* by 'fornication'. In its present context it means 'incest', and therefore the prohibition refers to marriage within the forbidden degrees (cf. J.A. Fitzmyer, *Theological Studies*, Vol. 37, June 1976, pp. 197 ff).

store to women their rightful and proper dignity, and so to raise the status of family life throughout the world for all time to come.

At that moment the Apostles could only see the difficulties in the way of the realization of this command, and expressed their dismay by saying: 'If the case of a man with his wife is like this, it is not expedient to marry!'. But Jesus had noted that they correctly understood him to say that marriages sanctioned and blessed by God cannot be dissolved. The evangelist did not allude to the assistance that the Lord would provide in his Church to make it possible for ordinary men and women to obey his teaching. Married Christians, in fact, receive through the sacrament of matrimony the special grace necessary to maintain lifelong fidelity to each other.

2) *Teaching on the Single Life (Mt 19:11-12)*

The Apostles' objection had unintentionally raised a point concerning their own special relationship to Jesus and his Kingdom. He therefore seized the opportunity to open their eyes to the value of celibacy for the sake of the Kingdom. He takes up their words 'it is not expedient to marry' to affirm that refraining from marriage for the sake of the Kingdom of God is not only honourable but is to be another notable mark of his Gospel, when he said to them:

> Not all can take this saying but to whom it has been given. For there are eunuchs who from the mother's womb were born so; and there are eunuchs who were made eunuchs by men; and there are eunuchs who have made themselves eunuchs for the Kingdom of Heaven.

Hitherto it had been regarded as a sacred duty on the part of all Israelites to marry and to raise children in order to increase the numbers of the Chosen People, who were in themselves only a small proportion of the total human race, occupying a small country surrounded by a hostile environment. But in the new Kingdom that Jesus had come to found, citizenship by carnal descent was to be replaced by spiritual membership of his Body, a membership open to all human beings. Nevertheless, though celibacy for the sake of the Kingdom is clearly encouraged and graciously advocated by Jesus, it is always to remain voluntary: 'He who can take it, let him take it' (cf. 1 Cor 7:7ff).

3) Jesus' Kingdom is for the Innocent
(Mt 19:13-15 = Lk 18:15f = Mk 10:13f)

It is surely not without particular design that Matthew placed this section immediately following the Lord's teaching on the Single Life. Devout and caring mothers of every race are always eager to obtain spiritual graces as well as temporal aid for their children; and the presence of Jesus drew them like a magnet to present to him their babes and youngsters for his blessing. Nevertheless the disciples, among whom were undoubtedly the Twelve, were anxious to protect him from being mobbed and over-zealously rebuked the mothers.

Mark tells us that Jesus was upset at the disciples' attitude and firmly bade them 'let the little children come and do not stop them, because of such is the Kingdom of Heaven'. Luke and Mark in fact not only quote these words but go on forcefully to add: 'Amen, I say to you, whosoever does not receive the Kingdom of God as a little child shall by no means enter into it'. And Jesus at once revealed his love for and desire to have the little children around him 'by embracing them, blessing them, and laying his hands upon them' (Mk 10:16). For he wished to hold up to his followers at one and the same time the total innocence, purity and guilelessness of such children as the ideal for all his followers, as well as the duty of the strong always to aid the weak and never to take advantage of them. Indeed, no one had ever before in human history spoken with such authority and compassion about children's need for care and guidance. His words: 'Whoever receives one such child in my name receives me', have been the fundamental charter for all child-care throughout the world ever since.

4) The Rich Young Man (Mt 19:16-22 = Lk 18:18-23 = Mk 10:17-22)

Jesus was further to elaborate his teaching on the demands of the apostolic life when a ruler of the synagogue enquired what he had to do to gain eternal life. When Jesus told him to keep the commandments of the Decalogue, he replied that he had always kept them, but felt that something more was necessary; and so Jesus said to him:

> If you wish to be perfect, go and sell your goods and give to the poor, and you will have treasure in heaven; and come follow me.

The Gospel relates that 'hearing this word the young man went away sad, for he had many possessions'. For reasons best known to himself he preferred to retain them rather than free himself in order to follow Jesus, who was swift to point out to his disciples that the possession of wealth is a grave handicap for anyone wishing to enter the Kingdom of God. The disciples registered severe shock which led Jesus to repeat that those who trust in riches will find it extremely difficult to enter the Kingdom. And to ram the point home he went so far as to add:

> I say to you, it is easier for a camel to pass through the eye of a needle than for a rich man to pass into the Kingdom of Heaven.

By using the language of hyperbole so forcefully, he intended to make this lesson unforgettable. The disciples were astounded by his words, since in the Old Testament ethos temporal prosperity was universally taken as a sign of God's approval of one's conduct. They had now to learn that there is no necessary connection in Christ's Kingdom between right conduct and temporal prosperity. For all those who wish to follow Christ closely must be prepared to give up everything as he himself had done. Hence their plaintive response: 'Who then can be saved?' was met with the uncompromising statement: 'With men this is impossible; but with God all things are possible'. Jesus wanted them to realise that he was teaching them a doctrine that neither they nor anybody else could live up to without a special grace from God, because no human being possesses the detachment necessary to resist the corruptive power of riches unless he be given strength from above to do so.

5) The Reward of Discipleship
(Mt 19:23-30 = Lk 18:24-30 = Mk 10:23-30)

This statement of Jesus worried Peter very much because in accepting the call to follow him, he and the rest of the Twelve had already 'left all things', had renounced all gainful occupation, had begun to practise the required detachment and were now dependent on divine providence in a spectacular way. Peter reasoned that if they indeed honoured their commitment to apostolic poverty until the day of their death, they had so far received no guarantee from him that in the next life they would regain the riches they had renounced in this one. So Peter as spokesman of the Twelve felt obliged to enquire: 'Behold we left all things and followed you. What then shall we have?' Jesus replied with his solemn affirmation: 'Amen, I say to you that when the Son of Man has taken his seat on the throne of his glory you who have followed me will be given in the Rebirth [by which he means the resurrection] twelve thrones for judging the twelve tribes of Israel'. By this he means them to understand that in heaven they will enjoy a place of unique dignity and authority. He adds furthermore that all those who in future for his sake follow their example and renounce their possessions and their right to raise a family and actually 'leave house or wife or brothers or sisters or children or lands for the sake of my Name and the Kingdom of God' will receive a hundredfold and inherit eternal life.

St Mark, or rather St Peter, if the Fathers are right that he is behind this Gospel, adds the paradox that the reward Jesus will give even in this life to all those who have similarly detached themselves will be a hundredfold recompense, that is, the true essence of all the good things of life on earth—with one qualification, that the promised happiness will be accompanied by 'persecutions'!

6) The Parable of the Labourers in the Vineyard (Mt 20:1-16)

Just in case the Apostles might get too elated by the fact of their selection by Jesus as founder members of his Kingdom, he tells them this parable, the moral of which is that he, its master and owner, is sovereignly free to give the same reward to those he engages at the 'eleventh hour', as he gives to those who have worked for him all day. As they progressed towards the city of Jerusalem, still continuing to believe that he would somehow achieve the success hitherto denied him, Jesus keeps on reminding them of the paradoxes involved in following him. For his followers, true greatness will consist in serving others, not in dominating them. 'He who wants to be first among them is to be the servant of all' (Mk 10:43-44). At the same time, since no servant is greater than his master, his servants too will have to expect persecution and endure ill-treatment and even death itself for his sake (cf. Mt 20:23f).

7) The Raising of Lazarus (Jn 11:1-44)

This is the last and greatest of the miraculous signs worked by Jesus. We know for a fact that he raised a considerable number of people from the dead (cf. Mt 11:5), but apart from the raising of Lazarus we learn details only of the raising of the daughter of Jairus (Mt 9:18-26 = Lk 8:40-56 = Mk 5:21-43) and that of the widow's son at Na'in (Lk 7:11-17). John alone records this story which forms the climax of the first part of his Gospel and throws much light on both the person and the message of Jesus.

The first thing to note is that Jesus has deliberately contrived this miracle in order to manifest and publicize his divine majesty and power on the eve of his voluntarily surrendering himself to his murderers.

We are next informed that the miracle was worked in favour of a family who lived in Bethany two miles from Jerusalem on the eastern side of Mt Olivet. Jesus regarded its three members, Martha, Mary and Lazarus, as his very dear friends, and he seems to have resided with them whenever he came up to the Holy City.

It was early spring in the year 30 and he and the Twelve were still on the eastern side of the Jordan, some two days' walking distance away, because the Jews had decided to arrest him whenever he next came up to Jerusalem. A message arrived from the two sisters to say that Lazarus was very ill. Jesus made no move to go and told the disciples not to worry and that Lazarus would not die. The disciples were later to realise that Jesus' words and actions, on this occasion, revealed that he knew all the time the actual condition of Lazarus in his home in Bethany forty miles away. In fact he deliberately delayed setting out for Bethany because he wanted in this instance not merely to restore physical health to the sick Lazarus but to raise him from the dead after his illness had killed him!

A couple of days later Jesus said: 'Let us go up to Judea again'. But the disciples remonstrated with him about the moral peril of such a visit. He then explained that Lazarus had gone to sleep and that he was going to wake him up. This remark led them to believe that this sleep was a sign of his recovery. But Jesus meant that it was the sleep of death. He said to them openly:

Lazarus is dead. And I am glad, because of you, that I was not there, so that you may believe. But let us go to him now.

The apostle Thomas then declared: 'Let us go that we may die with him'. When Jesus and his disciples arrived at Bethany, Martha got wind of his coming and went out to meet him, while Mary stayed at home. 'Lord, if you had been here', she pleaded, 'my brother would not have died. But now I know that whatever you will ask of God, God will give you'. Martha here revealed her faith in the healing power of Jesus and silently hoped for a miracle. Jesus replied, 'Your brother will be raised'. 'I know that he will be raised up in the resurrection on the last day', she answered, thus showing that she had accepted his teaching (which was also that of the Pharisees) that the just would one day rise again bodily.

By a further and extraordinary condescension Jesus now invited her to an even greater act of faith in him:

I myself am the resurrection and the life. He who believes in me, even if he has died, will live. And everyone who lives and believes in me does not ever die. Do you believe this? (Jn 11:25-26)

Martha's response was as full and satisfying as Peter's great confession that led Jesus to confirm him as the rock on which the Church would be built. 'Yes, Lord', she said, 'I fully believe that you are the Christ the Son of the Living God, the One who is come into the world'.

And now Martha realized that he was all set to manifest that he is the Lord of the dead as well as of the living (just as he had proved his power to forgive sins by attaching it to the healing of the paralytic). So she sped off to fetch her sister Mary to come and witness what he was about to do, and whispered into her ear that the Lord was ready and waiting for her.

Mary all the while had been waiting quietly at home for the summons of Jesus, surrounded by her friends who had come to commiserate with her and console her. These mourners were surprised when Mary, instead of going down to the tomb, went up the road to find Jesus who was still in the same place. By this time a considerable number of people had gathered round him waiting for something to happen. Like her sister, she fell weeping at his feet, repeating her sister's theme that Lazarus would not have died if he had been there, for she did not yet understand why he had delayed so long.

Jesus was so deeply moved by her tears that he had great difficulty in containing himself and he too shed tears of sorrow and compassion. The bystanders from Jerusalem were equally touched and were asking one another why this man who had given sight to the man born blind had not rather saved Lazarus from dying. They had not long to wait for an answer to their question, for Jesus told them to lead him to the place, a rock tomb hewn out underground with a large flat stone laid over the opening. When Jesus ordered them to lift off the stone slab, Martha complained: 'Lord, he will be stinking, because he has been already four days buried'. But Jesus brushed aside her protest, saying: 'Did I not say to you, If you believe you will see the glory of God'. So they lifted off the stone. Then in the presence of all Jesus raised his eyes upwards and uttered this prayer:

> O Father, I give thee thanks that thou hast heard me. And I know that thou hearest me always; but I have spoken because of the

crowd standing around, so that they may believe that thou has sent me. (Jn 11:41-42)

Then in a commanding voice he ordered: 'Lazarus, come forth'. And as they all looked on in amazement the dead man came out unaided, just as he had been laid in the tomb four days earlier, tied up in an enveloping sheet. 'Loose him and let him go', said Jesus. Willing hands untied him and handed him back to his sisters.

This amazing miracle was witnessed not only by the Twelve and the family of Lazarus but also by a large number of sightseers, and in next to no time the news was all round the Holy City.

The enemies of Jesus had several times asked him for a sign that would prove once and for all the validity of his mission, and in the raising of Lazarus he had fulfilled their request in a spectacular manner. Not only had he demonstrated his power over death itself and his power to give life to a body already starting to decay, but at the same time by his prayer immediately before restoring Lazarus to life he had proclaimed his intimacy and full equality with his Father, something no prophet had ever claimed. Finally, in this striking way he taught the faithful people of all future ages not to fear death, as for them it is to be but the stepping-stone into everlasting life.

8) *The Sanhedrin condemns Jesus*
(Mt 26:1f = Lk 22:1f = Mk 14:1f = Jn 11:45f)

The news of this fantastic sign soon reached the chief priests and the Pharisees, who were so alarmed that they at once summoned the Sanhedrin to decide what was to be done to neutralise its effect on the people. Blinded by their materialistic and worldly outlook these myopic clerical politicians could see nothing but the threat to their regime that had arisen from the enthusiasm of the people for Jesus. In spite of the fact that he himself was not putting forward any claim to revive the Hasmonean kingdom, his universal popularity gave him the power to make himself king if he so desired. They felt that they could not afford to take the risk of letting him remain at large;

the issues were too serious and alarming to contemplate. In the final analysis their own security and political survival depended on the support of Rome; any support they might show for Jesus would be regarded as a threat to Roman sovereignty, and Pilate would have deposed them at once, as other prefects within living memory had already treated former high priests.

Moreover the ideas of Jesus were in conflict with the character of the present regime, as he had shewn by his action in driving the buyers and sellers out of the Temple only some two years before. The most important and influential among the scribes and Pharisees hated him because he had challenged and dismissed their own interpretations of the Law with regard to such fundamental matters as his way of keeping the Sabbath and his prohibition of divorce. And he was above all insisting on an inward conformity with the spirit of the Mosaic Law as being more relevant than the details of its outward observance. In fact, they regarded him as the most dangerous kind of reformer, the type who is utterly radical and uncompromising in his pursuit of virtue and justice. Since the dominant voices in the Sanhedrin all thought about him along these lines, it did not take long for them to arrive at a decision. The leading men had already privately come to the conclusion that Jesus would have to die, and he himself had been fully aware of their intentions for some time and had publicly exposed them in his discourses in the Temple. The time had now come for them to act officially. The fourth evangelist succinctly describes what took place, for he seems to have had privileged access to the high priests' palace at this time (unless he learned the details from Nicodemus or Joseph of Arimathea, both members of the Sanhedrin).

> Now a certain one of them, Caiaphas, being the high priest of that year, said to them: "You yourselves know nothing, nor are you considering that it is expedient for you that one man should die for the people and that the whole race should not be destroyed" (Jn 11:49-50).

It is clear from this statement of Caiaphas, that other voices had been considering alternative ways of ridding themselves of Jesus without taking the drastic decision to have him put to death. But the voices of the partisans of Caiaphas prevailed over the objections of councillors like Joseph of Arimathea and Nicodemus. In his comment on these words of Caiaphas, John the evangelist pointed out that God's plan for Jesus to become the Saviour of the world would be fulfilled and that Caiaphas would be the unconscious instrument and prophet of its fulfilment:

Caiaphas did not say it of himself, but being high priest of that year he prophesied that Jesus was going to die for the race, and not for the race alone, but also that he might gather together into one the children of God who have been scattered (Jn 11:51-52).

The effect of this decision was to make Jesus an officially proscribed person, and prudence required him to take normal human steps to avoid capture until the time appointed by his heavenly Father. When that time came he would go up openly to Jerusalem to complete the sacrifice of his life. So he now left the neighbourhood of the Holy City and retired to a place northeast of Jerusalem called Ephraim, where he would be free from molestation for the time being (Jn 11 :54).

9) The Third Passion Prediction
(Mt 20:17f = Lk 18:31f = Mk 10:32f)

The excitement caused throughout Judea and Galilee by the meteoric passage of Jesus during the previous two years was now mounting to fever pitch as he once more drew near to the Holy City. It was the custom of many Jews to travel up a week or so before the Passover to prepare themselves by prayer and fasting for the most important feast of the year, and Jesus was no exception. It was of course by now well known that the chief priests and the Pharisees (Jn 11:57) had made up their minds to arrest him as soon as he appeared, and their only worry was whether in these circumstances he would dare to come up openly or at all. Jesus had however long before set his face to come up to the Holy City at this Passover to complete the task given him by his heavenly Father.

Leaving Ephraim he made his way first of all southwards to the city of Jericho, situated in a fertile oasis close to the River Jordan. For a third time he foretold to his twelve disciples even more explicitly than before what was going to happen to him. He declared that he was going first to be betrayed to the high priests and the scribes and then handed over by them to the Romans, who would scourge him and mock him and crucify him; and finally that he was going to rise from the dead on the third day. But the minds of the Twelve were still so set on the notion that his Kingdom was about to be inaugurated in a blaze of earthly glory that, as Luke wrote, 'they did not understand what he said to them' (Lk 18:34). Nor did they penetrate into his meaning when he again reminded them that 'whoever wanted to be first among them should be their slave, just as the Son of Man did not come to be served but to serve and to give his life a ransom for many' (Mt 20:27-28).

10) Jesus calls Zacchaeus (Lk 19:1-10)

A further event occurred while Jesus was at or near Jericho that still more inflamed the expectations of the crowds that now surrounded him all the time. As he passed through its streets the crowds had grown so dense that it was exceedingly difficult to get near him or even to see him. One of those who feared that he might never even glimpse him as he passed by was Zacchaeus, the chief tax collector for the Romans, a very rich and important man, but also very short of stature. Casting his dignity to the winds Zacchaeus raced on ahead along the route that he knew Jesus would have to follow, and climbed up into a sycamore tree in order to see him. Much to his surprise and amazement, Jesus looked up as he passed below and called to him: 'Zacchaeus, get down quickly for today I am happy to stay at your house'.

Zacchaeus got down as quickly as he could and received Jesus into his house with great joy. But the many bystanders who had heard Jesus call out to him were shocked that he had gone to stay at the house of a man who was publicly labelled a sinner because his occupation was not only unpopular but proscribed by the Pharisees on account of its connection with the Roman domination. Some of those who had followed Jesus into Zacchaeus' house were openly complaining: 'Why is he lodging with a sinner?' Zacchaeus however defended himself vigorously: 'Lord, please take note that I am now this very day giving half my possessions to the poor; and if I have defrauded anyone of anything I will repay him fourfold'. Jesus in reply declared to the accusers: 'Today salvation has come to this house because he too is a son of Abraham. For the Son of Man has come to seek and to save what has been lost'.

In fact as a tax collector he had been remarkably honest despite the temptations of his profession, and when he heard about Jesus he was determined to see him because he recognised the power of his teaching and wanted to hear more. The call of Jesus completed his conversion, and from that moment he determined to follow him as soon as possible. If he had in the course of his duties exacted too much from anyone, he would repay, he said, the debt fourfold, more than three times as much as the Law of Moses required. Later Christian tradition was to relate that he became the Bishop of Caesarea, though much against his will. On the part of Jesus, we see him going out of his way to recognise the merit of one of a despised class, for he looks at the heart rather than the face.

11) The Parable of the Ten Minas (Lk 19:11-28; cf. Mt 25:14-30)

While staying with Zacchaeus Jesus again attempted to allay the excitement of his disciples who were still expecting him to inaugurate his Kingdom in some dramatic way, and he did so by telling them the parable of the Ten Minas (a *mina* being worth 50 shekels). By means of this parable Jesus once more tried to impress on his disciples that he was shortly going to leave them and that he expected them, during his absence, faithfully to make proper use of the gifts and graces he would meanwhile entrust to them. In the parable the nobleman goes off on a journey of unknown duration and returns after a long absence to find out what his servants have done with the money he has put in their charge. The faithful ones are rewarded with a correspondingly generous gift, whilst the lazy servant is deprived of everything. Jesus of course used the story to point out that popular expectations of an early messianic triumph were quite wrong, although when the nobleman returns from the far country, he will call all his servants to a rigorous but just account, amply rewarding faithful service but inflicting condemnation and death on the embezzlers and defaulters.[29]

12) Jesus restores Sight to Bar-Timaeus
(Mt 20:29f = Lk 18:35f = Mk 10:46f)

The third fateful prediction of his passion was however for the time being driven out of the minds of the disciples by the miracle in which he restored sight to the blind son of Timaeus, Bar-Timaeus. This blind beggar had been sitting by the roadside when he heard the sound of voices as Jesus walked past surrounded by a large crowd talking excitedly about what they thought he would do when he got to Jerusalem this time. He had heard that Jesus claimed to be the Son of David, and began to cry out with a stentorian voice: 'Jesus, Son of David, have pity on me'. How amazing and encouraging it must have been for Jesus to hear himself called 'Son of David' by this wayside beggar, when the chief priests and the Pharisees obstinately refused to recognise his royalty! The crowd tried to shut him up, but he was not to be put down and shouted all the louder: 'Son of David have mercy on me'. Jesus heard his shout and stopped, and said: 'Call him'. And they did. When Bar-Timaeus heard them tell him: 'Cheer up, get up, he is calling you', he sprang to his feet, threw off his cloak and ran towards the sound of the voice of Jesus who said 'What do you want?' And he asked: 'Rabbi, that I may see again'. Jesus replied: 'Go, your faith has saved you'. At once he saw and followed Jesus on the road to Jerusalem, with all the people praising God for his cure.

---

29 Many commentators have suggested that this parable of the Minas is a reference to the contemporary real life story of Archelaus, the son of Herod the Great, who inherited Judea from his father in BC 4, and who made a special journey to Rome to try to persuade the emperor Augustus to give him the title of king. He was such a cruel and tyrannical ruler that his citizens sent a delegation after him to beg the emperor not to do so, and to free them from him. It was because of his evil reputation that Joseph returned to Nazareth instead of Bethlehem with Mary and Jesus. Archelaus was in fact deposed a few years later for his excessive cruelty. If there is any parallel, it is one in which the actual roles of the ruler and the citizens have been reversed.

13) Jesus is anointed in Bethany (Jn 12:1-8)

It seems that Jesus made his final journey up to Jerusalem by the scenic route from Jericho, a distance of nearly twenty miles in the course of which the road climbs from 900 ft below sea-level to some 2,200 ft above it. He arrived a week before the Passover and stayed in Bethany with the raised-up Lazarus and his sisters. There is no record of his ever having stayed in Jerusalem itself; always at the end of his daily sessions in the Temple he had gone out to Mt Olivet and passed the night there. Certainly he had friends in the City who would have been delighted to accommodate him and his disciples (witness the ease with which he was given the Upper Room for the Last Supper); but the danger of secret arrest by the Temple police was always too great to risk, and he did not wish to compromise his hosts.

The whole locality rejoiced at his presence and there was a general expectation that something great was about to happen. His many friends in Bethany organised a banquet in his honour at Simon's house (Mt 26:6) and Lazarus was one of the specially invited guests, among whom of course were also the twelve Apostles. Martha had charge of the provision of food and drink, but Mary her sister had ideas of her own how to celebrate the occasion. She wanted to show her love and veneration for the one she believed to be the Son of God, who had so recently raised her brother Lazarus from the dead, and whom unbeknownst to her the high priests were also plotting to kill, as the living subject of the miracle.

While the men were reclining at table in the usual way, Mary entered and poured over his feet a whole pound of the most precious ointment that money could buy and proceeded to wipe them with her hair.[30] The whole house was filled with the scent of the perfume. Everyone was delighted except Judas Iscariot who grumbled audibly that it was worth three hundred denarii

---

30 This Mary is identical with the Mary, the sister of Martha and Lazarus, mentioned in Jn 11:2. But her identification with Mary Magdalene and/or the unnamed woman of Lk 7:36-50 is problematical.

(the equivalent of a workman's wages for a whole year) and that the money ought to have been handed to him to give to the poor. John, writing his Gospel long afterwards, commented that Judas said this not because he cared about the poor but because he was a thief and had charge of the common purse holding all the alms given to Jesus and his disciples (Jn 12:6). Jesus overheard his criticism and swiftly responded in her defence:

> Why do you trouble her? For she has worked a good work for me. For the poor you have always with you, but me you do not always have. For when she poured this perfume over my body, she did it for my burial. Amen I say to you, wherever this gospel shall be preached in the whole world, so too what she has done will be spoken of as a memorial of her. (Mt 26:10-13)

The response of Jesus to those who honoured him without fear of human respect was always immediate and the reward he bestowed on them totally unexpected. His recognition of her good deed was to have her remembered by all future generations for anticipating the anointing of his sacred body soon to be entombed without any preparation for burial.

This was the last occasion on which Jesus was able to relax among friends, but the surly remark of Judas, whose depravity was already known to him introduced an unwelcome discordant note into an otherwise happy occasion.

14

The Propagation of the
Gospel Message

Jesus had introduced his twelve disciples in two stages to the arduous but rewarding task of proclaiming his Gospel:

1) The first stage (Mt 10:6-15) had been simple and practical and had been concerned with the situations that they had to cope with during the first trial exercise that he gave them to undertake in Galilee; this has already been discussed in our account of his missionary discourse in the earlier part of the Galilean Ministry above (see Chapter 9). On that occasion he only briefly referred to the possibility that some people would refuse to listen and would thereby suffer the dire consequences of rejecting the Word of God. This preliminary exercise lasted only a week or two, and after their return he helped them to evaluate it for the future (Mk 6:30).

2) But Jesus knew that he would not live to see his Apostles carry out the second and final stage which began immediately after the descent of the Holy Spirit on them at Pentecost (Ac 2:1ff). Nevertheless from the information that Matthew has recorded (10:16-42) we learn that he furnished them with a great number of valuable insights regarding the problems they would then have to face and how best to prepare for and overcome them.

When Matthew came to write his Gospel a few years after the resurrection the leaders of the Mother Church of Jerusalem had already suffered severe persecution and he accordingly in-

corporated further apposite prophetical words of Jesus for the
comfort and encouragement of the Church in its trials. Jesus
had foretold that after his departure his missionaries would not
only from time to time have their witness abruptly rejected, but
would also have to face active persecution of a cruel and heart-
rending kind. They would be arraigned before local Jewish
councils and even before the Sanhedrin; they would sometimes
find themselves betrayed by members of their own Church, and
parents would even be betrayed by their own children. They
would be unjustly accused before pagan rulers and tribunals for
adhering to Christ, and it would seem to them that they were
hated by all men because of their devotion to the name of Jesus.

Unlike the soldiers of secular governments who come armed
with weapons for attack as well as for defence, the soldiers and
missionaries of Christ are not to take weapons even to defend
themselves against unjust attack, and so will appear to onlookers 'like sheep in the midst of wolves'. However, they are not
to be afraid to put their case and defend the truth; indeed 'they
are to be wise as serpents and as simple as doves'. God's grace
and the wisdom of his Spirit is to be their sole weapon for confronting and convincing their adversaries. They are never to
worry what to say when questioned about their witness to Jesus
because the Holy Spirit will put into their mouth exactly what
to say, words which their persecutors will not be able either to
oppose or to contradict.

Although they are to forego the means of protecting themselves from physical violence, the Lord will make sure that they
will be 'saved', that is to say, come to no harm so far as their eternal destiny is concerned, even though they may suffer physical
injury and even death itself. For the Lord categorically guaran-
tees that 'he who perseveres to the end will be saved'. If persecuted in one city they are to flee to another. They are never to
be surprised at being victims of persecution and of calumnies,
since their divine Master has already endured the same injustices on their behalf, and 'the servant is not above his master'.
To fail to confess Jesus when challenged by their accusers and

judges will mean that Jesus in turn will not confess them before his heavenly Father at the Day of Judgement. To confess Jesus at the risk of one's life is to find true life, eternal life. On the other hand, the recipients of the Gospel message are to understand that therewith they are actually receiving Christ himself. Finally, this missionary activity is to go on until the end of time; for 'the Gospel of the Kingdom will be proclaimed in the whole inhabited world, as a witness to all the nations, and then the end will come' (Mt 24:14).

There are two further points that Jesus emphasised in this connection. Firstly, his preachers are to speak up and to speak out fearlessly; they are to preach the message of the Gospel 'from the housetops' (Lk 12:4f), and they are not to fear those who can only kill the body but are not able to kill the soul; indeed they are to fear only those who can also kill the soul. For the time will come when whatever is covered up will be uncovered and whatever is hidden will be made known, and their task is to make sure that the Gospel is made known now and not when it is too late. And so at the Last Day they will be fully vindicated in the sight of all.

Secondly, they are not to be deterred from preaching the Word simply because it will divide members of the same family from one another, 'setting a man against his father and a daughter against her mother' (Mt 10:35); for anyone who loves father or mother or son or daughter more than Jesus and his Word is not worthy of him. The supreme value for the Christian is to obey the Word of the Gospel. Jesus has promised that whoever loses his life by obeying the Word for his sake will actually receive it back again and be abundantly rewarded.

Whereas Matthew's Gospel was primarily written for Palestinian Jews, Luke's was composed twenty years later with Paul's Gentile converts in mind. Luke differs from Mt and Mk by inserting between its two narrative parts (Lk 1:1-9:51 and 18:15-24:53) a Central Section, containing what appears to be a random collection of stories and sayings, which takes up more than a third of the total length of the Gospel. A great number of these sayings and stories are parallel to those we find in the six great discourses of Matthew, but there are also a number not found elsewhere and which complement Matthew's. The new material that Luke was able to recover as a result of his researches was specially appropriate for Paul's churches, and much of it is found in this Central Section (9:52-18:14).

In this Section, for instance, Luke informs us that Jesus, in addition to his inmost circle of Twelve, commissioned another seventy-two to whom he gave similar instructions. These were as follows:

1) To be seen to rely on the providence of God for all their temporal needs; and so they are not to take money or provisions for the journey. Their act of faith would be rewarded by their hearers giving them freely everything they needed for their well-being (cf. Lk 10:19-20), and their trust in divine providence will encourage others to do the same.

2) Not to let themselves get side-tracked by irrelevances but to stick rigorously to their principal task, the proclamation of the Gospel (Lk 10:4).

3) They must be seen to be disinterested purveyors of the truth and single-minded servants of the Lord. It was important that they should be seen to be dedicated to the cause that they were proclaiming and preaching, and not like the teachers and philosophers of Greece and Rome who had the reputation of being very avaricious, and who usually demanded payment in advance for the wisdom they professed to impart.

The duty of his followers is to remind all who will listen to them of the existence of the Living God, and to persuade them to enter God's Kingdom by submission to the two great commandments of the Law: 'Thou shalt love the Lord thy God with all thy heart and soul and mind and strength, and thy neighbour as thyself' (Lk 10:25-28). Baptism by water and the Spirit confessing belief in Jesus as the Son of God was the title for admission into the Kingdom. It has to be remembered that the task of the Twelve and of the seventy-two was altogether different from and much easier than that of Paul who would have to convert pagans who were totally ignorant of God's Law; for the minds of all Jews had already been moulded for more than a thousands years by the Law of Moses, and the Apostles' Jewish audiences knew that they were God's people and that they had always been obliged to perform as perfectly as possible the Works of the Law.

The Twelve therefore had the task of reminding their fellow Israelites of their sins of omission and commission with respect to the Law, because they already had a basic knowledge of the existence of God and of God's dealing with their race, and the purpose of their preaching was to enable the people to recognise their guilt and repent. They had also been furnished with special insights to comprehend the new Law of Love with which he was infusing the Old Law of Moses. Their aim was to impart by precept, example and illustration this new spirit. Above all they had to make sure that all their hearers understood that Jesus had the authority of the Lord God of Israel, the God of Moses, for the new way in which he was treating such questions as the use of the Sabbath rest and the withdrawal of the permission to divorce wives. The first and the essential requirement for their conversion was to accept the divine authority of Jesus Christ whose spokesmen the Apostles had been constituted, because in his coming God was fulfilling the promise made to the prophets in past ages in their holy books.

The narrow contemporary views about who was or was not one's neighbour were to be replaced by the recognition that in the New Dispensation one's neighbour is the first person one comes upon who needs assistance, which Jesus so graphically described in the parables of the Good Samaritan (Lk 10:29-37) and the rich man and Lazarus (Lk 16:19-31). The imperative command to aid the sufferer transcends all bounds of race or caste or station in life. To avoid giving such assistance is to court eternal damnation.

Jesus is also hard on the sin of avarice, because 'a man's life is not in the abundance of his possessions' (Lk 12:15). The parable of the rich Fool illustrates that the accumulation of wealth without thought of 'the world to come' is the utmost folly because one never knows how long one will enjoy it or who will succeed to it after one's death (Lk 12:16-21). The true follower of Christ never worries about any lack of the necessities of life in the matter of food or drink or clothing, because he knows that his heavenly Father who also feeds the birds will not allow him to die of hunger. 'Rather seek his Kingdom, and all these things will be added to you' (Lk 12:32). Moreover, do not hesitate to give alms, 'make for yourselves purses that do not wear out', and through good deeds pile up treasure in heaven where there are no thieves to break in and no moths to consume'(Lk 12:33-34).

An outstanding characteristic of the follower of Jesus is his desire to be in constant communication with his heavenly Father, which takes place principally through prayer, its highest form being contemplation. The importance that Jesus attached to contemplative prayer is best seen in the story of Mary sitting at the feet of Jesus and absorbed by his presence, while her sister Martha bustles around (Lk 10:38-42).

As regards the prayer of petition, when we pray for our various needs for ourselves and for others, Luke gives two examples of the importance that the Lord attached to perseverance in prayer however hopeless the likelihood of our petition being granted. The first example he gives is that of the householder in bed asleep late at night with his family beside him, when a neighbour comes to his door and disturbs him by knocking loudly and long. Eventually in exasperation he rises and opens the door to find that his friend has only a trivial request to make—a loaf of bread to entertain a friend! But all the same he gives him what he wants in order to get rid of him and get back to bed. The moral is that *a fortiori* our own personal requests, provided they are good in themselves and good for us, will be answered by the Lord in due time if we persevere in knocking! The other example is a droll one; that of a judge who 'neither feared God nor respected man' who was besieged by a poor widow demanding redress for a grievance. For a long time he refused to listen to her but she refused to go away. So in the end, out of exasperation and the desire to get rid of her moans and groans, he gave her what she wanted. The moral here is that if even a tired householder and a wicked judge will act thus, how much more effectively will the all-just and all-loving God vindicate his elect who cry to him for justice (Lk 18:1-8).

The Lord also holds out hope to the sinner who has thrown away all his opportunities of leading an upright life and keeping God's commandments; it is never too late to repent and God is always ready to extend his mercy and his peace to the truly penitent sinner however black his sins. In the parable of the prodigal son (Lk 15:11-32) the errant son, who has wasted and thrown away the whole fortune left him by his father, knows that he has no longer any claim on his father's generosity; nevertheless the misfortunes that he has brought on himself bring him to his senses and cause him to realise that he must at least beg pardon and try to make a new start. But he greatly underestimates the depth of his father's love and desire to forgive him everything. At the first sign of repentance, his father reinstates him without a word of reproach, rejoicing that 'this son of mine who was dead has come to life'. The sequel of the parable is the contrasting haughty behaviour of the 'good' elder son, who though he never kicked over the traces, yet failed to realise his father's deep compassion and equal love for him too.

Luke notes and emphasizes the urgency of repentance for transgression of God's law, because there are two things that nobody knows: the day of his own death when he will be called to a final account, and the day of the second coming of Christ when all injustices will be corrected and crimes expiated. Two examples must suffice. In the first, some people reported to Jesus that Pontius Pilate had caused a wave of horror in Jerusalem by sending in his soldiers to slaughter some Galileans while they were actually sacrificing to God in the Temple. Jesus replied that these Galileans were no worse sinners than all the other Galileans, and that the eighteen Judeans, killed when a tower collapsed in Siloam, were no worse than the rest of the inhabitants of Jerusalem. And he added, 'But you will all likewise perish, if you do not repent' (Lk 13:1-5). A strong incentive to undertake repentance is the expectation of the sudden return of the master and the undoubted need for constant watchfulness. Jesus instances the case of the slaves of a household waiting for the reappearance late at night of their wealthy and powerful master after a night out. It is their duty to be ready and properly equipped with lamps lit to welcome him. In the same way the Christian must always be prepared for the return of the Son of Man who will come at an unexpected hour, like a thief in the night (Lk 12:35-40). All the while the Master is absent they must be faithful, even in little matters, to the tasks assigned to them (Lk 16:8-13).

Finally, Luke tells the parable in which the Lord reminds his followers that the possession of all the privileges that membership of the Kingdom confers on them, makes it the more incumbent to practise the virtue of humility. They are never to think of themselves as better than other men, 'for everyone who exalts himself will be humbled, but he who humbles himself shall be exalted'. The example he gives is the story of the Pharisee and the tax collector (Lk 18:9-14). The Pharisee proudly faces God in the synagogue and 'thanks the Lord he is not like other men',— and turning round and noticing an opulent tax-collector at the back adds, 'and not as that tax collector!'. The latter however has a very different prayer; he feels unworthy to come forward, and standing at the back strikes his breast and confesses inwardly, 'O God, have mercy on me, sinner that I am'. And Jesus concludes the parable with the words: 'I say to you, this tax collector was the one who went down to his house justified', that is, forgiven by the Lord, rather than the other, the self-righteous Pharisee.

In the light of the foregoing we can see that evangelization meant for the Apostles to preach the crucified and glorified Christ and to be the agents for arousing in the souls of all willing to listen both faith in Jesus and the desire for baptism. Today all baptised Christians have the same duty of passing on this Good News to all willing to listen.

15

The Last Days in Jerusalem

1) The Triumphal Entry into Jerusalem
(Mt 21:11 = Lk 19:29f = Mk 11:11 = Jn 12:12f)

According to the chronology which we are following, in the year in which Jesus died on the Cross the Passover fell on the Sabbath (probably 7 April AD 30). The previous Sabbath was spent in all likelihood at Jericho, and then on the first day of the week that would end with the Passover feast he started for Jerusalem, a steady ascent of twenty or so miles, in order to arrive at Bethany in time for the festive dinner that his friends Martha, Mary and Lazarus had prepared for him at their home (cf. chapter 13.13). With him were his twelve disciples and the entourage of women whose privilege it was to look after the material wants of the whole group. He spent the night in Bethany as usual, as it was too dangerous for him to stay in the capital. Indeed the news of his arrival in Bethany reached the Sanhedrin that same evening and so alarmed them that they were planning to have Lazarus also murdered. For the raising of Lazarus a few weeks before was still fresh in the minds of everyone and support for the high-priests' policy of implacable hostility was visibly crumbling (Jn 12:9-11). It had become clear to his enemies that there was a vast underground swell in his favour and they were now mortally afraid that the large numbers of enthusiastic pilgrims in the Holy City might easily trigger off a popular uprising that would put Jesus into power and

bring about their total disgrace in the eyes of the Roman governor.
In the events that were now to follow we are faced with the
mystery of the human mind and heart of Christ who had already prophesied clearly three times to his disciples that he was
going to suffer a cruel death in the near future. And so we have
the paradox that on the one level Jesus knew exactly what was
going to happen to him, and yet on the other level he went to his
death allowing everything to happen to him as if he had not
known it all the time in advance. No other human being could
ever behave in this way, but though like us in every way except
for sin, he was able to reconcile such opposites in himself
without any difficulty, because he was truly God as well as truly
man. For God knows all future things and allows them to happen according to the free play of human forces, though all the
time the whole world is moving steadily and inexorably towards
the predetermined consummation. That is to say, Jesus faced
and lived through the dangers and trials he had to undergo for
our sake with unflinching courage and determination, as if they
were previously unknown to him, whilst in fact seeing and
knowing everything in the light of eternity. What he underwent
was truly real, and we can therefore genuinely admire his fortitude and patience in not evading the tortures he knew were
awaiting him.

It was the Person of God the Son, possessing a complete
human nature and soul like ours, who of his own free will came
up to Jerusalem in order to make a final bid to get his claim to
be the true Messiah-King recognised by the high priests, a
priesthood originally appointed by his heavenly Father to be
the spiritual leaders of his people. He was indeed the royal Son
of David, whose destiny it was to set up on earth, indeed in
Jerusalem itself, the long-prophesied Kingdom that would last
for ever. None but he realised that the Kingdom could and
would only be established by the sacrifice of his life and through
his death and resurrection from the dead. In the events that
now follow he reveals his complete command over each and
every situation, and demonstrates his full knowledge of his own

dignity and authority. His actions were to speak louder than words, but only after his resurrection were his disciples able to evaluate his claim and recognise the magnitude of his achievement.

Jesus' claim to be the true Messiah of God's Chosen People had been rudely rejected by the high priests, and the eloquent speeches that he had made in the course of his subsequent visits had been brushed aside with death threats. On the other hand he had always firmly resisted the attempts of the people to proclaim him as a political messiah and an earthly king. He now clearly sees that the moment has come when he must either yield to the forces opposing him or risk a final demonstration to the whole nation of his claim to their allegiance. He will for the last time demonstrate in a peaceful way his messianic role and his royal power. To signal this he adopts a precedent set by his ancestor king David, who in order to defeat the attempt of his son Adonijah to usurp the throne had his favourite son Solomon placed on his own royal donkey and led in procession to be consecrated king at the Pool of Gihon (1 Kg 1). For on a mission of peace this was in any case the most acceptable way at the time for a dignitary to travel, since this animal signified the peaceful intent of the rider, the horse being the mount for fighting men.

Jesus therefore commandeered a donkey on which to ride into the City, in procession with his disciples in order to demonstrate his right to their recognition of his spiritual authority. Matthew, Luke and Mark all remembered very clearly the order given by Jesus to two disciples to go into the neighbouring village and to commandeer the first donkey they saw. If questioned they were simply to say that the Master had need of it, but would return it afterwards at once. When the disciples brought back not only the dam but also her foal upon which no man had yet sat, it was only fitting that while they put their garments on both, the Lord should be the first person ever to sit on the foal.

This incident notably increased the excitement of both the disciples and the crowd who at once realised that Jesus had some special intent. Meanwhile his numerous well-wishers in Jerusalem had got wind of his approach and had come out to meet him. The crowd coming up from Jerusalem and the crowd following him met on the brow of Mt Olivet just where the spectator enjoys the full view of the Holy City and its Temple spread out below. They all now spontaneously acclaimed him as their Messiah-King and made a processional way for him by spreading not only palm branches on the road but also their garments, praising God for all his miracles and shouting out: 'Hosanna to the Son of David; blessed is he who comes, the King of Israel, in the name of the Lord'. There was no restraining the extravagance of the joyous welcome given him by the crowd, aware of the recent raising of Lazarus from the dead; so much so that some of the Pharisees in the crowd bitterly complained: 'Teacher, rebuke your disciples'. But Jesus firmly replied, 'I say to you, if these keep silent, the very stones will cry out' (Lk 19:40).

Thus two years after his first unsuccessful appearance in the City, Jesus returns to receive a thunderous welcome from the whole population as he enters riding on the donkey, to the intense chagrin of the high priests, scribes and Pharisees. It was a spontaneous and genuine tribute to his power to convince all men of good will. Yet the sight of Jerusalem with its glorious Temple, his Father's House, all spread out beneath him—the joy and pride of every Jew and especially of Jesus himself— filled him now with poignant sadness rather than gladness, for he foresaw that within forty years it would be entirely blotted out in the most disastrous siege the world has ever known. Ignoring the delirious excitement all around him, Jesus drew rein on his donkey, and burst into tears, as he prophesied:[31]

> If you had known in this your day, the things for your peace. But now they are hidden from your eyes. For days will come upon you and your enemies will invest you with a rampart and will encircle you and compress you on all sides. And they will level you and your children in you, and they will not leave a stone upon a stone in you because you did not know the time of your visitation. (Lk 19:41-44)

31 This prophecy of the siege of Jerusalem is such an accurate and vivid forecast of what actually occurred forty years later that many modern exegetes argue that it must be a prophecy after the event. But the Two-Gospel Hypothesis claims that Luke's Gospel was published nearly ten years before the disaster of AD 70.

The evangelist John points out two interesting facts in connection with this triumphant entry. Firstly, at the time none of the disciples realised that Jesus was literally fulfilling a prophecy of Zechariah, 'Rejoice, daughter of Son, behold your king comes, seated on the foal of an ass' (Zech 9:9). Secondly, the Pharisees remained unimpressed by the enthusiasm of the crowd, which merely hardened their resolve to do away with him, although they were none the less scared by the strength and depth of his popular support.

2) The Barren Figtree (Mt 21:18-22 = Mk 11:12-14, 20-27)

It was probably some time during the weeks following his surprising cleansing of the Temple two years before that Jesus first noted a figtree with much foliage but no sign of fruit by the side of the road between the Temple and Mt Olivet. His heart was still heavy with the bitter experience of being rejected by his Father's priests, and he told his disciples a parable that reflected the situation as he saw it at that moment.

> A certain person had a figtree planted in his vineyard, and he came seeking fruit on it and did not find it. And he said to the vine-dresser: Look, for three years I have been coming seeking fruit on this figtree and have not found it. I will therefore cut it down. For why should it waste the ground? But he answering says to him: Sir, leave it just for this year, whilst I dig round it and spread manure. And if it should bear fruit in the coming year...? And if not, you shall cut it down. (Lk 13:6-9)

In this parable he was prophesying the lack of success in his efforts to win the support of the high priests, whose co-operation he rightly sought to enable the Word of the Lord to go forth from the Temple in Jerusalem. Many times since that day he had passed by that tree and seen the efforts of the owner to persuade it by the use of water and manure to bring forth fruit. And now on this final visit he noticed that the figtree had failed to respond to its owner's endeavours and in the style of the ancient prophets of Israel Jesus gave his disciples an 'acted parable'. For finding that the figtree had still failed to respond he withered it with a word: 'May no one eat fruit from you ever again'. The disciples heard him say it, and wondered.

The next morning as they again passed by on their way up to the Temple, Peter was the first to note that the figtree had entirely withered up from its roots to its crown, and pointed it out to Jesus, who replied:

> Amen, I say to you, if you have faith and do not waver, not only will you do it to the figtree; but if you were to say to this mountain, [and he gestured to Mt Olivet], "Be lifted up and cast into the sea", it will be done. And all things whatsoever you ask in prayer, when you believe you will receive.

With these words Jesus was giving his disciples an introduction that would enable them later to see the meaning of his life in proper perspective and to understand why Jerusalem and its Temple would have to be destroyed; for having failed to recognise the Messiah it had outlived its usefulness and had now become an encumbrance to the spread of his Gospel. They were about to learn that his own glorified Body was to become the new Temple for all nations and the vehicle for the fulfilment of Isaiah's prophecy. More striking still was the importance he attached to the all-powerful prayer of the man of faith, and he assured them that in response to their prayers God would grant favours that would be utterly impossible to human endeavour. It was a lesson that they would recall in later times, when their failure to believe in the possibility of his resurrection from the dead would be a thing of the past.

3) The Woman taken in Adultery (Jn 7:53-8:11)[32]

A very ancient tradition situates this incident during the course of the eight-day feast of Tabernacles (Jn 7-9), but it seems to fit

---

32 The history of this particular pericope is obscure. The Council of Trent (1545-1563) confirmed that it is an authentic part of the New Testament, but did not determine whether it is by John himself or by some unnamed disciple. Though it is omitted from our Gospel text by the majority of the great uncial manuscripts of the fourth century, a very early tradition assigned it to this part of John's Gospel; a few manuscripts however place it at the conclusion of his Jerusalem ministry at Lk 21:38. And because of its unusual mode of transmission there are a large number of variants in the text, though they are all of minor significance. I place the incident here because it belongs to the same type of story that we find in Mt 22.

in rather better with his last days in the Temple. The passage opens with the persistent interrogators of Jesus, the scribes and Pharisees, each returning to his own house after a previous encounter with him, while he repairs to his usual lodging on Mt Olivet. It has to be remembered that Jesus had made it clear to his hearers time after time that he had come to fulfil the Law and not to destroy it; and they now try to trip him up by evolving a stratagem that would compel him to act as good as his word. Overnight these rabbis had thought up a scheme whereby they felt sure they would be able successfully to accuse him of breaking the Law and so destroy his reputation and his ascendancy over the people. Their ruse was to find a woman in the act of committing adultery (they seemingly knew exactly where they would find one to fit their plan) and then present her to him to test his fidelity to the Law; because the Law of Moses clearly laid down that the penalty for adultery was death by stoning for both parties, for the man as well as for the woman (Lev 20:10; Dt 22:24). Since the couple would have been caught by the rabbis in the act, there would be no need for a formal trial to prove her guilt (the guilty man is however for some reason or other kept out of sight). They thought that they had Jesus cornered. If he told them to go ahead and stone her, her death would be attributed to him; the Romans could then accuse him of causing a riot and of having blood on his hands. But if he were to quash the death penalty in favour of a lesser punishment, they could justly accuse him of flagrantly failing to uphold the Law of Moses in the matter of a grave sin. This—they thought—would create an impossible dilemma for him.

So when he came into the Temple the next morning and sat down to teach the people, they accosted him and watched him intently as they demurely recited to him the woman's crime and then suddenly fired at him the cunning question: 'What therefore do you yourself say?' Jesus gave no immediate reply; he simply bent down and began to trace patterns in the dust with his finger. The instigators, believing that they at last had him at their mercy, began urgently to insist upon an answer. The tension mounted as he still kept silent and continued to write, or to draw patterns, in the dust, whilst they exchanged triumphant glances. At last after what seemed an age Jesus stood up and quietly said: 'Let him who is without sin among you be the first to cast a stone upon her'.

The circle of her accusers stood in shocked silence, trying to decide what next to do or to say. For Jesus by a word had transferred the whole case from the Temple courtyard into the secret tribunal of the conscience of his questioners, making the decision their own personal responsibility. Each one of them, trained in the knowledge and spirit of the Law, knew that he was in his own way as grievous a sinner as this woman. The words of the Master bit deep into the consciences of all. Not only were they gathered here in the Temple of God whose all-seeing eyes were ever upon them, but they now became acutely aware of their own sins and the sins of their companions. Was there among them anyone sufficiently hypocritical to undertake to cast the first stone? No, none of them dared to. They had no option but to slink away silently lest Jesus, who read the hearts of them all, should brand one of them with hypocrisy. He did not need to look up at them as once more he bent down and continued to write in the dust. And then the most senior of the accusing elders edged quietly out of the circle of onlookers and withdrew, followed silently by the others, until the woman was left alone standing in front of him. Slowly he straightened up and, looking kindly upon her, said: 'O woman, where are those accusers of yours? Has nobody condemned you?' And she said: 'Nobody, Lord'. And Jesus, knowing what was going on in her heart and perceiving her readiness to repent, said: 'Neither do I condemn you; go, and from now on, sin no further'.

In this way Jesus, the true Messiah and interpreter of the Law, changed in a moment of time the whole nature of the sanctions imposed in the Pentateuch, overruling the directions laid down with the authority of Moses. He now established that the punishment of physical death by stoning is no longer the appropriate measure for dealing with sins that bring spiritual death to the soul. Henceforth in such cases the culprit's life should not be forfeit, and the sin is to be forgiven, provided the sinner repents. However, Jesus in no way condones this woman's sin, but he has read her change of heart and sincere purpose to amend, and sanctions mercy replacing justice.

4) The Tribute to Caesar (Mt 22:15-22 = Lk 20:20-26 = Mk 12:13-17)

Matthew, Luke and Mark now add a series of four attempts by the various factions opposed to Jesus to disgrace him and bring him down. Matthew has placed them in his own literary order and we cannot be sure that they all took place during the final week of his life, but they form a fitting climax to his Temple preaching. Considered together these stories clearly reveal the bitter enmity of the forces that Jesus had to cope with throughout his two years of public life. Each story represents a particular aspect of his opponents' desire to belittle and humiliate him and shows how in every case they were themselves confounded and put to confusion.

The Pharisees are the first to take the initiative and, as Luke records (20:20), 'having carefully watched him they sent spies pretending that they were just, so that they might entrap him in speech so as to betray him to the government and to the authority of the governor'. That is to say, they pretended that they were honest inquirers in the hope of catching him off his guard and getting him to utter some sentiment that could be construed as disloyal either to the Roman emperor or to the Sanhedrin. For in those times there was a grave tension between the political domination of Rome and the hurt pride of the Jews smarting under the fact that they, the People of God, had become subject to a foreign pagan power. The symbol of their humiliation was the poll-tax levied by the Romans on every male Jew in Judea and Samaria. Moreover this tax had to be paid in a silver coin that bore the image of the Caesar inscribed as if he were God. This made its payment all the more galling. It seemed to Jesus' questioners that they could put him on the horns of a dilemma; if he approved of this payment they would condemn him as unpatriotic, and if he disapproved they would report him to the Romans as a disaffected person inciting others not to pay the tax. On the level of politics as they saw it, he could not escape blame one way or another. Jesus at once took up their challenge with his usual directness. 'Bring me a denarius [the coin of the tribute]', he said, 'and tell me whose image and title it bears'. And when they admitted that it was that of the Caesar himself he proceeded to give them a brief but salutary lecture. For from the higher level on which he moved, he was able to make a real distinction of which they had never even dreamed.

Every lawful government has the authority to levy just taxes for the common good, and the citizen has a duty in justice to pay them; and to do so is also to act in conformity with the Law of God. Thus there cannot be any clash between a state law and the Law of God if the law of the state is in conformity with the Law of God. Since the Pharisees had paid the tax and were in fact in collusion with the Roman administration, it was for them the lawful government and they could not question the logic of Jesus in telling them 'to give to Caesar what was Caesar's and to God what was God's'. They were completely baffled by the simplicity of his answer and were at the same time furious at the ease with which he had escaped their trap.

The profounder significance of this statement no doubt eluded them, but it was to become for the Christians a key-distinction in the long struggle to free the Christian Church from the control of the State. In the ancient world it was universally recognised that national unity permitted the state to determine the religion of its subjects. However, the coming of the Kingdom of Jesus Christ was to change everything. Henceforth while the state could demand from its subjects the support necessary for the attainment of their material welfare, all people of all nations were to learn that the Law of Christ transcends the laws of all the kingdoms of the earth and that these laws ought in due course to be brought into conformity with the Law of God. While the laws of the state and the Church are to remain distinct and independent in their respective spheres, the follower of Christ has now a double allegiance, which pays due deference to both, but at the same time allows him to retain his full spiritual freedom.

5) The Stratagem of the Sadducees
(Mt 22:23f = Lk 20:27f = Mk 12:18f)

In this section Matthew shows us the Sadducees' involvement in the general attack of the priests and the Pharisees on Jesus and his mission. They were an influential political group in the Sanhedrin and in the country and supported wholeheartedly the suzerainty of Rome. Theologically speaking they were very liberal; they accepted the authority only of the Pentateuch, and denied the new doctrine of the Pharisees that the dead will rise again at the great assize of the Lord at some distant date. They knew that Jesus accepted the Pharisaic doctrine of the final resurrection and their object was to make this doctrine look silly, and Jesus too for adhering to it. For their assault they invented an extreme case of the Levirate Law in which seven brothers married in turn the same woman, but each died before she had given him a child. They argued therefore that in any resurrection she would be married to seven husbands simultaneously which would clearly be contrary to the Law of Moses which imposed monogamy. There must have been a general laugh when the Sadducee interrogator concluded with the cunning question: 'Whose wife of the seven deceased husbands shall she be in the resurrection?' For he saw the Levirate Law as excluding the possibility of a resurrection.

Jesus now revealed his anger at this perverse misunderstanding of the relationship between this life and the life to come. 'You are wrong', he said, 'neither knowing the Scriptures nor the power of God'; and he went on to lift a tiny corner of the veil that obscures this life from the life to come and continued:

> The sons of this world marry and are given in marriage. But the ones deemed worthy to obtain that world and the resurrection from the dead neither marry nor are given in marriage; neither indeed can they die any more, for they are equal to the angels and are Sons of God, being sons of the resurrection.

Here we have the Lord of life himself revealing that the life of heaven is everlasting and that marriage and procreation only happen in this life and play no part in eternity. For there all human beings will be like the angels. That is to say, we shall then be as much at home in the world of spirit as the angels, whom the prophet Isaiah revealed as glorious beings surrounding the throne of God and singing his praise. Thus far Jesus has refuted only their very material ideas about the nature of the after-life. He then reminded them that they have also totally failed to understand the Pentateuch, which alone they still revered and which taught the doctrine of the resurrection of the dead. For when in the Book of Exodus (6:2-3) the Lord God declared to Moses that he had appeared 'to Abraham, to Isaac, and to Jacob as God Almighty' during different generations, he was clearly intimating his timeless and everlasting nature, thereby revealing that these patriarchs also 'live to him' (Lk 20:38) and that God now has them with him. Mark then concludes with Jesus' terse condemnation of their error: 'You are very wrong'. He is justly angry that they have not only misunderstood the doctrine of the resurrection but have tried to make fun of it. The crowds were ecstatic at his victory and even some of the scribes, the professional lawyers, admitted: 'Teacher, you have done well'.

It is, however, worth noting that the evangelists' accounts do not directly deal with the question of the bodily resurrection at the last day but only with the survival of the entire human person after death. The doctrine of the resurrection of the body will be finally established by the resurrection of Christ's body from the grave as the pledge of our own future bodily resurrection.

6) The Lawyer's Question (Mt 22:34f = Lk 10:25f = Mk 12:28f)

The Pharisees were delighted that the Sadducees had now been firmly put in their place; but despite their own previous discomfiture they themselves made another attempt to trip him up and so subvert his teaching. For at that time there was a serious debate among the rabbis as to whether there was one fundamental commandment of the Law that comprised all the others; and they were hoping that Jesus would say something that they could twist so as to make it possible for them to accuse him of speaking against the Law of Moses.

Matthew, Luke and Mark each relate the anecdote, namely the request of a lawyer (Luke's synonym for a scribe) who asked: 'Which is the great commandment of the Law?'. Jesus answered without hesitation in the words of the Pentateuch (Dt 6:5; Lev 19:18), ignoring whatever ulterior motive the question might have had:

> Thou shalt love the Lord thy God with thy whole heart and with thy whole soul and with thy whole strength and with thy whole mind, and thy neighbour as thyself (Lk 10:27).

This appear to have been the very first time that these two commandments of the love of God and one's neighbour had been linked together in this fashion. According to Mark, the lawyer was so pleased with Jesus's answer that he repeated it, adding that love of one's neighbour is 'more important than all the holocausts and sacrifices' (1 Sam 15:22). Jesus commended him for his answer by saying to him: 'You are not far from the Kingdom of Heaven'.

Furthermore, Luke alone adds a fascinating sequel. The lawyer decided to probe Jesus's mind further and asked: 'And who is my neighbour?'. Jesus at once responded with his own special insight, the parable of the good Samaritan (Lk 10:29-37), which teaches that for the true follower of Christ one's 'neighbour' is whoever one comes across in daily life who is in grave need of help and has been neglected or deserted by others. This was a lesson which the disciples of Jesus never forgot and which has been the hallmark of Christian civilization ever since.

7) How is Jesus David's Son?
(Mt 22:41f = Lk 20:41f = Mk 12:35f)

In this story Jesus again takes the initiative by summoning the Pharisees and putting to them a question that will finally expose their refusal to admit the truth about him. First of all, he gets them freely to admit that according to the prophecy of

Nathan (2 Sam 7:12) the Messiah is to be the son, i.e. a direct male descendant, of king David. He then points out to them that Psalm 109 [110] states that the Messiah is not only 'David's Lord' but also sits at the right hand of the Lord God. Thus two inspired texts of Scripture declare the Messiah to be both the equal of the Lord God and at the same time a creature, a man who is a prince of the house of David. Jesus then asks them to explain this paradox, namely how the Messiah will in fact be both God and Man. The Pharisees remain silent because Jesus himself standing before them is the living answer. They know that John the Baptist had declared him to be the Messiah; they also know that through Joseph he was a direct descendant of king David and, of course, his many miracles support his claim to have been sent by the Lord God. They are unable to deny that he has all the qualifications necessary for them to accept him, but self-interest forbids them to do so. And so from that moment the Gospels record that they dared not ask him any more questions.

16

Jesus' Final Assessment of the Situation

1) Jesus laments the Hypocrisy of Scribes and Pharisees (Mt 23:1-36)

At this point the enemies of Jesus had come to realize that far from being able to get the better of him in argument and confrontation, they invariably came off worse, each time losing more and more prestige in the estimation of the people listening to their debates. Yet now he was resigned to the fact that their attitude had hardened against him and that he could not win them over to accept his witness; but he was determined all the same to restate his position and vindicate his authority in unmistakable fashion for the benefit of his followers and all future generations. We have seen that his brilliant mind had laid before them every conceivable argument on behalf of his position as Messiah during his previous visits to the Temple; but to no avail. The time had come for plain speaking and for him to act 'like a refiner's fire'. It was his duty once and for all to make it clear to his disciples and to the people of Jerusalem that he was in the right and that priests, scribes and Pharisees had betrayed their trust by refusing to submit to his authority as Messiah.

Addressing the crowds within the Temple precincts in the presence of his disciples he laid bare the hypocrisy of the nation's religious leadership. He cited the following eight illustrations of their infamous behaviour which would bring on them 'Woe' as well as total exclusion from his Kingdom, just as earlier in the Sermon on the Mount he had declared 'blessed' those who adopted the Spirit of his teaching (Mt 23:1 3f; 5:2-12):

1) Their hypocrisy consists in 'praying with great pretence', and at the same time in 'devouring the houses of widows'.

2) They prevented the people from entering the Kingdom of heaven, his Kingdom, and by themselves refusing to enter it they were piling up terrible retribution for themselves.

3) Furthermore, they 'went about land and sea' in their zeal to make even one disciple and then make him worse than they are.

4) They swore false and hypocritical oaths, for they said, 'Whoever swears by the Sanctuary, it is nothing; but whoever swears by the gold of the Sanctuary is bound to keep his oath'.

5) They were hypocritical legalists tithing 'mint and dill and cumin' while neglecting the 'weightier things of the Law'; and they 'strain out the gnat and swallow the camel'.

6) They were like tombs that had been cleaned up outside for the Passover feast day but which were inwardly filled with rottenness and decay.

7) They were like cups and dishes that are clean on the outside but within are filthy with greed and intemperance.

8) They ornamented the tombs of the prophets, boasting that if they had lived in their day they would never have killed them; yet at that very moment they were planning to assassinate him, and thus fill to overflowing the cup of their iniquity.

They were indeed the 'offspring of vipers' (23:33), as John the Baptist had prophetically declared, and their wicked behaviour had now doomed the Holy City and its Temple to utter destruction in God's own time. The reader of this chapter of the Gospel of Matthew cannot but wonder at the depths of depravity to which these priests and Pharisees must have sunk in order to draw down such categorical denunciation of their attitude from the lips of the Saviour who was about to offer his life for them as much as for the rest of the world! Though he is truly the Rock of Salvation for all, he becomes for them the Stone of Stumbling! Jesus offered them this last chance of repentance by explicitly confronting them with their crimes; if they still continued in their sins, then in the Day of Judgement he would be bound in justice to condemn them for failing to repent.

2) The Parable of the Wicked Tenants
(Mt 21-33f = Lk 20:9f = Mk 12:1f)

And then he clarified their situation with regard to his own by relating in the presence of the chief priests and the scribes the parable of the wicked tenants.

There was a landowner who had a beautiful vineyard on which he had spent a great deal of money and which year by year produced a fine vintage as the result of the hard work of the tenants, the employees, to whom he had entrusted its working while he went off on a long journey abroad. As the vintage season drew near, these workmen yielded to avarice and greed as they saw the produce piling up and decided to repulse the agents of the landowner and keep it for themselves. So when the envoys arrived to collect the harvest, they ejected them from the vineyard, killing some and wounding others. However instead of sending in the bailiffs the owner sent other representatives whom they treated in the same way. Once again he refused to match force with force, but this time decided to appeal to their better feelings by sending his only son and heir, feeling sure that they would treat him with respect. But on the contrary, when the workforce heard that the owner was sending his only son they reasoned that if they were to despatch him too, the vineyard would be theirs for good. And they did so, as soon as he appeared; they threw him out and murdered him on the spot.

The chief priests and the Pharisees had listened intently and sympathetically throughout; and when he had finished, Jesus suddenly turned to them and asked: 'What action will the owner of the vineyard take when he learns what the tenants have done?'. Without further thought they spontaneously

replied: 'He will put those bad men to the death they deserve
and will let out the vineyard to other more trustworthy people'.
No sooner had they blurted this out than their faces revealed
that they understood Jesus had been referring to them. But it
was too late for them to draw back, for he cut in with the words:
'Amen I say to you, the Kingdom of God shall be taken away
from you and shall be given to a nation that will bear good fruit'.
This was plain speaking indeed! Every one gasped. They
bristled up at once and would dearly have liked to arrest him
there and then, but were afraid to do so because they had no
answer to the charge, and in any case the crowds were supporting him, believing him to be God's prophet. So once again the
chief priests and the Pharisees withdrew in sullen silence in
order to plot the best way to destroy him.

3) The Discourse on the Last Things (Mt 24 & 25)

But Jesus had more important matters to ponder over than to
worry about the secret machinations of his adversaries. On the
one hand there was the pressing need to prepare his disciples
for the shock they would experience when he, their hero, their
invincible leader, their great hope, who had so far led a charmed
life in the midst of terrible dangers, would be suddenly kid-
napped, tried and executed all within the space of twenty-four
hours. And on the other hand he had yet to make the arrangements necessary to ensure his saving presence in the world
until the end of time.

It was of fundamental importance for his disciples to realize
that this seemingly calamitous end to his life was indeed his
own deliberate choice and that of his Father in heaven, that he
would in due time return in glory to judge the world and reward
the good and punish the evil, and that the vicissitudes and trials of his disciples following upon his death were all part of
God's salvific plan. As they left the Temple on one of his last
days they admiringly pointed out to him its beauty and mag-
nificence, the pride of every Jew, and they were shocked by his
matter-of-fact rejoinder that before long it would be reduced to
rubble and flattened to the ground. So disturbing was this

prophecy that while they were resting for a moment on the slope of Mt Olivet looking across towards the Temple, Peter and Andrew, with James and John, the four leading Apostles, came up to him privately to seek an explanation; for to speak of the Temple in such terms was regarded by the authorities as blasphemy and punishable with stoning.

St Matthew in his account of the end time shows that Jesus was fully cognisant of all that was to come after his death, and his teaching can be summed up in three main points:

1) The pattern of world events between his death and his final return would severely test both the faith and the fortitude of his faithful on account of the success of false prophets; in fact this background of spiritual turmoil would increase in intensity as the time of his return drew nearer.

2) Jerusalem and its Temple would be blotted out within forty years, within one generation in fact.

3) After many further convulsions, and at an unspecified time in the future after the Temple's destruction, the end of the age would come both suddenly and dramatically with his return in power and glory.

Peter and his companions did not doubt that Jesus was prophesying truly, but quite understandably they asked him to enlighten them on two matters in particular:

a) the time of the destruction of the Temple and City, and the warning signs of its happening;

b) the time of his second coming in glory to inaugurate the new era and also the signs that would herald it.

Jesus responded by announcing that the age following his departure would be very disturbed, full of upheavals of many kinds, that many false messiahs would appear deceiving millions of people, and that it would be characterised by wars of terrifying magnitude between different nations and kingdoms, and that the distress of the peoples would be further magnified by plagues and famines and earthquakes. Worst of all, his own disciples would for no good reason come to be hated by whole nations and there would be treachery even among their own brethren. He foretold that nevertheless the Gospel of the Kingdom would eventually come to be preached to all the nations, and only then would this present age come to an end. His disciples were therefore never to lose heart but were to persevere confidently in the knowledge that the Holy Spirit would be actively with them in all their trials and sufferings (Mk 13:11f).

As regards the destruction of the Temple itself, it would indeed be flattened to the ground within forty years, i.e. some time during that present generation, and the siege of the Holy City would be one of heart-rending and unparalleled savagery. According to Matthew the sign that it was about to happen would be the profanation of the Temple, which actually occurred when the Zealots made it into a fortress against other factions there. St Luke added that another sign would be the investment of Jerusalem by hostile armies (Lk 21:20).

With regard to the time of his second coming (his *Parousia,* as it is called, his return in glory with all his angels and saints), all he would say was that it would undoubtedly come to pass after the destruction of the Temple, but how much later in time it was not in his power to reveal to them. Therefore his followers must be continually on the watch since the time and the hour are known only to his heavenly Father. The Gospels of Luke and Mark join with that of Matthew in reiterating the importance of being constantly on the watch in expectation of the return of the Lord (Lk 21:34-36; Mk 13:33-37). We further read in Matthew that when Christ finally comes in glory the whole world will at once realize it, for it will be as conspicuous as the 'lightning coming out of the East and appearing in the West'. The whole world will be taken completely by surprise; it will be as sudden as the coming of a thief in the night, as sudden as the flood that overwhelmed the contemporaries of Noah as they were eating and drinking, as sudden as the unexpected arrival of the bridegroom who thereby caught unawares the improvident virgins.

At the same time Matthew, Mark and Luke also emphasize

the importance of not wasting time while waiting for the second coming; the faithful steward must watch carefully over the household while the Master is absent on a long journey of unknown duration (Mt 24:45-51) and must not permit disorderly behaviour. In fact all those entrusted with some portion of the Master's goods during his long absence (that is, the time between the resurrection and the second coming) must make fruitful use of the talents entrusted to them so as to be able to show the Master a good profit when at length he comes back (Mt 25:14-30).

An influential modern school of biblical exegesis holds that there is evidence in the Gospels that Jesus himself expected to return very soon indeed in order to establish the definitive Kingdom of God. It also asserts that the Apostles themselves for many years after the resurrection were under the impression that Jesus might return at any moment, and that this expectation had a very unsettling effect on the first communities of Christians. On the surface this hypothesis is attractive, since there can be no doubt that there were little pockets of early converts to Christianity who mistakenly thought along these lines. Nevertheless, there are adequate reasons for continuing to hold the time-honoured view that at no time were either Paul or the evangelists misled into thinking that the second coming might occur before the destruction of the Temple.[33]

There is, of course, no doubt that among the first converts of Paul at Thessalonica there were some who decided not to work on account of this expectation, but who were quickly disabused by Paul (1 Thess 4:15f). That is to say, Paul and the Twelve knew Jesus' prophecy that he would not return until some date after the destruction of the Temple, an event which he had foretold would take place within that same living generation (i.e. by AD 70). They also understood that after its destruction the Church and the world would be in the Last Age and that the end might then come at any time, whenever the signs given by the Lord could be said to have been fully verified. However it is

---

33 I have shewn elsewhere that Paul was well aware of the eschatological teaching of Matthew (cf. 'Thessalonians and the Synoptic Gospels', *Biblica* 1938; Orchard & Riley, *The Order of the Synoptics*, p. 118).

clear from Matthew's parables of the faithful steward and the talents, and other indications, that the delay might be considerable and tiresome, because the servants of the master are expected to settle down to work for an extended period (Mt 24:45f) Hence it is certain that Paul's various references in his Letters to the return of the Lord need not and should not be taken to imply that he was unaware of the qualifications expressed in Matthew.

Jesus never concealed from his faithful disciples, but made it very clear to them, that they would have to endure persecution even unto death for preaching in his Name. At the same time, he promised that his Holy Spirit would always be with them to give them the courage to speak out boldly. 'I will give you', he said, 'a mouth and wisdom which all those opposed to you will be unable to withstand or contradict... The Spirit of your Father will teach you in the very hour of trial the things you are to say... for he who perseveres to the end will be saved' (Lk 21:15, 18; Mk 13:11-13). This prophecy will continue to be fulfilled in each generation till Christ comes again.

4) The Parable of the Last Judgement (Mt 25:31-46)

Finally Jesus wanted to impress indelibly on the minds of his followers that the world would one day come to an end in a day of judgement and that this judgement would be a matter of vital concern for every single member of the human race. In the parable of the last judgement the humble and self-effacing Son of Man openly describes himself as the king of the universe before whom his angels will marshal for reward or condemnation all the peoples of the world of all times and nations drawn from the four quarters of the globe. On his right side are the just, and on his left are the sinners and reprobates.

In this parable the judgement has already taken place; Christ Jesus, now revealed as the king, has summoned the assize in order to manifest the justice of his judgements according to the criterion he has laid down. The criterion is utterly simple: have those arraigned before him shewn real love for their neighbour? For according to his teaching, love of God is shewn in love of one's neighbour, as exemplified in the parable of the good Samaritan. All those who have demonstrated in some way their love of God either by feeding the hungry or giving drink to the thirsty, or aiding the refugee or clothing the naked, or visiting the sick or the imprisoned—all these, on his right hand, will in some way or other have qualified to hear the blessed sentence: 'Come ye blessed of my Father, inherit the Kingdom prepared for you from the foundation of the world'. But those on his left, who have failed to act with compassion when they had the opportunity, will hear the dread sentence: 'Depart from me, you cursed ones, into the eternal punishment prepared for the devil and his angels'.

These are the stark alternatives pronounced by the King—eternal life or eternal punishment. However, many modern people feel uncomfortable with these words of Jesus, but there is no way of avoiding their impact. These alternatives are existential and real; and this is why he himself entered this world at the bidding of his heavenly Father, namely to re-open heaven by freeing mankind from the power of the Devil who dwells in hell and wants everyone to join him there. The difficulty for us moderns is to be able to accept with heart as well as mind God's plan for the salvation of the world. In rejecting the existence of hell men are rejecting God's plan. In fact by so doing they are asserting that God should have 'known better' than to allow people to disassociate themselves from him voluntarily. Such persons are in fact claiming to know God's plan better than God himself. But if some, rejecting God's grace, use their free will to opt out of God's orbit and in consequence suffer eternal loss, it is their own free choice. Only the proper exercise of our free will can enable us, with God's grace, to enter into eternal life with him. The faithful Christian must nevertheless bow his head and humbly accept the mystery of God's plan as he finds it, including hell—the eternal separation from God. As Simeon had foretold at his presentation in the Temple, Jesus was to prove a sign of contradiction!

Jesus had now come to the end of his public ministry and had equipped his followers with all the information about himself that they were capable of absorbing at that time. Between his resurrection and ascension he would fill out his teaching on the Kingdom still further to prepare them for the proclamation of his Gospel after Pentecost. The Holy Spirit would then recall to their memory all the details they would need in the days to follow. And so in a last public statement in the Temple in the presence of an attentive crowd of worshippers Jesus will now declare his readiness to seal his witness with the sacrificial death for which his whole life had been one long preparation and to which everything was leading up.

5)Some Gentiles ask for Jesus (Jn 12:20-50)

The occasion for his last public oration was the arrival in the Holy City of a group of 'Greeks', seemingly 'God-fearers'. The name of Jesus was on everybody's lips; and these Gentiles were anxious to meet the man believed by so many to be the long-awaited Messiah. When Andrew and Philip came and informed him of their interest, Jesus took it as a sign that his sacrifice would not be in vain but would be welcomed by the Greek-speaking world. So he exultantly proclaimed: 'The Hour has come for the Son of Man to be glorified'. And he attached the condition for his glorification, namely: 'Amen amen I say to you, if the grain of wheat does not fall on the ground and die, it remains alone; but if it dies, it bears much fruit'. However, the thought of this death, which would bring him infinite glory and eternal life, also reminded him of the terrible agony that he needed to undergo to attain it; and his sensitive human nature recoiled from it instinctively. But in the same breath he mastered his fear and renewed his resolve to go through with it. Nevertheless at the same time his dilemma surfaces in his next utterance:

> Now my soul is troubled. And what should I say? O Father, save me from this Hour? But for this, I have come to this Hour. O Father, glorify thy Name!

And as he uttered these words, there came a mighty voice from heaven (Jn 12:27-29):

> Indeed I have glorified it, and will glorify it again.

Only the Apostles understood its significance, the crowd either thinking that it was a clap of thunder or that 'an angel had spoken to him'. A second time Jesus called out still more exultantly:

> Not for my sake has this voice occurred, but for yours. Now is the judgement of the world; now shall the ruler of this world, Satan, be cast out; and I, if I be lifted up from the earth, will draw all peoples to myself.

Jesus knew that his ministry had been well and truly accomplished and that nothing would prevent his re-opening the gates of Paradise at the coming Passover. Yet in outward appearance his mission had been a complete failure. Despite all his miracles, despite even that thrilling voice from heaven, the Temple worshippers as a whole refused to recognise the long-promised Messiah in the person of the humble carpenter from Nazareth. They were further alienated by his prophecy that the Romans would crucify him like a common criminal; and they could not reconcile this with their belief in the Messiah as a glorious and conquering figure. But though the clique of chief priests and Pharisees, who effectively controlled the Sanhedrin, were determined to destroy him, there were in fact not only a small number of just men who openly believed in him but also a good number who secretly believed but were unwilling to admit it in public through fear of being excommunicated from the synagogue and thereby losing their civil rights. The evangelist John explains their attitude by recalling that 'they loved the glory of men rather than the glory of God' (12:43), and that Isaiah had prophesied centuries before that this was how the Messiah would be treated when he finally came:

> [The Lord] has blinded their eyes and has hardened their heart lest they see with their eyes and understand with their heart and be converted and I heal them (Is 6:10).

Yet Jesus remained serenely confident in the justice and value of his mission, since he was doing no more than repeat with absolute fidelity whatever the Father had given him to speak; and he continued unshaken to promise eternal life to all who believe in his Name. His twelve Apostles would form the nucleus of his

Kingdom and would be the first members and leaders of his glorified Body when fully constituted. In the few hours that remained to him he would concentrate on the final in-depth formation of these chosen men and entrust them with all that he had received from his heavenly Father.

17

Jesus Prepares for his Sacrificial Death

1) The Betrayal by Judas (Mt 26:14-16 = Lk 22:3-6 = Mk 14:10-11)

It is true that the Sanhedrin had already decreed that Jesus had to be got rid of as soon as possible (cf. chapter 13.8); but it is difficult to find an adequate motive and still more difficult to find any extenuating circumstance for the behaviour of Judas in going secretly to the chief priests and offering to betray him to them for the paltry price of thirty silver pieces, a sum no more than the price of a slave in the bazaar. Was it his inability to accept the notion of a suffering Messiah? Or was it his realization that Jesus had no intention of leading a crusade against the Roman domination, on which Judas had set his heart? Or had he as the result of many minor infidelities seen himself as unworthy of being in the company of such holy men and then in a sudden fit of depression yielded to a bout of hate and despair? Though Judas was the only non-Galilean among the Twelve, Jesus seems to have had complete confidence in him and shewn it by having made him the treasurer of the party. Furthermore the Gospel tradition seems to suggest that Judas was 'the bosom friend in whom he trusted, who ate his bread and yet lifted up his heel against him' (Ps 40 [41]:8). Therefore whatever his motivation was, the hard fact remains that he repaid the love and trust and confidence that Jesus reposed in him by the most callous act of treachery imaginable. What he did was to go

secretly to the chief priests the day before Jesus was to eat the
Passover with his disciples and for that pitiful sum promise to
let them know when they could arrest him at a time when he
was without the safeguard of the presence of the crowds who
adored him. The priests rubbed their hands with glee at this unexpected help and sat back awaiting the call from Judas to send
round their armed retainers to seize him.

2) Preparations for the Last Supper
(Mt 26:17f = Lk 22:7f = Mk 14:12)

For all Jews the Passover was not only the most important feast
of the year but also a family gathering at which they thanked
God for delivering them from the power of their Egyptian slave-
masters and for making them into his holy people. More than
twelve hundred years before it had required ten plagues to force
Pharaoh to allow the Israelites to leave Egypt, the tenth being
the midnight slaughter of the firstborn child of every Egyptian
family. The Israelites were of course spared because they had
obeyed the instruction of the Lord to substitute the blood of a
year-old lamb in place of their first-born son and to smear the
blood of this lamb on their lintels and doorposts as a sign to the
destroying angel to 'pass over' their houses. The Lord God had
chosen to save his people from Pharaoh's tyranny by means of
this ritual which was to be understood as a type of the bodily
death that the Messiah would undergo one day at the time of
another Passover in order to free not merely the Jews but the
whole world from the power of Satan. In fulfilment of this plan,
Jesus, the true Messiah, was now going to master-mind this
particular occasion of the performance of this ancient ritual in
order to make it into an everlasting memorial of the once-for-all
physical sacrifice of his life that he was about to accomplish.

Jesus knew exactly when, where and how he was going to arrange this turning of the ancient rite into concrete reality. He
had never had any lodging in the Holy City itself where he and
the Twelve, who were his own spiritual family, might now
celebrate the Passover together. So when the Apostles came and
asked him where he was going to celebrate it he gave them

directions for finding the place he had chosen, telling them that he was going to celebrate it that very evening, that is to say, to anticipate the celebration of this national feast by twenty-four hours.[34] This alteration of time caused them little surprise since they had by now got used to his habit of updating the Law of Moses. He then detailed Peter and John to go into the City and make the usual preparations.

Thus he did not leave it to them to make the decision where they were to eat; he himself had determined on the house and the room he deemed to be suitable for the institution of the New Covenant in his Blood, the Holy Eucharist. 'Go into the city', he said to Peter and John, 'and a man will encounter you carrying a pitcher of water; follow him into the house into which he enters. And you shall say to the master of the house: The Teacher says to you, Where is the dining-room where I eat the Passover with my disciples?' (Lk 22:8-12). His words recall the incident when a few days earlier he had sent two disciples into Bethany to commandeer the donkey on which he rode into Jerusalem.

Again everything happened exactly as Jesus had foretold. As only women normally carried water-jars, they at once spotted the man carrying one and followed him to his destination. The owner of the house showed them a magnificent upper room beautifully prepared for their meeting, and handed it over to the disciples. This man must already have been a convinced follower of Jesus in his heart, because of the risk he ran if the chief priests had discovered what was going to take place that evening.

The preparations the disciples had to make included the provision of sufficient cushions for Jesus and the Twelve to recline on, the provision of enough wine for the four cups that the whole ceremony required, the preparation of the dishes that

34 Jesus died on the afternoon of Good Friday; and the Jews celebrated the Passover that evening (Jn 18:28). But Jesus anticipated it by twenty-four hours, celebrating it in his own fashion on the Thursday evening. There is no clash if we recognise that Jesus substituted his own flesh and blood under the appearance of bread and wine for the lamb, a substitution that only he, the Messiah, could make.

formed the hors d'oeuvre, a selection of vegetables and bitter herbs with sauces to suit, and some unleavened bread. Normally after the second cup of wine had been drunk the year-old lamb that had been carefully roasted over a fire without breaking any of its bones would have been consumed. However, since he was anticipating the whole ritual by twenty-four hours there could be no roasted lamb, because the priests would not be slaughtering the paschal lambs until the afternoon of the next day (our Good Friday). As we shall learn shortly, this time Jesus would be substituting his own Body and Blood under the appearance of the unleavened bread and wine. We may assume that the householder put at the disposal of Jesus all his domestic staff to make sure that everything was just right. When all the arrangements were complete, Peter and John reported back to Jesus, and at sunset they all repaired to the Upper Room[35] they had been lent for the evening.

3) The Last Supper (Mt 26:21f = Lk 22:15f = Mk 14:18f = Jn 13)

At long last, after more than two years of ceaseless and arduous activity and a whole lifetime spent in preparation, Jesus comes to the hour when he is going to seal with his own blood the covenant he entered upon at the moment of his Incarnation nearly forty years before. His opening remark to the Twelve, when they had settled down in the traditional reclining position, gives us some inkling of the depth of his joy and contentment at now being able to give them himself in a unique and permanent way for all time to come. 'With desire I have desired to eat this Passover with you before my passion', he said, as he looked around at their expectant and yet somewhat apprehensive faces. For by now they realized from the unusual form that this meal was going to take—no roast lamb to be eaten—that this was going to be no ordinary Passover.

We need to recall that the Twelve were among the few fol-

---

35 The traditional site of the Upper Room lies in an area just outside the walls of modern Jerusalem and quite close to the Benedictine Abbey of the Dormition on Mt Sion. In the time of Jesus it was within the precincts of the Holy City. It is possible that it was the house belonging to Mary, the mother of John Mark, the future evangelist (cf. Ac 12:11; Mk 14:51).

lowers who decided to stay with him after his discourse on the Bread of Life, delivered at Capharnaum shortly after the feeding of the five thousand. But though they now understood that this was to be the moment when he was going to fulfil his promise to give them himself to eat, they would be as yet unable to associate this new symbolical sacrificial sign of his death with his physical death on the Cross the very next day. His sudden ignominious end was to be a shock that only his Resurrection could overcome. All four Gospels agree in relating the total unpreparedness of the Twelve for his death despite his repeated warnings.

We must also remember that our Gospels are simply apostolic reminiscences of what Jesus actually said and did and were never meant to offer explanations of what took place. They were intended to be supportive of the oral tradition of the Apostles. Thus the Gospels do not specifically tell us that Jesus replaced the paschal lamb by consecrating the bread and wine already provided by the rite, but this has to be inferred from the fact that the lambs were slaughtered by the priests in the Temple only on the afternoon of the Passover meal itself. It is true that medieval exegesis of the Last Supper texts assumed that Jesus gave the Twelve the roasted year-old paschal lamb before consecrating the bread and wine. But there is nothing in the sacred texts to demand our acceptance of this interpretation, and modern exegesis now favours the view that there was no lamb eaten at the Last Supper. Of course the Gospel of Luke says that Jesus 'ate the Passover' and this is true. For he would have eaten some herbs and drunk the first two cups of the Passover rite. He did not himself eat and drink his own body and blood at the third cup, but, as the Gospel texts say, 'he gave It to them'. The Passover that he gave them was in fact the substitution of his own flesh and blood under the appearance of bread and wine, that is to say, the reality that the year-old lamb had symbolised from time immemorial. In this way Jesus transformed the ancient rite into a symbolical sacrifice of his life to his heavenly Father.

In the time of Jesus the Passover meal was no longer precisely performed as described in the Book of Exodus (Ex 12), but, while preserving the essentials, it had been transformed into an elaborate family ritual.[36] A first cup of wine, together with some dishes of herbs, had been introduced as a preliminary to the rite proper, and it was often consumed in an anteroom. The Passover meal as such began when the whole party—no larger than the number needed in ordinary circumstances to consume the roasted lamb—took their places in the dining room.

When they had taken their places at table in the order prescribed by Jesus, he noted that they had started to argue among themselves as to which of them was the greatest.

They had observed that he had placed John nearest to himself on his right hand, thus giving him preference over Peter. Jesus broke firmly and at once into their altercation, by saying:

The kings of the nations lord it over them and those in authority over them are called Benefactors. But this is not to be so with you. Let the greatest among you become as the junior, and the ruler as the servant. For who is greatest, the one who reclines or the one who waits on him? Is it not the one who reclines? Yet I myself am in the midst of you as the one who serves.

And at once suiting the action to the word, he rose from the table and began to do something that the Apostles would never forget.

He removed his outer tunic, tied a towel round his waist and taking a bowl of water knelt in front of each disciple in turn and washed his feet—they were all barefooted as the custom was. They watched in embarrassed silence as he made his way steadily round the room. Peter however could not stifle his protest when his own turn came and argued: 'Lord, are you washing my feet?' Jesus replied: 'What I am doing now you don't understand, but you will later'.

But this did not satisfy Peter, who exclaimed: 'You shall never

36 The description of the Passover meal that follows is based on rabbinic traditions compiled several hundred years after the time of Jesus, and recorded in the *Talmud-Mishna;* but although the basic facts are certain we cannot be quite sure how accurately the details reflect the practice in pre-70 Judea.

wash my feet!' And so Jesus firmly told him: 'If I don't, you will have no part with me'. Greatly dismayed, Peter then demanded: 'Lord, not only my feet, but also my hands and my head.' Jesus patiently replied: 'It is enough for me to wash your feet, and you will be wholly clean, except for one of you'—referring of course to Judas.

When he had completed the round of the Twelve, he again put on his outer garment, and returning to his place said to them all:

> Yes, I am in your midst as the one who serves. Yet you rightly call me your Teacher and your Lord, for so I am... If you follow the example I have just given you, you will be fully blessed (Jn 13:13).

And then a sadness came over him as he reflected:

> However I am not speaking of quite all of you. I myself know all the ones I have chosen, but as the Scriptures have foretold, there is one among you who has gone against me although he has eaten bread with me. I want you to know that I know all about him, so that you will not lose faith in me when it happens (Jn 13:19).

This speech both astounded and perplexed the disciples, and after looking blankly and unhappily round the table at one another and finally at Jesus, they began to say one after the other: 'It isn't me Lord, is it?'. Then Peter nudged John and whispered, 'Ask him whom he means.' And so in a low tone John asked, 'Who is it, Lord?' Jesus forthwith replied:

> It is the one to whom I shall dip a morsel of bread in the sauce and give it to him. And the Son of Man will indeed go in this way, but woe to that man by whom the Son of Man is betrayed; it would have been better for him if he had not been born' (Lk 22:21f; Jn 13:26).

The other disciples did not, it seems, hear what Jesus said since there was other conversation in progress and so they failed to understand the significance of his next action which was considered a sign of special regard. Before the eyes of all he handed the morsel to Judas, who as he took it looked Jesus in the face and asked: 'Is it I Lord?' and Jesus answered: 'You have indeed said it'.

The Gospel of John tells us that at that moment Satan

entered into Judas, who at once got up; and, as he made for the door, Jesus called out to him: 'What you are doing, do quickly'. Without a word Judas went out into the night to warn the high priests that if they were prompt they would find Jesus still in the Upper Room.

When Jesus said 'What you are doing, do quickly' he was not of course encouraging Judas to betray him; Judas had already decided to do so. It simply indicated that he was humanly anxious to complete his own oblation in good time, the task for which he had entered this world.

The departure of Judas seemed to take a great weight off the mind of Jesus, for he then spoke his mind joyfully as he looked into the future:

> Now is the Son of Man glorified, and God is glorified in him. And you, you are the ones who have stayed with me in my trials. And I bequeath to you, as my Father has bequeathed to me, a kingdom. You will therefore eat and drink at my table in my kingdom, and you will sit on thrones judging the twelve tribes of Israel' (Jn 13:32; Lk 22:29-30).

Jesus thus reveals that he has no fears for the future despite the frightful death he was then awaiting. He is confident that there will one day be a gloriously happy reunion for them all, and that they are already destined for glory in the sight of God.

When they had all settled down again and the second cup of wine had been served, Jesus delivered the customary Haggadah, the recital of the story of their liberation from the Egyptians, of God's subsequent goodness and their election as the People of God. Then, in accordance with the ritual, they sang the first part of the Hallel (Ps 113 [114]—117 [118]) and drank the second cup.

The first stage of the rite was now ended and Jesus was ready to enter upon the actual Passover meal which commemorated not only their liberation from slavery but the establishment of God's holy Covenant with them on Mt Sinai through the mediatorship of Moses. In this present instance we must recall that the Mosaic Covenant was itself only a type of the definitive Covenant that Christ was now going to institute, the New

Covenant of God with mankind in his blood. So he now proceeded to replace the old rite by the new one that he had spoken about when he had prophesied that he would give them his own flesh and blood to eat and drink (Jn 6).

Taking into his hands the platter of unleavened bread (in place of the lamb) he blessed it and, raising his eyes to heaven, said:

Take this and eat, it is my Body,

and gave each a portion. Then he took up the cup of wine, the third cup, and having blessed it in the same way he gave it to them, saying:

Drink from it, all of you; this is my Blood of the New Covenant, that is being shed for you unto the remission of sins. Do this in my remembrance.

In this simple fashion, Jesus instituted the New Covenant, the Holy Eucharist, the 'Breaking of the Bread' as the Apostles were to call it; and by the words, 'Do this in my remembrance' he empowered them to re-enact this ceremony in his Name, thus making them his priests. This bestowal of himself under the appearances of bread and wine was, and is, the supreme gift of his love for the whole human race. It was in this Upper Room that for the first time in the history of the world the Lord God himself took up his dwelling in human breasts in this new way, making each one his Temple. The God of Love was within each of them as well as present in their sight, and their hearts were full of a joy beyond all words, as they adored him, their Lord and their God.

In the centuries following the resurrection the Fathers of the Church were to work out the full significance of the realities hidden in this simple rite. What Jesus did at the Last Supper was to offer to his Father, in advance of its accomplishment, the whole of his passion and death, the sacrifice of himself. All the events of the succeeding day were encapsulated in this new rite. It was nothing other than the symbolical but real pre-presentation of his passion and death under the appearances of bread and wine. Because he was God as well as Man, the words he pronounced at this rite were immediately and totally effective, symbolically and really, and the bread and wine became his body and blood in virtue of his divine power and the power of his resurrection. Thus he performed symbolically and really at the Last Supper in an unbloody manner the death that he was to undergo the next day. In fact, the Last Supper and the Cross form one grand whole. At the same time he had deliberately handed on to his Apostles the power to re-present what he then did (before it physically took place); and the Sacrifice of the Mass is in fact the re-presentation of what he then did once and for all.

While they were silently communing with him in their hearts, Jesus gave them this commandment of love:

> A new commandment I give you, that you love one another as I have loved you; and if you do so, all men will come to know that you are my disciples' (Jn 13:34).

At the same time he remained entirely realistic in his appraisal of their strength and their weakness. On the one hand he warns them that though he is going to leave them soon for a short time, he will see to it that during his absence they will suffer no lack of any kind (Lk 22:35). On the other hand, to check their present euphoria, he informs them that he is going to be struck down that very night and that they will all run away like cowards. However, he will quickly restore their morale by re-uniting them with him again in Galilee (Mt 26:31-32). Unfortunately, this foreknowledge in no way prevented them from being scandalised that very night, but at least they were later to recall and to rejoice in his prophetic knowledge and in his full command over all that was about to happen to him.

Jesus then noticed that Peter had become restive and anxious to break in, and so he forestalled him by saying very solemnly in the presence of the others:

> Simon, Simon, behold Satan has begged earnestly for you to sift you like wheat; but I have asked for you that your faith should not fail; and do you, when you have come to yourself, confirm your brethren (Lk 22:32).

Here again Jesus showed his knowledge of the future and of

Peter's brash over-confidence. Unhappily, this new promise made Peter so swell with pride that he rashly promised: 'Lord, with you I am ready to go both to prison and to death'. Jesus' reply was to look hard at him and say:

> Amen I say to you, that today, in this very night, before the cock crows twice you will deny me thrice.

Peter, however, was undeterred by this warning and repeated even more emphatically: 'If I have to die together with you, I will not deny you!' And the others concurred with him, so little did they realize their own frailty and how soon they would fall from grace.

4) The Last Will and Testament of Jesus (Jn 14-17)

We cannot be totally sure of the order in which the events and the dialogue between Jesus and his disciples took place during the Last Supper. But it is reasonably certain that the discourse recorded in the Gospel of John took place after the institution of the Holy Eucharist and that John wrote it in the light of the text of the other three Gospels. Hence we may assume that, at the end of the quiet time they enjoyed after receiving the Holy Eucharist from him, he judged the moment ripe for giving them his last will and testament. In spite of his comforting words and actions during the supper they still remained uneasy and anxious at the very thought of losing him, for they were certainly not yet psychologically prepared to live without his human presence.

His first concern is to assure them that where he is now about to go, they too will follow without fail in due course; indeed he is leaving them precisely in order to provide a home where they will come to share his glory for ever in the company of his Father. And where his Father is, there he is too, for the Father is in him and he is in the Father. But in the meantime he is not going to leave them orphans, for he and the Father are going to send them another Comforter, the Paraclete, the Holy Spirit. When the Holy Spirit comes they will realize that Jesus himself too will then be abiding with them, though unseen by human eyes. Nevertheless, he has first to return to receive from his Father in heaven his glory, that is, full recognition of his achievement, and so his return there is the condition for sending the Holy Spirit.

He repeated that they must understand that in order to extend the benefits of his earthly mission to all future generations, it is necessary for him to die and return in glory to his Father and thus receive the reward due to him. He will then be able to send the Holy Spirit and release the riches of his sacrifice to the whole world. In this new era of the Spirit, Jesus will be able to operate through his grace, not as formerly on earth with respect to the chosen few with whom he was then in personal contact, but upon all peoples. By means of his mystical Body, the Church, he will be able to be present and act effectively in and upon all human beings in all ages and climes, provided only they believe in him and obey his commands, which the Holy Spirit through the Church will make known to them. This is the reason for his departure, and it should lead them not to sorrow but to gladness, because his salvation will then be made available to the whole world.

They must also remember that they did not choose him but that he chose them for their glorious destiny. It is high time for them to realize that they are not like slaves in the house of the master, for the slave does not know what his master is doing; but they are his friends and active agents because he has given them full knowledge of the working of his mind and his Father's mind too. However, he is aware that they are not able at the moment to take in everything that he wants them to know, but when the Holy Spirit comes, he will fill up all the gaps in their understanding of his Gospel.

Nevertheless they must not forget that by becoming his friends and equals, persecution is awaiting them in the same way that he himself has had to suffer. They will be expected to bear witness to him even unto death for his sake. Indeed a time will come, as he said, when 'everyone who puts you to death will think he is giving glory to God' (Jn 16:2). But they may rest assured that because he, Jesus, is the Way, the Truth and the Life, they will receive from him, when he is in glory, all the spiritual strength needful to cope with the trials that will come upon them.

He then gives them the simile in which he is the vine (Jn 15), the Father is its cultivator, and they are the branches; from him they will receive the sap of grace to enable them to bear much fruit. Only the branch that is cut off from the vine can wither, so they must make sure that they remain attached to him, the vine, in order to share his divine life. Whatever persecution they may suffer is to be regarded as no more than the pruning of the branches which the Father, as the vine-dresser, does to make them bear more fruit. They should further remember that no one comes to the Father except through him, Jesus. And because the obedience of faith is the true sign that they love him, if they keep his commandments, the Father will make them fruitful and give them everything they ask for (Jn 14:14).

Finally before leaving the supper table to go to his passion, Jesus directed his supplication once more to his heavenly Father, uttering the most sublime prayer ever offered by man to God (Jn 17). It is his prayer for the unity of the assembly of believers that will come into existence as the result of his life-work; it surveys his life and sums up all he has done to fulfil the will of his Father. Jesus is conscious that he has perfectly fulfilled the task he has undertaken, and that he will therefore be correspondingly glorified. This task was in the first place to make known the Name of the Father to the Eleven whom the Father has given him and who are now listening to him. He has kept them safe and prepared them for the mission on which they are to be sent and prays the Father to protect them from the Evil One by sanctifying them in the truth. In conclusion he asks that their mission to the world be fruitful and that all who through them come to believe in him will be one, just as he and the Father are one. This unity will be the sign that the Father has truly sent him and that he is dwelling in their midst. His high-priestly prayer ends on this note.

Jesus is aware that he has done no more than lay the all-important foundation of the work that is to commence with the coming of the Holy Spirit. He will now go gladly to his self-imposed immolation and return only briefly for the forty days after his resurrection before at last ascending to heaven to prepare a place for his Apostles and for all who through them will come to believe in his name. He, the supreme prophet, knows that what he has started will come to a glorious conclusion in God's own time. And though he would like to linger on at table in the company of his beloved disciples and friends, the hour is late and time is pressing. They are all weary and he is not going to keep Judas waiting! So having sung the second part of the Hallel they leave the Upper Room together, and by the light of the full moon make their way through the deserted streets to the city-gate, left open during the Feast, and downhill to the Wadi Kidron. Crossing over it they enter the Garden of Gethsemane, where Jesus intended to spend the night, and where Judas would eventually find him.

18

Jesus in the Power of the High Priests

1) Jesus at Gethsemane
(Mt 26:36-46 = Lk 22:39-46 = Mk 14:32-42 = Jn 18:1)

Gethsemane (the name means 'oil-press') is usually spoken of as a 'garden', whilst it was probably an extensive estate beautifully situated on the lower slopes of Mt Olivet, with a breathtaking view of Jerusalem and the Temple. Its owner had permitted Jesus to use it whenever he wanted to, and so in the past he had often gone over there with his disciples and relaxed in its tranquillity and seclusion.

Arriving at the entrance to the estate, he waited for his eleven disciples to gather round him. He then ordered them to sit down and wait for him while he went further in to pray. Inviting Peter, James and John to accompany him, he started to walk up the path between the olive trees. After some paces he turned to them and said: 'My soul is very sad and dismayed; stay here and watch with me.' He then went forward alone for what Luke calls 'a stone's throw', before falling on his knees and bowing his head to the ground in prayer. And then the full apprehension of the ordeal that was to come began to weigh upon him.

As he knelt there, oblivious of his surroundings, the bright full moon shone through the sparse foliage of the trees, making a chequered pattern on the ground and over his spotless white robe. In the silent stillness of the night every sound and every movement was audible and magnified, and the three disciples clearly heard the cry of distress, wrenched from his lips as his imagination vividly pictured the burden he was assuming:

Abba, my Father, if it is possible, let this cup pass away from me; yet not as I will but as thou.

What is the significance of this heart-rending appeal? What was the burden that he was assuming that, as St Luke tells us, was beginning to weigh him down to the point of the actual sweating of his blood? To understand, we must remind ourselves that he had come into the world to redeem sinful mankind, and in order to accomplish this task he had to assume the guilt of all the sins of the human race from the beginning to the end of time. Because he was the sinless Son of God as well as the Son of Mary, the New Adam, he alone was capable of destroying sin in his own flesh and presenting a purified humanity to his heavenly Father by incorporating this sinful humanity into his own sinless body. He was in fact making himself the scapegoat for all mankind. As St Paul wrote, 'He became sin for our sake' (2 Cor 5:21).

Throughout his life he had of course experienced, had been the witness of, the object of, and, in one sense, the 'cause' of men's sins. That is to say, 'He was set for the rise and the fall of many in Israel and for a sign spoken against', as Simeon had prophesied (Lk 2:34). It was his coming to earth that led Herod to murder the innocent babes of Bethlehem; at Nazareth his outspokenness led his own fellow-citizens to attempt to lynch him; it was the priestly hierarchy of his Father's Temple who deliberately refused to honour him as the Messiah and had plotted his annihilation; it was the Pharisees who accused him of working his miracles by the power of Satan, God's principal adversary; and it was 'his own bosom friend in whom he trusted, who ate his bread' who had just betrayed him to his enemies. There had never been a time in his life when he had not had to endure these and many other blasphemies, insults and injustices, all these without reckoning the extra burden of the folly and stupidity of even the best of those he had chosen to accompany him during his ministry. But he was now to endure a testing far severer even than that to which Satan had subjected Job.

Now in the Garden, in the final moments before he was seized by evil-doers to begin his actual immolation, there came upon him the realization of the enormity of his task, one that would have crushed any ordinary man. For not only was he there to atone for his neighbours sins—more than enough for anyone but still more for the sins of the whole world from the time of Adam to the end of the Age. Upon his shoulders alone now came the horrible sins, cruelties and vices of all the peoples of the world, their private sins, their public sins, their social sins, the result of all the unjust regimes that man in his pride and depravity has set up in different ages and places. This indescribable pool, nay this ocean, of moral filth had to be taken over by him and expiated, for in him alone could the world find the purification that it had to have in order to be made pleasing in the sight of Almighty God. For God has decreed that no man can be saved unless he be first incorporated into Christ's Mystical Body; and in order to be thus incorporated, one must first be purified by faith in him and by the spiritual waters of Baptism.[37] So then at that moment in the Garden the cost of incorporating every single human being into his pure mystical Body came upon him and the intensity of the struggle between his sensitive nature and the fulfilment of the Father's will almost tore him apart and caused that sweat of blood. And furthermore,

37 The Mystical Body of Christ is of course more extensive than the visible Church of Christ, which has been given by Christ himself the task of incorporating into itself all men and women of all ages and races, and membership of which is mandatory for all who have received the light of faith (Mt 28:16-20). Yet since 'God wills all men to be saved and to come to the knowledge of the truth' (1 Tim 2:4), the uncovenanted grace of his Passion is also being mediated continuously in secret ways to all true lovers of Jesus in other Christian denominations and also to all those multitudes of pagans who are lovers of truth and justice and who are therefore truly though unconsciously being led towards Jesus, the Way, the Truth and the Life. Karl Rahner has dubbed these good people as 'anonymous Christians', but this epithet is not entirely acceptable without some qualification.—On the meaning of the Agony in the Garden, see also H.U. von Balthasar, *Mysterium Paschale* (Engl. Ed.), Edinburgh 1990, pp.71f.

would there not be some for whom he knew that he would die in vain because they preferred in their pride to follow Satan in rejecting God? Indeed Satan, knowing that he had so far utterly failed to gain any hold over Jesus, was permitted by God the Father to employ all his malicious powers in one last attempt to break down the resolution of the Son of God and to provoke him to despair.

It is this spiritual battle against Satan and Jesus' ultimate victory that is recorded in such matter-of-fact terms in our Gospel accounts. Neither the eight Apostles left sitting at the entrance to the Garden nor the three whom he invited to watch with him could then comprehend the reason for his agony, to which they were quite indifferent, actually dozing off after his exhortation to keep awake and out of temptation. His willpower to go ahead and pay the price for the salvation of the world was tested up to breaking point, but he did not waver in the least. His words, 'My Father, if it is possible, let this cup pass away from me, yet not as I will but as thou', do not signify his capitulation to the temptation to escape from his passion, but are indeed a revelation that what he was doing was meritorious because done of his own free human will. It indicates that as man he had a human will distinct from the will of his Father but at the same time it indicates the impossibility of this human will of his being other than absolutely one with the Father's will.[38] The clause 'If it is possible' is rhetorical and highlights the unity of Father and Son. It is not possible for this cup of suffering to pass away from him because he has agreed from all eternity to accept it in free agreement with his Father. And Jesus wanted us to know it. His human will remained fixed in union with his Father's will; and his sacrifice of himself was acceptable on behalf of the human race because he was truly man, representing the human race in its perfection. At the same time his sacrifice was only acceptable to his Father because, being the Son of God, his offering was not only voluntary but of infinite value. Yet so great was the pres-

---

38 For an important discussion of the free human will of Christ cf. R. Kereszty O.Cist., *Jesus Christ—Fundamentals of Christology*, New York 1991, pp.208-210.

sure on his human nature that the Father had to send him an angel, the Angel of the Agony, to strengthen him and prevent him from passing out completely. Three times did Jesus make this appeal to his heavenly Father, and in between each appeal he returned to seek comfort and support from Peter, James and John, and each time they let him down. He had never before felt so alone, but they were too feeble to sustain him.

The first time he returned he gently reproached Peter for his inability to watch for even one hour, but excused him on the grounds that 'the spirit was willing but the flesh was weak' (Mt 26:41). When he came back the second time hoping to find the three supporting him in prayer, they were again dozing, and Mark says that 'they did not know what to answer him' (Mk 14:40). When he returned the third time he told them that he had overcome the temptation and recovered his serenity and was ready for the ordeal awaiting him. He added in gentle rebuke that they could now go on sleeping if they wanted to, because his betrayer was arriving and his arrest was imminent.

2) The Arrest of Jesus
(Mt 26:47f = Lk 22:47f = Mk 14:43f = Jn 18:2f)

It is difficult to estimate from the evidence of the Gospels just how long a time Jesus spent making his own the dreadful burden of human depravity that he had undertaken to wipe out once and for all; it was perhaps no more than an hour, 'the hour of darkness' as he himself described it. But during that hour Judas had not been idle. He had gone to the house of Caiaphas and succeeded in convincing him that Jesus could be spirited away that very night either from the supper room or the garden of Gethsemane. However, by the time that Judas had managed to persuade Caiaphas and his cabinet to take action, Jesus and the Eleven had left the supper room. Not finding them there, Judas, knowing that they must have gone on down to the garden, hastened after them with his accomplices as fast as they could lest Jesus again escape capture. For if he failed to catch him then, his trap would be sprung and the followers of Jesus would have been fully alerted and would have rallied to his protection.

Judas' last minute nocturnal call on the high priest on the very eve of the great feast meant that there would have to be a lot of improvisation if Jesus was to be taken and eliminated in the course of the following day. So the traitor had been given an odd but overwhelming assortment of followers to facilitate rounding him up in the expectation that his disciples would fiercely resist his arrest. The mob that arrived at the entrance to the garden had been got together by order of the Sanhedrin (Mk 14:43) and seems to have consisted only of employees of the high priests and other members of that body. They were a rabble of a score or more, armed with a variety of swords and clubs, but there were no professional soldiers of the Roman garrison with them; their intervention was to come later. Judas had been put in charge by the high priest, and before setting out had given them careful instructions to avoid arresting the wrong man in the darkness. He had not only ordered them to bring lanterns and torches, but had arranged to identify Jesus personally by kissing him in front of them, thus singling him out for capture.

As they hesitated at the gate before entering to apprehend the man whom up to that day everyone had been acclaiming, except the entourage of the priests and Pharisees, Jesus himself approached them, as they stood there with Judas in the forefront, and quietly asked them whom they were looking for. When they answered 'Jesus of Nazareth', he replied, 'I am he'. The evangelist John tells us that as he said this, they all shot backwards and fell sprawling to the ground, felled by a supernatural awe. Jesus gave this miraculous sign to his followers to cause them later to recall that he was to be taken only because he himself willed it, and for no other reason. When they had had time to pick themselves up and scramble to their feet, he again asked them, 'Whom do you want?'. Again they said 'Jesus of Nazareth', and again he replied, 'I tell you that I am he; if therefore you seek me, let these go away', and pointed back to his bewildered disciples. For he was determined to face the enemy alone and not to involve any of the Eleven in his death, since they were not yet spiritually prepared to follow him; and in any case he alone could offer the sacrifice that would redeem the world.

It was at that moment that Judas came forward as pre-arranged and embraced Jesus, saying in a loud voice, 'Hail, rabbi'. Jesus did not recoil from the embrace, but gave him one further chance to abandon his treacherous act by saying to him, 'Judas, dear friend and colleague, what have you come for? Are you going to betray the Son of Man with a kiss?' But by this time Judas' heart had wholly hardened against the appeal, and he made no response.

The crowd behind Judas now closed in on Jesus and started to lay their hands on him. Until that moment none of the Apostles except perhaps Peter and John had any real reason to suspect Judas of this horrible treachery. But Peter suddenly woke with a shock to the realization of what was about to happen and rushed forward drawing his sword from its scabbard. Determined to implement his oath to die with Jesus if necessary, he shouted, 'Lord, shall we strike with the sword?'. The assailant of Jesus whom he happened to strike was a certain Malchus, a slave of the high priest. Either through his bad aim or Malchus' skilful sidestep Peter was spared from killing anyone, but as the blade whistled past Malchus' head it cut off his right ear. Jesus said sharply to Peter,

> Put your sword back into its sheath, for all who take the sword will perish by the sword. Did you not realize that if I wanted to I could appeal to my Father, and he would instantly put at my disposal more than twelve legions of angels? For what is now happening has to happen so that the Scriptures may be fulfilled. The cup that my Father has given me, shall I not drink it? (Mt 26:52f; Jn 18:11).

And then, turning to Malchus standing beside him and clutching his wounded head, he touched his ear and it was immediately restored. That night Jesus would not permit any blood but his own to be shed (Lk 22:15).

Peter, nonplused and confused, drew back to the line of the other Apostles as the servants of the high priest surrounded Jesus and tied his hands. But Jesus, with his majesty un-

diminished and facing his foes with equanimity and serenity,
perceiving in the background some members of the Sanhedrin,
who had come to witness the capture, called out to them:

> Have you come out as if against a robber or a terrorist with swords and
> clubs to seize me? Day by day I have been sitting among you teaching
> in the Temple and you did not raise your hands against me. But this is
> your hour and the power of darkness (Mt 26:55; Lk 22:53).

Silence fell on the bystanders as the words of Jesus rang out, for
no answer was possible. There was a muttered word of command from Judas, and then those holding Jesus got going, with
him in their midst, and made their way back to the house of
Caiaphas where other members of the Sanhedrin were
anxiously awaiting the result of the sortie. As they did so, his
disciples panicked and ran away among the olive-trees.

The evangelist Mark reports one other strange occurrence
that night as they left the Garden. He relates that a youth,
whom he refrains from naming, and not one of Judas' gang,
started to follow Jesus. He was spotted and seized by some of
Jesus' captors. But as he was only wearing a sheet over his
nakedness, he managed to wriggle free and get away naked.
Readers of the Gospel of Mark continue to be intrigued by this
episode. One possible explanation could be that the youth was
our evangelist Mark, none other, in fact, than the John Mark,
son of a certain Mary, at whose house Peter called after his
miraculous release from prison some ten years later (Ac 12:12).
If this identification were secure it would seem possible that the
Last Supper was held in John Mark's home, and that the young
lad, excited by the feasting and singing of Jesus and the Eleven,
followed them down to the garden too late to warn them, but in
time to see Jesus being led away.

3) Annas questions Jesus (Jn 18:19-23; cf. Mt 26:57f)

The mob holding Jesus made straight for the palace of the high
priest, the exact location of which is still disputed, but which,
according to an old tradition, was situated not far from the
modern Abbey of the Dormition. Though Caiaphas was the official high priest, who had been imposed on the Jews by the

Romans some years before, it seems that the Jews themselves still regarded his father-in-law Annas as the lawful one. The two shared, it seems, the same residence.

Meanwhile the first of the Eleven to recover from his fright and flight was John, who crept up from behind and joined the procession of those guarding Jesus; for strangely enough he was known to the high priest and was on excellent terms with his servants. Peter too had had the same thought, and seeing John followed him. Arriving at the palace, John was admitted without question but Peter was not and had to stand outside the gate in the street. When John realised Peter's predicament, he went and spoke to the portress, who then admitted him on John's recommendation. History does not tell us the reason why John, despite his intimate connection with Jesus, was trusted by the high priestly family, the most exalted in the land. One reason, it has been suggested, may have been that the sons of Zebedee had formed a consortium with their partners Peter and Andrew, and had a long-term contract to supply fish from the Lake of Galilee to the high-priestly household. Whatever the reason, the presence of these two within the palace at this crucial moment was to provide the Church with a firsthand account of the disgraceful treatment Jesus was to suffer at the hands of the Sanhedrin.

In the great courtyard of the palace, which gave access to the surrounding offices and apartments, the servants had lit a fire to warm themselves, since the night was cold. John was well enough known to be able to go wherever he wanted without raising suspicion; but Peter decided to join the throng round the fire and try to keep warm.

Protocol dictated that Annas, the former high priest, should be the first to interrogate Jesus, for he was the patriarch of the family, although the Romans no longer recognized his authority. While Peter stayed in the courtyard by the fire, John was able to slip into the hall where Annas was awaiting the arrival of the prisoner. Jesus was brought in with his hands still bound and made to stand in front of Annas, with guards on either side. This high priest, still believed by the people to be God's representative on earth, demonstrated his contempt by compelling him to stand there in this humiliating posture. Jesus was innocent of any crime, and Annas had no charge to bring against him; it was a travesty of justice. Indeed, if only Annas had had the grace to realize it, the man in front of him was the Messiah of his people and the one and only true High Priest of mankind.

Annas was a wily old politician and could see that his son-in-law Caiaphas would need all possible help to manage the dangerous business on which he had started by bringing in so famous a person as Jesus. For his part, Jesus had no intention of accepting his jurisdiction and submitting to his interrogation, and deliberately refused to answer his questions. Instead Jesus reminded him that he had given all his teaching in public either in the synagogue or in the Temple and had taught nothing in secret. It was all available to Annas and verifiable; he had nothing more to add and he was not going to repeat it for Annas' benefit either! The independent attitude of Jesus provoked the anger of Annas, who raised no objection when on his behalf one of the guards struck Jesus in the face, thus condoning his cowardly behaviour. Jesus, in fulfilment of his own teaching about 'turning the other cheek', calmly rejoined: 'If I have spoken wrongly, justify your action; but if not, why did you strike me?' Annas made no recorded response. Indeed, in no way could he justify such a shameful action; so he swiftly brought this embarrassing episode to a close by sending Jesus still bound across the courtyard to Caiaphas.

4) The Sanhedrin seeks Evidence against Jesus
(Mt 26:57f = Lk 22:54f = Mk 14:53f = Jn 18:24)

By this time it must have been well past midnight and Caiaphas had done his best to gather as many members of the Sanhedrin as possible in order to debate informally the fate of Jesus. The problem before him was to try to give a show of legality to the crime he was about to commit, namely to have Jesus put to death. Of course, for him the end now justified the means; he was already on record as having declared that it was better for one man to die for the people than for the whole nation to perish at the hands of the Romans. But there were many obstacles to be overcome to achieve this objective. In the first place, he had to find some colourable excuse in the eyes of his own nation for demanding the death penalty. The only way to accomplish this would be to prove Jesus guilty of blasphemy— the very man who had gone about for the past two years doing good to everyone, working countless miracles of healing and who had proved his equality with God his Father. Hence Caiaphas had to find the right indictment and then obtain his Council's agreement. The next task would be to secure the approval of Pontius Pilate, the Roman Prefect then in residence in the Holy City, whose consent for the execution was mandatory as the law stood. But one step at a time. The members of the Sanhedrin whom Caiaphas had managed to get together met behind closed doors in a chamber leading off the courtyard. Their endeavour was to find persons of repute who would bear witness that Jesus had blasphemed. But as Matthew records, 'they sought false witness against Jesus to put him to death and they did not find any, many false witnesses coming forward' (Mt 26:59-60).

5) Peter's Three Denials of Jesus
(Mt 26:69f = Lk 22:55f = Mk 14:66f = Jn 18:17f)

While Caiaphas and his supporters were engaged on this task indoors, Jesus was kept waiting outside in a cold corner of the courtyard with his guards, some way from the fire and from Peter. The latter had not been long there when the same portress came up again and, having stared at him, announced to the bystanders: 'This one too was with him', and turning to Peter she added: 'Are you not one of the disciples of this man?' But Peter loudly declared: 'I do not know him, O woman'. And then a cock crowed. Peter started guiltily, and quietly slunk out of the circle and into the forecourt to avoid further attention. But he was not to escape sharp and prying eyes. Another servant-girl noticed him and remarked to one of the men: 'This man was with Jesus the Nazarene', and he in turn said to Peter, 'You too are of them'. Again Peter denied, this time with an oath, 'O man, I am not'. Those around looked incredulous but held their peace for the moment. But about an hour later he was recognized by a relative of the Malchus whose ear he had sliced off, who asked him: 'Did I not see you in the garden with him?' And another bystander added: 'In truth this one too was with him; for even his speech betrays him to be a Galilean'. But Peter, by now in complete panic, began to curse and to swear, 'I know not the man'. As he uttered those words the cock crowed a second time, and Jesus 'turning looked on Peter, and Peter recalled the word of the Lord how he had said to him: Before the cock crows twice, you will deny me thrice' (Lk 22:61). And Peter broke down, weeping bitterly, and went out sobbing, for the glance of Jesus suddenly brought him to himself and he realized the depth of his cowardly betrayal of his Master and the truth. For Jesus this was another stab in the back, this time from one in whom he had placed the greatest trust. For the moment he no longer had a single friend in the world on whom he could rely for either help or collaboration.

6) Jesus condemned to Death for Blasphemy
(Mt 26:59f = Lk 22:66f = Mk 14:55f)

Within the hall of Caiaphas the argument went on for hour after hour until dawn was about to break. After failing to find any two witnesses to agree on any charge against Jesus that could be considered blasphemy—for the Law required that at least two witnesses must agree on the same charge—they finally led in Jesus to answer a charge brought under pressure by two further witnesses. One witness was prepared to testify that Jesus had said: 'I can destroy the Sanctuary of God and after three days rebuild it'. The second witness was willing to swear: 'We heard him say, I will destroy this Sanctuary that is built with hands and after three days I will build another not made by hands' (Mt 26:60-61; Mk 14: 57- 59). But they had no sooner uttered their respective statements than they started to argue with each other. Ignoring their disagreement, the high priest demanded to know from Jesus: 'Are you not answering any-thing to these charges against you?' But Jesus remained silent, saying nothing.

The high priest was now completely nonplused, because the lack of agreement of these two witnesses meant that he could not ensure the near unanimous vote from the Sanhedrin he needed to solicit the death penalty from Pilate. Nevertheless it was necessary to come to a decision as soon as day dawned and to arrive at a formula that would secure the condemnation of Jesus that very morning. And then Caiaphas had a brain-wave. He said to himself, 'This man claims to be the voice of truth. Per-haps because he claims to be a pious Jew who upholds the Law of Moses, he will admit under oath in court his claim to be the Christ the Son of God, if I adjure him by the God he professes to serve. In this way I could succeed in condemning him out of his own mouth'. It was a last desperate gamble and it might succeed where every other stratagem had failed. For he felt sure that if in his capacity as God's high priest he could put to him on oath in the supreme court the lawful question to declare his true identity, Jesus would unfailingly respond and commit himself irrevocably.

With this plan in mind, shortly before dawn Caiaphas led the members of the Sanhedrin, priests, elders and magnates, with Jesus their captive, along the still darkened street up to the Temple and the Chamber of Hewn Stones, their official meeting place (Lk 22:66). By the time all had arrived and were in their places it was dawn and the official session could commence. Caiaphas drew himself up and in slow and measured terms ad-dressed Jesus, standing bound in their midst: 'I adjure you by the living God that you tell us if you are the Christ the Son of God.'

And then Jesus, acknowledging the authority of the high priest to put this question to him in this legal assembly, responded in ringing tones (Lk 22:67f):

If I tell you, you will not believe. And if I question you, you will not answer me or let me go. But from now on the Son of Man will be sit-ting on the right hand of the Power of God.

By these words Jesus identified himself with the Son of Man

who appears in the prophecy of Daniel as the divine person who receives the everlasting kingdom from the Lord God of Israel. And so they all lent forward eagerly saying: 'So then you are the Son of God'. And Jesus replied: 'You have said it.' Jesus, as we see, phrased his admission in terms revealing that he fully understood their malice in asking this question at that time and place, and was fully aware that he was now putting his life into their hands. However, he also prophesied that this confession would result in his glorification at the right hand of the Lord God himself.

At long last the members of the Sanhedrin had got the words they wanted to hear from out of his own mouth, in a form which would enable them to accuse him of blasphemy. He had admitted in court and on oath that he was truly the Son of God. It was now clear to them that he, a mere man in their eyes, had made himself equal to the Lord God of Israel. With dramatic skill Caiaphas seized the moment, and foregoing any further discussion, and tearing his outer robe at the neck, shouted: 'What further need have we of witnesses? For we have heard the blasphemy from his own mouth. What do you all think?' And as with one voice the whole Court cried out: 'He is guilty of death'.

A blind madness then seized these normally grave and grand citizens as they maliciously watched the captors of Jesus start to maltreat him by spitting in his face and blindfolding him and calling out as they buffeted him, 'Who is it who is striking you now?'

It was then just after sunrise, about six o'clock in the morning, and time to make for Pilate's palace, the Praetorium, where the day's work always started at that hour. Caiaphas and his confederates had triumphantly achieved their first objective by securing an immediate condemnation of the 'upstart Christ' and had managed to do so outwardly at least in legal form.

19

Jesus Before Pilate

A number of modern scholars have argued that it was not possible for all the events described in the Gospels to have happened to Jesus in the twenty-four hours between the beginning
of the Last Supper and the deposition of his lifeless body in the
tomb just before sunset on the following evening. It is therefore
worth discussing this question briefly at this point, prior to the
last phases of his passion. In the first place the distances
covered by the chief protagonists were not great; Jerusalem has
always been a compact city. The house of Caiaphas was not
more than fifteen minutes' walk from the ancient entrance to
the Temple across the bridge that spanned the Tyropoeon Valley which in Jesus' time separated the eastern from the western
side of the City but has since been filled in. The official meeting
place of the Sanhedrin, the Chamber of Hewn Stones, where it
met at dawn on that Good Friday was near this entrance.

When the City was levelled to the ground in AD 70 the old street
plan was lost, and the modern layout of the City is based partly on
the emperor Hadrian's plan for Aelia Capitolina (c. 130) and partly on the emperor Justinian's ambitious rebuilding scheme in
the sixth century. As a consequence the site of Herod's palace is
unknown. Latterly the experts have differed as to whether Pilate interrogated Jesus in the Antonia fortress that overlooked
the Temple domain or whether his Praetorium was in fact at the
Citadel beside the modern Jaffa Gate, from which the hillock of

Calvary is no more than ten minutes' walk. However the Christian Via Dolorosa, from the site of the Antonia to the Holy Sepulchre, has a venerable history going back before the Crusades, so that the Antonia is still to be regarded as a likely site for Pilate's interrogation of Jesus. It is therefore impossible to map with certainty the steps of Jesus as he was dragged from place to place on that fateful morning. However, when all the various permutations are added up, they do not amount to as much as two hours of walking, which still leaves two hours for Pilate's two interrogations and a further hour for the visit to Herod. We may now leave the problem of Jesus' itinerary for that day, and turn our attention to the unfolding drama.

1) The First Questioning
(Mt 27:11f = Lk 23:2f = Mk 15:2f = Jn 18:29f)

The Gospels of St Luke and St John tell us that Jesus was handed over to Pilate by the whole body of the Sanhedrin early on the morning of the day when the Passover was to be eaten. Arriving at Pilate's hall of audience the members of the Sanhedrin refused to enter for fear that they might have some contact with a pagan official or soldier and so become unclean and unable to eat the Passover that evening. Pilate must have been warned of their approach, and to make speedy communication possible he decided to comply with their request that he should come out to them, although he may have regretted this later on, because by this concession he immediately put himself at a disadvantage in the subsequent negotiations.

Pilate's first words indicate that he guessed that their real charge against Jesus might be concerned with their own religion rather than political subversion and reveal a certain wariness. He had just moved up from his headquarters at Caesarea on the coast to Jerusalem with a large force because, as the Roman governor, he had to be ready for the possibility of disturbance when great numbers of patriotic Jews congregated for this great annual feast. And his guess was correct. However, the Jewish spokesmen truculently replied that they would not have troubled him if Jesus were not a criminal. They cunningly made no mention of the charge of blasphemy but framed three diverse political charges all within Pilate's competence. They accused him of disloyalty to Caesar, forbidding to pay him tribute, and claiming to be Christ a king (Lk 23:2).

Pilate initially ignored their accusations and, determined to get at their real motivation, riposted by telling them to take Jesus back and judge him according to their own Law of Moses. This compelled them to reveal that they had brought Jesus along precisely in order to extract from Pilate the death penalty which the Romans invariably retained for themselves alone in all subject territories. His suspicion was soon confirmed that they wished him executed not for breaking the law of the Romans but for having committed a capital offence against the Law of Moses. The high priests wanted Jesus put to death legally, but since they were not permitted by Roman Law to execute him themselves, they had to persuade Pilate to do so. Crucifixion was the most painful death imaginable and was reserved by the Romans for murderers and enemies of the state and restricted to slaves and provincials. Roman citizens could neither be scourged nor crucified. But Jesus, being a provincial, one of a race subject to Rome, was not protected by Roman law against such treatment. Nevertheless the high priests had first to produce convincing evidence that Jesus was a traitor to Rome and a rival to Caesar in order to win Pilate's consent.

Jesus had meanwhile been kept inside the Praetorium under guard by Roman soldiers. So leaving the menacing and clamorous crowd out in the street, Pilate went in to interview him and ask him the direct question: 'Are you the King of the Jews?', to find out whether he was indeed a king. Before answering, Jesus demanded a clarification. He wanted to be certain that Pilate was asking the question in a neutral and unbiased sense: 'Do you say this of yourself or do others say it to you about me?' So Pilate replied: 'Am I a Jew? Your own race and the high priests have handed you to me. What have you done?' This of course revealed that the only factual knowledge he had of Jesus was what his enemies had so far told him. Jesus responded with a statement on the true nature of his kingship. He declared categorically that his kingdom was not of this world; that it was no rival to the Roman empire; if it were, he would not now be in the dock, for in that case his followers would never have let him be captured.

But this statement puzzled Pilate. Jesus was obviously thoroughly sane, so what did he mean by saying that his kingdom was not of this world? In his perplexity Pilate enquired: 'Are you not then a king?' The answer of Jesus explained the paradox. His kingdom is not of this world because he himself is not of this world but has come down from heaven to reveal the truth about life to the whole human race. And all who love the truth are his subjects. His authority is a spiritual authority, and not a political or a physical one. But this concept is too new and too profound for Pilate to grasp. 'What is truth?' he snorted, and, as Francis Bacon wrote, 'he did not stay for an answer', but went outside again to the waiting Sanhedrin to tell them that he could find no reason at all to condemn Jesus. He was clearly shying away from the recognition of the truth but also wanted to avoid a manifest injustice. But the high priests undeterred continued to develop their accusations against him, so that Pilate went in again and urged him: 'Do you not hear how many things they testify against you?' Jesus maintained a dignified silence from that moment onwards, leaving Pilate to the dictates of his own conscience. Meanwhile the crowds continued to chant: 'He disturbs the people, teaching throughout all Judea, and beginning from Galilee to here', and Pilate, goaded by Jesus' silence and almost demented, once more went out to them.

2) Jesus brought before Herod Antipas (Lk 23:6-12)

Pilate now thought himself to be in an impossible situation, and was looking round anxiously for a way of escape. The mention of Galilee as the place from which Jesus had begun his teaching meant that he must be a Galilean, thus incidentally revealing Pilate's ignorance that Jesus was known already to many as Jesus of Nazareth in Galilee. Since this made him a political subject of Herod, Pilate hastily decided to send him off to be dealt with by this tetrarch who was also in Jerusalem for the Feast in order to give the impression that he was a true Jew at heart despite his matrimonial troubles. Nevertheless this move boded no good for Jesus because of his connection with John the Baptist, who as we saw earlier had been first imprisoned and then barbarously executed to satisfy the spite of Herod's second wife whom he had enticed away from his half-brother Philip. Herod, a man now in his late fifties, still had a bad conscience about the murder of the Baptist and had been troubled with the nightmare that Jesus might be 'John risen from the dead'. Nevertheless the news that this wonder-worker was now a prisoner of the Sanhedrin, who were baying for his blood, made him anxious to see him in the expectation of his working some special miracle for his delectation. If Jesus were willing to grove at his feet for mercy he might even consider treating him magnanimously!

Jesus was led off under guard of Pilate's soldiers and accompanied by the high priests and the scribes who were determined not to let their prey out of their sight. They wanted a quick decision because time was running out and it was necessary to get Jesus condemned and crucified by midday and finished off before the Feast intervened.

Herod, it seems, made a pompous speech intimating that if Jesus would work a miracle or two he would see what he could do to secure his release. But Jesus stood silent and impassive and totally unimpressed. He did not even deign to answer a single word or to show any sign of compliance whatsoever. He knew that this interlude was just a tiresome irrelevance; he was not contemptuous but merely sorry for this poor lost soul. When Herod realized that Jesus was not going to reply and saw that his oratory was making him look rather ridiculous, his anger suddenly blazed up and his mood changed to one of mockery of the meek and silent figure in front of him. The high priests saw their chance to fan the flame of Herod's fury by renewing their accusations of Jesus' supposed subversive activity in

Galilee. So in order to have some sport at the prisoner's expense and mock his claim to be the Messianic King, Herod called for a splendid and glittering robe to be thrown around his shoulders, and for a few minutes he and his bodyguard with the high priests reviled and ridiculed him. But Herod did not dare to ill-treat further the silent prisoner, as he still feared his 'occult' powers. He was therefore glad to dismiss him after a short time and return the responsibility to Pilate. There was however one unexpected side-effect of this visit; Herod was greatly flattered at the consideration shewn him by Pilate for inviting him to examine the prisoner, and Luke tells us that it changed their former enmity into warm friendship that very day!

3) Pilate tries to free Jesus
(Mt 27:15f = Lk 23:17f = Mk 15:6f = Jn 18:39f)

By the time Jesus was brought back about an hour later, Pilate had made up his mind that Jesus was innocent of all charges and was set on releasing him. But he knew that he would have to battle with the Jews and that they would not give in easily. He therefore summoned them to meet him—still out in the open—and bluntly told them that neither he nor Herod had been able to find any wrong-doing in this man, and that it would be totally unjust to put him to death.

Then Pilate recalled that he had still one more expedient available. This was to invite the crowd outside to invoke the so-called 'paschal privilege' by which at this Feast he, as the prefect and supreme judge, and as a great favour on account of the Feast, was at liberty to release to them any criminal they were prepared to designate. Now it happened that on that very morning he had condemned to death a few minutes prior to Jesus' appearance three terrorists who had been convicted of riot and murder in the City. Their leader was named Barabbas, who had in fact achieved a certain notoriety on account of his opposition to the Romans.[39] So he summoned them again and

---

39 Barabbas means 'Son of the Father' and a few Gospel manuscripts actually call Barabbas 'Jesus Barabbas'. This strange coincidence has led one scholar—probably mistakenly—to assume that Pilate got the two names confused and asked the crowd to decide which one they wanted him to release.

gave them the alternative: 'Which of these two do you desire me to release to you, Barabbas or Jesus who is called the Christ?' He then left them for a little while to give them time to make up their minds, a time which the high priests and the elders used to persuade the crowd to ask for Barabbas. What Pilate failed to perceive was the length to which the Jews were prepared to go to secure the condemnation of Jesus. When he returned he was both startled and dismayed by the roar of their response: 'Away with this man and release us Barabbas'. Pilate tried to persevere by reminding them that Jesus claimed to be a king: 'Surely', he said, it must be your wish that I release to you the king of the Jews'. And again came the savage roar: 'Not this man but Barabbas'. Pilate was now thoroughly intimidated, and in full retreat could only weakly reply: 'What then shall I do with Jesus ? What evil has he done?'

At that moment one of his servants came up to him and drew him aside with an urgent message from his wife Procula,[40] saying: 'Have nothing to do with that just man; for I have suffered greatly today in a dream because of him'. This message almost froze his blood, for he now realized that he was entangled in some way in a cosmic struggle between the forces of good and evil. For his wife's appeal proved that powers from another world were fighting on behalf of this man against the Jews. What was he to do? What indeed could he do? Well, at least he could gain time and a breathing space by having Jesus scourged. And here Pilate made a fatal mistake out of a craven deference to the feelings of the high priests. For he thought— quite wrongly as it turned out—that he could pacify them and

40 According to the 2nd cent. apocryphal gospels her name was Claudia Procula.—It is also worth noting here a statement of Tertullian about the Roman government's knowledge of Jesus. Tertullian (*Apologeticus,* 5) wrote: 'Tiberius, in whose time the Christian faith (*nomen*) came into the world, having received information from Palestine of the events there, which had revealed the truth of Christ's divinity, brought the matter before the Senate and gave his vote in favour of setting Christ among the gods. The Senate rejected the proposal because it had not given its approval of its own initiative. Caesar maintained his opinion and threatened the accusers of the Christians that they acted at their peril.' (cf. Eusebius, *The History of the Church,* II. 2 , Penguin Classics 1965, pp. 65f)

head them off if he were to reduce Jesus to a pitiful figure by administering a severe scourging instead of the death penalty. Such a compromise was of course grossly unjust because, as he himself had said, Jesus was innocent of any crime whatsoever and should therefore have already been unconditionally released. But the crowd continued to chant implacably: 'Let him be crucified'. To his credit then, let it be acknowledged that Pilate made one further effort as he again faced that murderous gathering and entreated them: 'But what evil has he done? I have found no reason to execute him. I will scourge him and let him go' (Lk 23:22). But the only effect of his words was to reveal his moral weakness and to step up the pandemonium to a still higher pitch of hysterical rage. The affair had reached an impasse.

While the soldiers gleefully took Jesus down to the torture chamber Pilate sat alone in his audience hall, sick at heart and listening to the shouts of the mob. He felt that he was doing something grievously wrong but did not possess the courage to act honestly and justly. When the soldiers brought Jesus back, Pilate saw that they had liberally interpreted his mind and had inflicted on him sufficient injuries and indignities to move to pity hearts of stone. They had first stripped him naked and then scourged him from head to foot with whips having small lead pellets on the end of each cord. They had then produced a wreath of thorns which they had pressed down on his head as if it were a crown. They had then 'roughed him up' and had made sport of him by putting on him a soldier's crimson cloak to suggest royalty and a reed into his hand as a sceptre. They then made mock genuflections and struck him as they rose. Pilate now hoped that these disfiguring injuries would be enough to satisfy the high priests and get them to call off their mob.

So Pilate went out again to prepare them for the sight of Jesus now reduced to a state which 'makes people screen their faces'. Once more he told them that he could find no wrong whatever in him, and then ordered Jesus to step outside for them to see. 'Behold the Man', said Pilate, unconsciously revealing Jesus as the Suffering Servant of Isaiah 53.

But the sight of Jesus humiliated in this ghastly fashion, far from pacifying the chief priests, only whetted their appetite for the final kill, and they roared louder than ever: 'Crucify him, crucify him'. Pilate, still hoping to avoid the ultimate responsibility for putting Jesus to death, retorted: 'Take him yourselves and crucify him, for I find no case against him'. In saying this Pilate was ironically inviting them to break the law of the Roman Senate which always insisted on the Roman authority retaining the exclusive right to inflict capital punishment; if they had dared so to act, they themselves would in fact have risked a heavy penalty from Pilate. There was however no need because they now knew that they could force him into compliance with their wishes by persevering a little longer.

Nevertheless this sally of Pilate forced them to disclose plainly the real reason for demanding the death penalty. 'He has got to die', they chanted, 'because he made himself the Son of God'. This remark served to confirm his wife's premonition and increased Pilate's fears. He was now beset on all sides, and in his extremity he was driven back to consult the prisoner himself.

Taking his seat again he appealed to Jesus, saying: 'Whence are you?' This time however Jesus did not answer but kept silent, for Pilate had already rejected his declaration that he was the Truth. More distraught than ever Pilate tried to cajole Jesus by a threat: 'Do you refuse to answer? Do you not know that I have authority to release you and authority to crucify you?' And now lest the bystanders and all future generations should ever doubt that he was going voluntarily to his death, Jesus responded (Jn 19:11): 'You would have no authority over me unless it had been given to you from above; for this reason he who handed me over to you has a greater sin'. Even in this last hour of his life Jesus remained in full control of his fate. He apportioned serious blame to Pilate for his death but even greater to Caiaphas and his fellow high priests who were the real instigators of his condemnation.

4) Pilate yields to the Jews

(Mt 27:24f = Lk 23:24f = Mk 15:15 = Jn 19:1f)

The Jews had noted Pilate's growing sympathy for the prisoner, and so they decided to play their own last gambit, which was to threaten to report him to the emperor if he failed to execute a man whom they could represent to Sejanus, his all-powerful minister in Rome, as lacking in loyalty and sense of duty. Hence they shouted back at him: 'If you release this man who claims to be a king you are not a friend of Caesar'. Owing to the morbidly suspicious nature of Tiberius, to be accused by powerful Jews in Rome of not being a friend of Caesar, would mean not only the end of his career as a statesman but even his death warrant. Pilate could no longer resist the pressure imposed by the high priests, and going outside in a state of near collapse sat on the judgement seat in the great courtyard known as the Lithostratos in order to pass sentence.

He now saw no chance of avoiding the unjust condemnation of Jesus to crucifixion, but he intended to make the Jews pay for it as heavily as possible by compelling them against their will to profess their total loyalty to Caesar for the sake of securing the judicial murder of their king. In the presence of the prisoner he sets out to provoke them by saying with mock gravity as he surprisingly sat Jesus alongside himself on the judgement seat: 'Behold your king'. The response of the crowd is to howl: 'Away with him; crucify him'. But Pilate stirs them further by repeating with subtle mockery: 'Shall I crucify your king?' And the high priests, willing to swear to anything in order to see the messianic claimant instantly condemned, forthwith deny not only Jesus but also the whole messianic idea by categorically declaring; 'We have no king but Caesar'. Pilate at least can now send back to Sejanus the message that he has not only put down this messianic claimant but has secured a statement of loyalty from the high priests such as they had never before given in the whole history of Romano-Jewish relations to any other representative of Rome!

Pilate had yet to give one final twist to this most extraordinary drama in order to bring to the attention of the whole world that he had been forced against his will to convict an innocent man. Instead of pronouncing sentence of death on Jesus, he sent for a bowl of water, and washing his hands in the presence of the persecutors of Jesus, he announced in a clear voice: 'I am innocent of the blood of this just man; look you to it'. This was the moment of truth for the high priests, the elders and the scribes with their attendants; for, exalted by their triumph over the prefect of Judea, they exultantly exclaimed: 'His blood is upon us and upon our children'(Mt 27:25), thus absolving Pilate from blame as far as it was in their power to do so and deliberately taking it upon their own shoulders. Pilate then without further word handed Jesus over to the centurion to implement without delay the process of crucifixion. Thus Pilate never actually uttered the dread condemnation to death; he could not bring himself to do so, but revealed by his silence that the Jews had uttered it instead.

20

The Death on the Cross

1) The Way of the Cross
(Mt 27:32 = Lk 23:26f = Mk 15:21 = Jn 19:17)

Jerusalem, like every important city had in those days its regular place of execution at a convenient spot outside its walls, one that was easily accessible to all the inhabitants. For the centurion and his squad of four soldiers a crucifixion was a routine job, in which everyone knew his part. The route taken by the detachment was well known to the public who were accustomed at frequent intervals to watch the doleful processions with horror or satisfaction or pity, as the occasion demanded.

The place of execution was a small bluff beside the road to Jaffa, set amid fields and gardens not far outside the walls. It was locally known as Golgotha (Heb., Place of the Skull, and latinised as 'Calvary') because from a certain angle it had the appearance of a skull. Prominent on the bluff were three stout upright posts each having a slot, about two metres from the ground, shaped to take the crossbar that each convict would carry. This crossbar would be a heavy plank two metres or so in length, and it is easy to understand that Jesus, weakened by his scourging and other tortures, was already too weak to carry it alone.

Barabbas had of course been reprieved and freed, but his two accomplices in crime, usually referred to as 'the two thieves', were now lined up in the courtyard with Jesus, each with his own crossbar.[41]

At the word of command the first soldier led off from the Lithostratos, the other three following in single file, with the condemned men roped to them and the centurion bringing up the rear. Even before they had issued from the parade ground the centurion's practised eye had noted that Jesus was already staggering under the weight of his crossbar and would never arrive at Golgotha. Since it would have been beneath the dignity of a Roman soldier to carry a felon's instrument of execution, the centurion, with the high-handedness of the master-race, stopped the first strong-looking Jew he met in the street and bade him share the burden with Jesus. Putting the bulk of the weight onto his own broad shoulders, Simon, a devout Jew, a Passover pilgrim from Cyrene, followed Jesus to Golgotha. Some thirty years or more later the Gospel of Mark was to inform the Church that this Simon was the father of two sons, Alexander and Rufus, who were then prominent members of the apostolic Church in Rome (Mk 15:21; cf. Rom 16:13).

The news that Jesus had been arraigned before Pilate had spread among the inhabitants of the City, and long before his final condemnation a large body of sympathisers had congregated silently behind the vociferous supporters of the high priests. The ordinary people were thoroughly shocked at the treatment meted out to Jesus, and many started to follow the pitiful procession as it wound its way through the streets to Golgotha. The women in particular gave vent to their feelings in loud cries and heart-rending lamentations. Before long Jesus turned to face them, knowing the fate that was to befall their city owing to the appalling miscarriage of justice of which he was the victim. It is true that his sufferings were to work the

---

41 The crossbar is a detail suggested by the Holy Shroud of Turin, which carbon-dating tests conducted in 1988-9 declared to be a cloth dating only from between 1290 and 1360. This dating however conflicts with a vast amount of accepted scientific and artistic evidence that it dates from New Testament times. It is certain that it cannot be a 14th century forgery. Moreover its history proves that it is not a suitable subject for carbon-dating, since it has been through too many vicissitudes ever to make it possible to ascertain its original carbon-content. Thus in fact its authenticity has not been seriously affected by the unfortunate carbon-dating experiment.

redemption of the world and would more than pay for all the moral evil of the human race. But since the City in the shape of its chief priests had officially and deliberately rejected the Messiah King sent by the God whose priests they were, this same God in turn had now rejected his City and Temple and would sanction its own self-destruction in forty years' time. Jesus had previously prophesied this disaster, and as a faithful Jew, proud of his City, it was for him an intensely painful thought. Indeed he had been overwhelmed with grief at its future fate as he sat on Mt Olivet a few days earlier, exclaiming:

> Jerusalem, Jerusalem, thou who killest the prophets and stoneth the ones sent to thee. How often I wished to gather thy children, just as a hen gathers her chicks under her wings, and you would not. Behold your House is left to you desolate. (Mt 23:37-38)

Jesus ignored his own physical condition, because he had fully and willingly welcomed his present fate. Though happy to acknowledge these women's compassion for him, his concern was all for them and their children. He prophesied that they must prepare themselves for the terrible disaster that was going to fall upon the City before their generation had passed away, a disaster, which would involve them all; they would then wish that they had never had any children. With a striking simile he indicated the depths of misery that would envelop them; namely, just as a fire made with green wood is mild compared with one made with dry wood, so, if his contemporaries committed such crimes when the times were still propitious, how much greater would be the intensity of the catastrophe when the time was ripe for judgement (Lk 23:29)! His words can also be understood in another way, viz. if they have treated the life-giving Jesus in this way, what hope can they expect to derive from those without any life in themselves? Motioning then to his guards to go forward, Jesus continued on his way to Calvary.

2) The Crucifixion
(Mt 27:33f = Lk 23:33f = Mk 15:22f = Jn 19:18f)

The news that Jesus of Nazareth, the miracle-worker and claimant to the messiahship, had been captured and condemned to death by crucifixion that very afternoon, had brought a large crowd to witness the calamitous end of the man whose name had been on everybody's lips for the past two years. Prominent among the spectators were the chief priests and other members of the Sanhedrin, but there were also a great number of sympathisers ringing the hillock at a respectful distance. As they watched, the procession came to a halt beside the upright posts.

Simon was ordered to slot Jesus' crossbar into the central upright and was then discharged. Someone in the crowd, perhaps a friend, produced a flask containing a narcotic drink, a mixture of wine and myrrh to serve as a pain-killer, and passed it to a soldier to give to the convicts. Jesus however refused to drink it, wishing to retain the full use of all his faculties until the very end, despite the excruciating pain that he would have to endure. The prisoners were then ordered to strip naked, because their clothing was the perquisite of their captors. Jesus likewise removed his seamless robe and stood naked before the mocking gaze of his tormentors, to the embarrassment of all his friends in the background. Meanwhile another soldier produced a bag of nails and a hammer. When Jesus' turn came, he was told to step onto the low block of wood fixed at the foot of the central cross, to face outwards and stand upright and spread his arms. The executioner proceeded to drive a single nail into each wrist in turn, and then told him to place his left foot on top of his right foot to enable a six-inch nail to be driven through the top of his left foot down through the right and into the wooden block on which he was standing. In this way they completed their assignment swiftly and with a minimum of physical effort. No word came from Jesus while they were performing their grisly task and laying their blood-spattered hands on him. But when they had finished, he turned his eyes of compassion on them and called out: 'Father, forgive them, for they know not what they are doing'.

Not infrequently the convict wore round his neck a placard informing the public of the reason for his condemnation. Pilate had not forgotten this detail, and in order to spite the high priests for forcing him into judicial murder, he personally chose as the text to pin to the Cross over Jesus' head the words: JESUS OF NAZARETH, KING OF THE JEWS. And to make quite sure that as many as possible should read it in that multilingual country, he had it written in Hebrew, Latin and Greek. This inscription greatly enraged the chief priests and they at once sent a messenger to Pilate to ask him to amend it to: 'This man said, I am the King of the Jews'. But Pilate had no intention whatever of altering what he had purposely written in order to revenge himself on them. Moreover the wording he had chosen was not only true but would also serve to prove to Tiberius Caesar that he deserved well for eliminating yet another rival to the emperor. So Pilate simply snapped back: 'What I have written, I have written'.

Mark tells us that Jesus was nailed to the cross some time during the 'third hour', that is between nine o'clock and the 'sixth hour' (midday), at which time Matthew relates that a 'darkness came over the whole earth' that lasted until he died at the 'ninth hour', about three o'clock in the afternoon. This darkness is to be regarded as a revulsion of nature itself witnessing to the death pangs of the author of nature. It would seem to have resembled the eerie half-light that comes over the earth during an eclipse of the sun. Meanwhile the four soldiers, whose task it was to guard the victims until they were dead, sat down in front of the crosses to work out the distribution of their victims' effects. They succeeded in making four parts of everything including their outer garments, their undergarments, their belts and sandals, but they could not agree on what to do with the seamless robe, the single most valuable item, undoubtedly made for Jesus by one of the faithful women of his entourage. To cut it up would have rendered it valueless, and at length they agreed to cast lots for it; and this they did. And St John notes that by doing so they literally fulfilled the words of the messianic Psalm 21 [22]:18:

> They divided my garments among them, and over my vesture they cast lots.

St Mark (15:28) also notes that another striking prophecy was fulfilled by the fact of his crucifixion between two malefactors, namely a verse in the fourth Servant Song of Isaiah which says: 'And with the wicked he was reckoned' (Is 53:12).

As soon as the soldiers had done their work and shared their booty, they allowed the friends of Jesus to draw near. St John certainly mentions three women, his mother Mary, her sister-in-law Mary of Clopas and Mary Magdalene, and one man, undoubtedly John, the disciple whom Jesus loved. Also close at hand, but gloating over the predicament of Jesus, were the chief priests, scribes and elders, a close-knit group standing well within earshot, making cruel and cutting sallies at his expense, and even daring him to come down from the Cross. They could not contain their evil joy at their triumph over him and they made no attempt to do so: 'Others he saved, himself he cannot save. If he is king of Israel, let him now come down from the cross and we will believe in him. He trusted in God; let him now rescue him if he wants him; for he said, I am the Son of God' (Mt 27:42-43).

Their mockery was so infectious that some passers-by who had stopped to see the spectacle, wagged their heads at him, adding: 'You who destroy the Temple and build it up in three days, come down from the Cross'. Furthermore the soldiers, tired and bored, now joined in by contemptuously offering him a drink of vinegar which he refused to take, and by mockingly inviting him to descend from the Cross. Finally even the criminals on either side of him joined in the ridicule.

3) Jesus commends John to Mary (Jn 19:26f)

Yet all the time his mother Mary, and the other three were listening with horror and revulsion to the malevolent pandemonium of insults, jibes and curses levelled at the meek and motionless Saviour as he stood exposed and vulnerable on the pedestal of his Cross. Few though they were, they supported him unflinchingly with their presence and mute sympathy until his tormentors got tired of abusing him and lapsed into silence. Jesus however continued to hold up his head and to look

out from the throne of his Cross over the City, and indeed over
the whole of his creation, confident in the love of his heavenly
Father. Then slowly turning his head he looked down on Mary
and John and said to her: 'O Woman, behold thy son', and turning to John, he said, 'Behold thy mother'.

The significance of these words, uttered so firmly and so succinctly, cannot be overestimated. In the first place, they are the
compassionate words of a dying son bequeathing the welfare of
his widowed mother, now deprived of her only earthly support,
to his beloved disciple. This disciple, traditionally believed to be
the evangelist John, is careful to note that he did exactly as the
Lord had commanded him, and 'took her unto his own'. And
there is a very ancient Church tradition that in due course she
went with him to Ephesus and lived there under his protection
until the time of her assumption into heaven.

However there is a far more profound meaning attached to
the simple words of the Saviour; 'O Woman, behold your son'.
For they are an integral part of his last will and testament, the
solemn and meaningful words of a dying man who is making
sure that his followers come to realize the new spiritual
relationships between all human beings that he is now setting
up as a consequence of his life, death and future resurrection.
From the time of his coming to the age of discretion at twelve
years, Jesus had been gently but carefully preparing his mother
for her role as the new Mother of all the Living. Her role as the
mother of his human flesh was only the necessary preliminary
to her role in the resurrection as the Mother of all the members
of his Mystical Body. Her Son Jesus always loved her with every
fibre of his Being for conceiving him through the Holy Spirit,
and now in reward for her faithfulness he transforms her role to
make it match his own. At his resurrection he will become the
glorified Saviour of mankind and be able to impart the benefits
of his humanity in a new way through his Sacraments. So
likewise her own role is to be transformed into that of being the
true spiritual Mother of all the Redeemed, the Queen of Heaven
and the Queen of All Saints and the supreme intercessor for us

all. John therefore becomes the first named of all her spiritual children, who will be the members of his Mystical Body. By these simple words Jesus has set up the new economy, that is to say the new order of salvation. The Kingdom of God is in fact to be a new family, the family of God the Father, with Jesus Christ his Son as the Redeemer and our brother, and Mary as the spiritual Mother of us all, in the unity of the Holy Spirit of Love.

4) The 'Good Thief' (Lk: 23:39-43)

Mark agrees with Matthew that for a while the two Jewish malefactors crucified on either side of Jesus openly allied themselves with those who reviled him. But Luke, who usually has additional information to add to the remarks and stories of Matthew, now adds a most poignant sequel. One criminal was honest enough to admit openly that he deserved to be crucified, and he had also by now come to realize that Jesus was not only entirely innocent but was in fact a hero of a very different sort. The futility and the stupidity of railing against Jesus seems to have forcibly struck this man (to whom an ancient tradition has given the name of Dismas), so that when the other again yelled out: 'Are you not the Christ? Save yourself and us', he was constrained to rebuke his fellow-sufferer: 'Do you then not fear God, because you are in the same judgement? And we indeed justly, for we are receiving back just what we deserve, but this man has done nothing amiss'.

The candid enunciation of this truth suddenly caused to well up in Dismas a new insight into the truth that Jesus was a true king and that his Kingdom must indeed be the one mysteriously foretold in Is 60. And making a great act of faith in Jesus, and turning his head towards him, Dismas blurted out: 'Jesus, remember me when you come into your Kingdom'. And Jesus looking round at him with eyes of joy and love responded: 'Amen I say to you, today you shall be with me in Paradise'.

There was nothing more to be said. Dismas had found his Saviour and could now bear his sufferings for the remaining hours with equanimity in the certainty that before the day was out he would be Jesus' companion for ever in heaven. But what extraordinary light this remark throws on Jesus himself! The recognition of the truth, and the will to do it, is all that he asks in order to associate with himself the most abandoned of sinners. His forgiveness wipes out a lifetime of ill-doing and brings the former sinner instantaneously into God's friendship and Kingdom. Thus even on his death-bed the Saviour is able to carry out one more act of his pastoral ministry.

5) The Death of Jesus
(Mt 27:45f = Lk: 23:44f = Mk: 15:33f = Jn 19:28f)

We have come to the final moments of the Saviour's life on earth in which he revealed his ultimate state of mind and provided us with the model of how to pass from this world to his heavenly Father and ours. Jesus had now been nailed to the Cross along with his two companions for nearly three hours. The gloom that had descended over Calvary at the moment of the crucifixion had intensified and the chattering of the crowds had hushed; only the moans of the two thieves could be heard. And then from the lips of Jesus there came loud and clear the first words of the 21st Psalm: 'Eli, Eli, lema sabachthani, that is, My God, My God, why hast thou forsaken me?'

This psalm is one of the great messianic psalms. It starts with this cry of distress. The psalmist, speaking in the person of the Messiah, declares that God, his God, the all-holy God in whom his ancestors trusted and who in fact delivered them from all their enemies, has left him alone to suffer the cruellest torture. These enemies now surround him like fierce bulls of Bashan, his blood has all been poured out, his strength is dried up like a potsherd, his tongue cleaves to his jaws, and he lies in the dust of death. They have pierced his hands and his feet; he can count all his bones, his foes stare and gloat over him, and they have cast lots for his garments. And then the psalmist announces that despite all appearances, he can confidently call upon the Lord God for help; in fact he has not really hidden his face from him, but has heard his cry. Indeed all the proud rulers of the earth will soon bow down before him and posterity will serve him, and his victorious deliverance shall be proclaimed to a people not yet born.

Jesus on the Cross is intensely aware that all these predictions have just been truly enacted. In uttering the first line of this psalm he made known to the world and to all his followers that the psalmist's prophecy had been triumphantly fulfilled in him, and in particular that the dereliction that he had suffered was all in God's plan.

Some of the bystanders misheard and misunderstood his Eli, Eli and thought he was calling upon Elijah, the prophet who is to return at the end of the world, to come and rescue him. And while they were pondering what to do, Jesus added: 'I thirst'. Such a thirst was one of the many tortures endured by crucified victims and was induced by the severe loss of blood from the wounds in the hands and the feet. The psalmist had prophesied this thirst when he wrote 'My tongue cleaves to my jaws'. At Jesus' words, a compassionate bystander rushed to the tub full of vinegar that stood beside the crosses and filling a sponge put it to the lips of Jesus, thus fulfilling the prophecy of Ps 69:21, 'For my thirst they gave me vinegar to drink'. His thirst was however still more a thirst for the souls for whom he was giving his life.

When Jesus had tasted the vinegar, yet without drinking it, he triumphantly exclaimed: 'My task has now been accomplished'. That is to say, he had now finally completed the work of redemption that his Father sent him to accomplish, and he had no further reason to go on living in this world. So calling upon his heavenly Father with the words: 'Father into thy hands I commend my Spirit', he breathed forth his soul by his own authority and died.

6) Witnesses of the Death of Jesus
(Mt 27:54f = Lk 23:47f = Mk 15:39f)

The radical critics of Christianity adopt one or other of two positions regarding the death of Jesus. Either they assert that he never really died but was carried away in a swoon and buried alive in the tomb from which his disciples stealthily removed him over the Sabbath weekend and he recovered sufficiently to have been seen by some of them; or else he really died and the disciples manufactured his post-resurrection appearances by some process of group hallucination. Both assertions are untrue, and their falsity is demonstrated by the events that followed his death.

The Gospel of Matthew records that Jesus had no sooner breathed out his soul than the veil of the Temple, the one that curtained access to the Holy of Holies, the innermost shrine, where the Jews believed that Yahweh, the Lord Gcd of Israel, dwelt invisibly among them, this very veil was rent in two from top to bottom[42] (Mt 27:51). The rending of course signified that the Old Dispensation was ended and that henceforth access to the Lord God would be by another way, in fact through the heart of Jesus. The rending became known that very evening when the priest, deputed to offer incense at the altar before the curtain, entered the shrine to officiate and saw what had happened.

However more immediately striking, because it affected all those watching the death of Jesus on Calvary, was the earthquake and the splitting of the rocks that took place at the moment of his death, including perhaps the cleft in the existing rock of Calvary. The Gospel adds that not only were the rocks split open but also that some holy persons of the Old Testament rose from their tombs, and that after the Resurrection 'they

42 The rending of the Temple veil (Mt 27:51) is strikingly attested in the so-called 'Slavonic Additions' to Book V, 214, of Josephus, *History of the Jewish War* (Loeb Classical Library, Heinemann, and Harvard University Press, 1957). Jewish scholars attribute this passage to 'Christian interpolation'. But critical examination of all the twenty-two so-called 'interpolations' reveal that only seven of them relate to Christianity, the remainder relating either to the iniquities of the Herod family or to the shortcomings of the high priests, or hostile and virulent criticism of Roman manners and behaviour. It would therefore seem that the interpolation explanation does not fit, and that all these twenty-two passages are the genuine work of Josephus, although they are not to be found in the Greek text that has survived and which was published in Rome about AD 79. They were discovered about a hundred years ago in Slavonic (Old Russian and Rumanian) translations. The interested reader will find them in the Appendix to G.A. Williamson's translation of the *Jewish War* (Penguin Classics, 1959). Josephus adds nothing to our knowledge of Jesus derived from the Gospels; but by their very brevity and restraint the references made to him make us realize what an enormous impact he made on his whole nation (see also *Appendix*).

entered the Holy City and appeared to many' (Mt 27:52). It is
the fashion among the majority of commentators on the Gospels
to describe these events as 'legendary', by which they mean that
they never really occurred but were simply 'apocalyptic
imagery' which the circle in which Matthew operated thought
appropriate to create as a concomitant of the death of the Son of
God. The view taken here is that Matthew was faithfully reporting what actually happened, and that he is truly recording what
the centurion and those with him experienced as they stood beside
the Cross of Jesus; for as the evangelist writes, 'the centurion and
those with him guarding Jesus seeing the earthquake and the
happenings were exceedingly afraid saying: 'Truly this was God's
Son' (Mt 27:54 = Mk 15:39). There is nothing unlikely in the mute
creation that owed its existence to Jesus, the Word of God, expressing its sympathy with its Creator, as well as its horror at the
dreadful crime committed against the Head of Humanity. Indeed,
all things created that can suffer pain suffered with him. As Julian
of Norwich wrote in her *Revelations of Divine Love*: 'The firma-
ment and the earth failed for sorrow in their nature at the time of
Christ's dying, for it belongs naturally to their character to know
him for their God, in whom all their strength is situated. When he
failed, then it was necessary for them out of nature to fail with
him, as much as they could, out of sorrow for his pains'. Magnificent too was the eloquent witness of this pagan centurion to
Jesus being truly God's Son. No greater tribute could he pay than
this, a tribute which with hindsight we can see that he was inspired to utter on behalf of the whole pagan world.

The Beloved Disciple and the women followers are the only
disciples of Jesus mentioned as witnesses of his agony and
death. The other Apostles had, it seems, been completely
stunned and overwhelmed by the speed and thoroughness with
which he had been disposed of and his life-work brought to an
abrupt end, seemingly for good. They were too dazed and dis-
consolate to think positively about the future or to make any
plans. They were unable to recall that he had many times
prophesied everything that had happened to him, including his

resurrection, and they had lost all hope. By contrast his enemies were very much on the lookout for counter action by the disciples and were prepared to forestall it. The first thing, however, for friend and foe alike was to get the bodies of all three victims taken down and removed, lest the Sabbath be defiled by the grim reminder of their bodies decomposing on the crosses during the most holy feast of the Passover.

7) The Deposition and Burial of Jesus
(Mt 27:57f = Lk 23:50f = Mk 15:42f = Jn 19:31f)

There was however one follower of Jesus who had his wits about him, a member of the Sanhedrin in fact, by name Joseph of Arimathea, who had not consented to their decision to put Jesus to death. By a special dispensation of divine providence he had recently constructed a new tomb for himself, hewn out of the rock in the garden that adjoined Golgotha. No one had as yet occupied it, and when he saw Jesus dying on the Cross, it seems that he at once went up to Mary and John and offered it to them as at least a temporary resting-place for the body of the Saviour, and they gladly agreed. Joseph hurried off to Pilate, who by that time had returned to his residence near the Jaffa Gate, and boldly petitioned to be allowed to take away the body of Jesus. Pilate was so surprised that Jesus had already died that he summoned the centurion to learn the truth of the matter. When the representatives of the high priests saw the centurion summoned by the messenger, they followed him back to Pilate; and when Pilate gave Joseph the required permission, they asked to have the two survivors finished off quickly and their bodies removed from the crosses before sunset. This was also granted.

On his return to Calvary the centurion ordered his men to break the legs of the two thieves. The reason for this action was that as long as they could stand up on the pedestals at the foot of their crosses they could survive, but they would die of asphyxiation as soon as the whole weight of their bodies came to depend on their arms. So the soldiers expertly smashed the shins of each in turn with the hammer used to crucify them and thereby caused them to collapse and die in a few minutes for lack of breath. But as Jesus was already dead, such action in his case was superfluous, and they did not break his legs.

John had been anxiously watching all this as it took place, and he was astounded to note that when the soldier, in order to make sure that Jesus was really dead, drove a lance through the rib-cage into his heart, there burst forth at once a jet of blood and water combined. Years later when he came to write about this event, John reminded his readers that two more prophecies were thereby fulfilled, namely, 'Not a bone of him shall be broken' (Ex 12:46), and 'They shall look on him whom they pierced' (Zech 12:10). This colourless fluid which he calls water was undoubtedly the lymph that collects in the envelope around the heart and which was discharged with the blood, symbolizing of course the saving grace that flows from the Saviour's glorified Body.

The Gospels do not tell us who took care of the removal of the bodies of the two thieves, but Joseph had worked out exactly what he had to do for the body of Jesus in the short time available before sunset when all work had to cease. He had already contacted Nicodemus, another member of the Sanhedrin who had become a follower of Jesus, and asked him to bring along as much myrrh and aloes as he could manage. For his own part he had just bought privately in the bazaar a winding sheet of the finest linen that money could buy in which to wrap the body of Jesus.

By the time that the centurion and his detachment had left the scene, it must have been about five o'clock, allowing Joseph just one hour before sunset in which to take down the body and lay it reverently in his own tomb. With the help of Nicodemus and John and possibly several others, a number of linen strips were laid down parallel to one another at intervals of about a foot and then the winding sheet was spread full length on the ground on top of them. Since his expiry the body of Jesus had been hanging solely from his wrists at the point where the nails had made their way through the complex of bone and gristle. It was necessary first to put a rope round the torso under the armpits and over the top of the cross to support the body while the nails were being removed. This done, the body could be gently lowered onto the winding-sheet with the head in the centre and the feet at one end. The crown of thorns was removed and the arms laid crosswise over the body. There was no time to wash off the blood stains or to comb the matted hair and beard; that would have to be done on the day following the Sabbath when the women would take over. The bags of aromatic spices brought by Nicodemus were laid on either side from head to foot and the far end of the sheet brought up over the head and down over the chest to meet the bottom end of the sheet at the feet. The strips of linen bandages were then brought over and tied across the body to keep the spices in place and shroud it completely. The final task was then to lift it and place it on a stretcher for the short journey to the tomb. Negotiating its low and narrow entrance was no easy matter, and by the time that the body had been properly arranged on the low rock shelf in the inner compartment of the tomb, the sun was on the point of setting. There was just enough time to roll the heavy stone across the entrance and depart for home before sunset and the start of the Sabbath Passover. Joseph of Arimathea and Nicodemus, advised by Mary, the mother of Jesus, had completed a stupendous task against great odds in providing a fitting though temporary resting-place for the King of the Jews.[43]

While the men were thus occupied, the other faithful women, led by Mary Magdalene. were carefully watching everything and noting the whereabouts of the tomb wherein Jesus had been laid, for there were also other tombs in the neighbourhood. They planned to return at the earliest possible moment after the Sabbath rest with the spices and oils they needed to wash and anoint the body for final burial.

The disciples of Jesus remained meanwhile in a sort of list-

43 The description of the deposition of the body of Jesus is based on a comparison of the Gospel evidence with that furnished by the Holy Shroud of Turin (see note 41 above).

less torpor, but the chief priests and the Pharisees were far from idle. One of the latter recalled that Jesus while still alive had prophesied that he would rise on the third day. Though they believed this to be impossible, the man had done so many marvellous things, like raising Lazarus from the dead, that they decided to take no chances. So they called on Pilate and asked him to have the tomb guarded for the next three days just in case his disciples were to come and steal his body and then claim that he was still alive and had risen from the dead! Pilate found their request unwelcome, and wanting to forget the whole affair, brusquely replied: 'You have got your own police; go and guard the tomb to the best of your own ability.' Having secured his permission they did so at once, setting guards and sealing the stone at the entrance (Mt 27:66).

During that great Sabbath, which was also in that year the feast of the Passover, the party of the chief priests quietly exulted over their successful elimination of Jesus of Nazareth who had been such a threat to their peace of mind and thorn in their flesh for the previous two years. Nevertheless they still had a niggling fear that this miracle-worker might somehow or other still spring a surprise on them through the machinations of his followers. But they were unaware that the death of the Master had in fact for the time being broken the spirit of his chief disciples and cowed the remainder. All that day the Apostles stayed at home in great dejection and without any hope, their minds dwelling on the dreadful events they had witnessed the previous day. His mother, however, secretly knew that her Son would in his own way and time keep his promise to rise again.

Part III

The Life of Glory

21

From Resurrection to Pentecost

1) The Meaning of the Resurrection

Christian theology has come to certain conclusions as to what happened to Christ's soul after his death. In the first place, a Christian believes that after death the soul, the human spirit, the unique and indestructible part of every person, does not cease to exist, but enters into another state comparable to that of the angels. Furthermore at the moment it leaves the body, because the body can no longer sustain it, its destiny is already in principle determined for all eternity. That is to say,

a) either it is entirely pleasing to God the Supreme Spirit and can enter into complete union with him at once;

b) or it is basically oriented towards him but still has certain defects that withhold it from such union, until they have been eliminated;

c) or it has exercised on earth its own free will to reject totally such union, and thus separates itself from God for all eternity.

In the case of the human soul of Jesus, at the moment of expiry it would have been instantly joined in a new dimension to the Father and the Holy Spirit in the Beatific Vision with an infinite elan. This is what Jesus meant when he told the Good Thief that he would be with him that day in Paradise, i.e. in heaven in the bosom of the Father. And though the human soul of Jesus had departed from his body, that body, as it lay in the tomb, still remained at the same time the sacrament of the divine presence, and could not suffer even the remotest beginning of the process of corruption that affects us all (cf. Ac 2:25-31).

Furthermore, time is 'the succession of before and after' and is a phenomenon that is peculiar to this world of ours in which everything is in movement in one sense or another. But the angels and the saints and the souls of the dead are beyond the reach of time. At death in principle our souls move into a timeless world and become attached to the timelessness, the infinite now of God himself. And so with the human soul of Jesus. The exact moment when he was to resume possession of his lifeless body, still sealed in the tomb, was a secret known only to the Blessed Trinity. It was in the early hours of the first day of the week that his human soul inseparably united with the Second Person of the Blessed Trinity again took possession of his body in the privacy of the tomb. And the life which his soul imparted to it, this new life was not the mortal life to which he had first subjected himself, but the eternal life of the Spirit of God. And then the body of Jesus infused with its new and everlasting life passed through the walls of his rock tomb into eternal freedom with all the qualities that we shall note in his glorified body when he manifested himself to his disciples.

While the body of Jesus lay lifeless in the tomb for the space of 'three days' (according to the Jewish method of reckoning) his human soul was nonetheless enjoying the Beatific Vision. Theologians tell us, however, that in the moment of the passing of his soul out of his body he made a proclamation to two categories of spirits in the course of his instantaneous ascent into union with his Father. His descent into the underworld is known as 'the harrowing of hell'. Firstly, he announced to Satan and all his wicked associates that he had triumphed over them all and had won the definitive battle for the redemption of the human race (cf. 1 Pet 3:18-22). And secondly, he was able to tell the souls of the just of former times, who had been waiting for his victory, that they were now to enter Paradise with him.[44]

Finally, what does the resurrection of Christ from the tomb signify for us? St Paul tells us plainly: 'He died for our sins and rose again for our justification' (Rom 4:25). It means that as soon as the soul of the deceased Christian has been purified from all stain of sin and has satisfied the requirements of divine justice with regard to the temporal punishment due to past sins, it will be introduced by the power of the resurrection of Christ into the Beatific Vision of God and enjoy the eternal happiness resulting from seeing him as he is. Furthermore, when Christ returns at the Last Day with all his angels and saints, he will give public recognition and just recompense to all mankind, to those alive at that moment and to all those raised from the dead (Mt 25:31-46; cf. 1 Thess 4:15-17). Then the souls of the Blessed Ones will be raised and reunited to their bodies, restored and glorified according to their spiritual capacity; and body and soul, as complete human beings, will share ever after in the happiness of the vision of God. In the case of the unrighteous their bodies will be raised but will also share in the unhappiness of being for ever excluded from the vision of God, because that was their own decision.

2) The Resurrection (Mt 28:1f = Lk 24:1f = Mk 16:2f = Jn 20:1f)

The office of making known the bodily resurrection of the Lord was entrusted to an angel, whose arrival was signalled by an earthquake, which was also the outward indication that the Lord Jesus Christ had risen from the tomb. Henceforth, no material walls could restrain his free movement.

And behold a great earthquake occurred, for an angel of the Lord came down from heaven and approaching the tomb rolled away the stone from the entrance and sat upon it. And his appearance was

---

44 The medieval theologians referred to the period between the resurrection and the second coming of Christ as the era of 'angelic time', because it is outside earthly time, whilst the final consummation of all things has not as yet taken place. H.U. von Balthasar (*Mysterium Paschale*, p.79f) however, argues very powerfully, in opposition to the concept of Christ's triumphal preaching to the dead, that in and by his death Christ experienced the pain of total abandonment by his heavenly Father. His dereliction was the ultimate experience of his *kenosis*, his self-emptying.

like lightning and his vesture white as snow. And the guards were seized with fear of him, and became like dead men (Mt 28:2-4).

Christian tradition supported by the Gospels, has proclaimed that Christ rose from the dead by his own power before dawn on the first day of the week—the day known ever since as the Lord's Day. For all Christians this day has ever since been the holy day of each week and has superseded the Sabbath, the holy day of the Jews, established by Moses a millenium and more earlier.

Nobody saw Jesus rise; but he was to give fully adequate proofs of the reality of his resurrected body during the forty days he appeared to the Eleven and to many other specially privileged witnesses. His resurrection is the best attested fact in human history, though it is a truly historical event only in the sense that the dead body of Jesus was placed in the tomb belonging to Joseph of Arimathea just before sunset on the eve of the Passover of AD 30, that the high priests' guards sealed it securely (Mt 27:65-66), and that early in the morning of the first day of the next week—some thirty-six hours later—the body had vanished without trace and has never been located since. The fact, of course, is that Jesus re-appeared mysteriously several times that very day with that same body which however now possessed something infinitely greater than the life he had lost on Good Friday. The Jesus who appeared that day to Mary Magdalene and some other women, to the two disciples on the road to Emmaus and to the Eleven, was alive with a new life whose source was out of this world. Yet the physical body was the same, for it still retained the marks of the Five Wounds, and its possessor was able to eat in normal human fashion. Thus the disappearance of his body at that particular moment of time is explained by his re-appearance at particular moments of time in the following days in Jerusalem and elsewhere, when he demonstrated to those who saw him the new eternal life with which he had now endowed his body.[45]

From the time of his death Jesus no longer belonged to the

---

45 The proofs of the resurrection have been set down in classical fashion in *Who Moved The Stone?* by Frank Morison, published in 1930; cf. J. Ratzinger, *Journey Towards Easter* (Engl. ed.), Slough 1987, pp. 114-116.

world perceptible to our senses but to the world of God; and therefore from the moment of the resurrection he can only be seen by those to whom he grants the sight. Furthermore, his death, followed by his resurrection, puts an end to death not only for his own body but also for the bodies of all those who are members of his Mystical Body. Just as his death opened the door for his body to enter into eternal life, so henceforward the physical death of all those who belong to him will usher them also into eternal life; and their bodies will be returned to them in like manner in the final resurrection. That is why St Paul could exult:

> O death, where is thy victory! O death, where is thy sting? For death is swallowed up in victory (1 Cor 15:54-55).

By his death and resurrection Jesus has withdrawn the 'sting of death', has conquered it and won victory over it and replaced it with everlasting life.

Mary is the one person in whom this destiny has already been fulfilled. The Catholic tradition now maintains as a dogma of faith that, though the sinless Mother of Jesus had to die like everyone else, yet at the moment of her death she received back her glorified body, which now becomes another pledge of the bodily resurrection of all mankind at the Last Day. The Catholic Christian sees in this fact the honour and the reward that she has received from her Son for her unique faithfulness and love.[46]

3) The Discovery of the Empty Tomb
(Mt 28:5f; Lk 24:11f; Mk 16:2; Jn 20:2)

The first of the disciples to return to the tomb early that morning appears to have been Mary Magdalene accompanied by 'the other Mary', the mother of James the Less and of Joses (Mt 28:1). It seems that they arrived soon after the earthquake and found the angel sitting on the stone that he had rolled back. The women were naturally terrified by this apparition, but the angel calmed them with the words:

---

46 As regards the assumption of the Blessed Virgin Mary into heaven at the time of her death, the tradition of the Church from earliest days was finally confirmed by Pope Pius XII in 1950 as a doctrine of the faith.

Don't be frightened; for I know that you seek Jesus who has been crucified. He is not here; for he has risen just as he said. Come, see the place where the Lord was laid. And go quickly and tell his disciples that he is risen from the dead. And behold he goes before you into Galilee, where you will see him. Behold I have told you! (Mt 28:5-8).

They were overjoyed by this wonderful news and ran off at once to find the disciples. But as they got nearer and nearer to their destination doubts and fears began to assail them. They had no evidence beyond their own unsupported testimony and felt sure that the Apostles would pooh-pooh their story and pack them off as hysterical women unnerved by the strain of their harrowing experiences. Indeed, as has already been noted, the disciples were in such a melancholic state of mind as to be psychologically incapable of visualising the possibility of the resurrection. And then, just as the women were on the point of turning back rather than face the ridicule of the disciples, Jesus himself suddenly appeared before them in the way and greeted them with 'Hail' in his old familiar voice. In great relief they flung themselves at his feet and worshipped him, while he assured them:

Do not be afraid. But go, inform my brothers, and tell them to go down to Galilee and there they will see me. (Mt 28:10)

On the strength of this reassurance they hastened to relay the angel's message and what Jesus himself had said to them. But their earlier premonition was correct; the disciples were not prepared to accept such startling news on the unsupported testimony of a bunch of pious women and, being quite unconvinced, thought they were talking nonsense and dismissed them summarily.

Meanwhile, according to Mark, another group of women had arrived at the tomb with all the materials ready to anoint the body of Jesus, and they too were surprised to find the stone rolled back (Lk 24:1-8; Mk 16:2-8). Timidly entering into the tomb they found it empty. As they came out they saw two men standing by them in dazzling attire who repeated the message given earlier to Mary Magdalene and the other Mary. They too rushed back to tell the Apostles, who again dismissed them, but perhaps not quite so summarily.

4) Peter and John inspect the Empty Tomb (Lk 24:12 = Jn 20:2-10)

Without delay Peter and John ran together straight to the tomb as fast as they could. John being considerably younger got there first, but, recognizing Peter's precedence as the leader, waited for him to come up and enter first. It was the all-important moment of the verification of the evidence for the empty tomb by two of the leading Apostles. John, it seems, at once perceived the significance of what Peter also saw, namely, the linen strips that had encompassed the body of the Lord lying collapsed but still tied and in their original order on the stone shelf. The shroud that had enveloped the body was itself neatly folded up apart from the linen strips or bandages.[47] John at once believed in the fulfilment of the prophecy because he realized that no earthly power could have extracted the shroud from the bandages and the body of the Lord from the shroud in that precise way. That is to say, it was clear to him that the body could not have been removed by anyone, neither by the Apostles nor by tomb-robbers nor body-snatchers, who would either have taken away the shroud and the bandages with the body or else left them in disarray on the floor. Peter however remained puzzled and not yet entirely convinced, when he and John returned to their own place for the time being (Jn 20:11-18). Peter seemed still unable to take in the full significance of what had he had just seen; and it was not until later that same afternoon when the Lord appeared to him in person that he too came to full belief in the resurrection of the Lord (Lk 24:34).

5) Jesus appears to Mary Magdalene (Jn 20:11-18)

From the account in the Gospel of John it might seem that Mary Magdalene was on her own when she informed Peter and John of the empty tomb; at least there is no mention of the other Mary being with her (cf. Mt 28:1). The evangelist implies that she was also by herself when she followed Peter and John back

47 See notes 41 & 43 above.

to the tomb, arriving after they had departed from it.

As she arrived and stood outside weeping, she stooped down and peered into the arched entrance of the tomb and saw two angels in white in the inner chamber where the body had once lain. In response to the angels' question why she was weeping she said that she was worried because someone had removed the body without letting her know. Then turning round she saw a man standing nearby and watching her; and she thought he must be the gardener. He in his turn asked why she was weeping, and she begged him rather peremptorily to tell her if he had removed the body as she wanted to recover it. When Jesus at this point revealed himself to her by 'releasing her eyes' she exclaimed '*Rabbouni*' (my teacher) and involuntarily moved forward to embrace him. But he at once forbade her, explaining that he had not yet ascended to the Father, thus informing her that he now no longer belonged to this world but only to the supernatural sphere.

It is perhaps worth noting about this story that the Lord accorded her precedence over the eleven apostles in seeing him in his new state of existence. And the Lord also imposed on her the duty of informing them that he had indeed arisen and had spoken to her in this way in the garden. Later on the same day he would also appear to the Eleven in the place where they were assembled for fear of the Jewish authorities (Jn 20:19).

6) The Reaction of the Sanhedrin (Mt 28:11-15)

When the Temple police appointed by the Saviour's enemies to guard the tomb had sufficiently recovered from their fright at the earthquake and the sight of the angel and found that it had been unsealed and opened by divine power, they ran back into the City and informed the high priests of this extraordinary intervention.[48] The high priests at once put a bold face on this—for them—shattering news and refused to panic. As the guards were obviously telling the truth there was only one thing to be done, namely to deny it strenuously and to take all the steps

---

48 It would seem that the soldiers guarding the tomb on behalf of the high priests were Roman soldiers whom they had specially hired for the purpose.

they could to reduce the impact on the people. And so, true to their policy of obliterating as far as possible every trace of the passage of Jesus through their land, they decided on a grand cover-up:

> The high priests, assembling together with the elders, made a plan, and gave a lot of money to the guards, saying: Explain that his disciples came by night and stole him away, while we were asleep. And if this should come to the ears of the prefect, we will persuade him, and make sure that you need have no worry.

The high priests were desperate to find some plausible explanation of the body's disappearance and this crude lie was the best they could think of. It continued to remain the official Jewish explanation of the events connected with the resurrection of Jesus despite all the evidence to the contrary.[49] Meanwhile, however, the true story was reaching the ears of the Apostles gathered together in gloomy conclave.

7) Other Appearances of Jesus

A comparison of the Gospel accounts reveals that it took more than a week to convince the Eleven as a group of the reality of Jesus' resurrection (cf. Mk 16:14). It was a gradual process; each time that he appeared to one or more of them, it was borne in on them little by little that, although he was indeed the same person who had walked and talked with them and had then died on the Cross, he now belonged no longer to this earth but to a new and heavenly world entirely beyond their experience. Among other things they had to get used to the fact that he could materialise whenever he pleased and then disappear as suddenly as he had come; as for instance when he walked and talked with Cleophas and his fellow-disciple on the road to Emmaus on the very day of the resurrection, and then vanished after breaking bread with them. But he had not hesitated to rebuke them severely for their slowness to appreciate what had happened: 'O foolish and slow of heart to believe all that the

---

49 In view of the shattering impact of Jesus of Nazareth on the fortunes of the Jewish people, it is altogether remarkable that the *Talmud* maintains what is in effect a complete silence about his life and ministry.

prophets have spoken! And beginning with Moses and all the prophets he interpreted to them in all the Scriptures the things concerning himself' (Lk 24:13-35).

Jesus' comprehensive commentary on the principal passages of the Old Testament books was never forgotten and was most carefully treasured and extensively utilised by the first Christians, as we learn from the numerous quotations and countless allusions in the Gospels. These ancient prophecies illumined their understanding of the life and ministry of Jesus, of which the Twelve in particular had been the privileged witnesses, and for this reason the details of this event were carefully preserved by the authors of the Gospels.

On that same first day of the week Jesus also appeared to the Eleven and specially invited them to inspect the marks of the wounds in his hands and feet to make sure that it was the same body that he had before and none other (Lk 24:39). Again, in order further to prove to them the reality of his bodily resurrection he went out of his way to eat some food in front of them (Lk 24:42) and once more opened their minds to understand the Scriptures that had foretold all these events (cf. Lk 24:45).

Though Thomas happened not to be with them when Jesus had appeared on the evening of that first Easter Day, Jesus was well aware of Thomas' subsequent comment that he would not believe it unless he could put his finger into the Lord's wounds to assure himself of the reality of his glorified body (Jn 20:24-29). Therefore one week later, on the next Lord's Day, Jesus appeared again to the Eleven, and after the greeting: 'Peace be with you' he turned reproachfully to Thomas:

> Bring your finger here and see my hands, and bring your hand and put it into my side and be not faithless but believing (Jn 20:27).

Thomas, overcome by embarrassment could only exclaim: 'My Lord and my God', thus being the last of the Eleven to be convinced and make his profession of faith in the divinity of the risen Lord.

Once Jesus had convinced them that he was the identical person in every respect except for the one vital fact that he was now in a new state and enjoying eternal life, he set about preparing them to continue his work on earth without them any longer having the assurance of seeing him with their bodily eyes. St Luke summarizes his activity during the forty days leading up to his ascension in these words:

> He presented himself alive after his Passion by many proofs, appearing to them during forty days and speaking of the Kingdom of God (Ac 1:1-3).

Jesus had always made it clear that the Jewish nation as such and its spiritual rulers, the Jewish hierarchy, had lost its status as representing the Kingdom of God on earth. Now, on the evening of that first Easter day in Jerusalem the time had come for them to realise their new status and so Jesus proceeds to give the Eleven the power to forgive sins in accordance with their own right judgement and likewise the power to impart the Holy Spirit. Breathing on them he said:

> Receive the Holy Spirit: Whose sins you shall forgive they are forgiven; whose sins you shall retain they are retained (Jn 20:22-23).

St Thomas Aquinas has explained that in breathing the Holy Spirit on the Eleven on this occasion, Jesus was personally giving them the power to perform his own specifically priestly acts in his name, viz. the conferring of his sacraments, the power of forgiveness, as well as everything that goes with them.

Later, when they had followed his call to meet him in Galilee by the lakeside and after a second miraculous catch of fish, Jesus rehabilitated Peter in the eyes of the other Apostles after his threefold denial during the passion and not only reinstated him, but also appointed him in his stead to be the Good Shepherd of the whole flock of Christ and the presiding authority among the Apostles (Jn 21:1-14). While Peter may so far have been sharing his responsibilities with John and the others, from now on he was to be their Good Shepherd too.

And while they were still in Galilee on the mountain whither Jesus had called them, perhaps the place known to them from his Great Sermon, he informed them that he was sending them out in exactly the same way as the Father had sent him, and that they were to be his plenipotentiaries in the fullest sense of the word:

All authority in heaven and on earth has been given to me. Go therefore and make disciples of all nations, baptizing them in the name of the Father and of the Son and of the Holy Spirit, teaching them to observe all that I have commanded you; and lo, I am with you always, to the close of the Age (Mt 28:18-20).

The double shock endured by the eleven Apostles, firstly the death of Jesus and subsequent desolation and secondly the overwhelming joy of the resurrection, had initially left them emotionally drained and for the time being disoriented. They needed everyone of the many appearances Jesus granted them during the forty days before his ascension to regain their mental balance. It was for them a period of transition between the physical intimacy of their common life with him during that glorious year, when he taught and befriended them and walked with them in Galilee, and the years to come, when they would have only their memories together with his unseen sacramental presence and the power of the Holy Spirit to lead them forward.

His appearances had served the purpose of assuring them of his continued surveillance of their welfare as well as the opportunity to ask questions that their future life was already raising in their minds. It also gave them the opportunity to learn to work with his invisible presence only. They had to learn that they would soon be in independent charge of the Church, with the whole inhabited world as their field of work, and at the same time to realise that they could do no good except by total reliance on his grace and by following the spiritual principles he had laid down.

Sooner or later there would have to be a positively last appearance after which they would know with certainty that they would not see him or hear his voice again. That moment was to be his ascension which he had spoken of as an event he longed for (Lk 9:51).

8) The Ascension (Lk 24:50-53; Ac 1:1-14)

By the time the fortieth day arrived Jesus had got the Twelve into a contented and expectant frame of mind, eager for the coming of the Holy Spirit and the opportunity to go forth to the ends of the earth in his name to make use of the powers he had promised them to win souls to his obedience. So he led them out to Bethany on Mt Olivet where he reminded them again that the fellowship of the Twelve Apostles was now to replace the leadership of the high priests. From now on, under the guidance of the Holy Spirit, they were to develop independently the new Kingdom of God, and to be his witnesses first of all 'in Jerusalem and in all Judea and Samaria and then to the end of the earth' (Ac 1:8). And having blessed them and once more assured them that he would send the Holy Spirit upon them, he rose bodily in the air and a cloud hid him from their sight. Nevertheless, waiting above to receive him was his heavenly Father and the whole court of Heaven in order to acclaim the successful completion of his world mission of salvation. The prophet Daniel in fact foretold in words of unforgettable splendour the scene as Jesus re-entered Heaven in triumph to receive the public approbation of his Father. He wrote:

As I looked, thrones were placed and one who was ancient of days took his seat; his raimant was white as snow, and the hair of his head like pure wool; his throne was fiery flames, its wheels were burning fire. A stream of life issued and came forth from before him; a thousand thousands served him, and ten thousand times ten thousand stood before him... And behold, with the clouds of heaven there came one like [the] Son of Man, and he came to the Ancient of Days and was presented before him. And to him was given dominion and glory and kingdom, that all peoples, nations, and languages should serve him; his dominion is an everlasting dominion which shall not pass away, and his kingdom one that shall not be destroyed (Dan 7:9-10, 13-14).

Meanwhile on earth below, while the Eleven were still gazing upwards, two angels stood by them announcing that he would thenceforth remain invisible to human sight until the moment of his second coming (Parousia), his return in glory to judge the living and the dead, a moment which he had told them was known only to his heavenly Father.

9) The Election of Matthias (Ac 1:15-26)

For the Eleven, there was still one task to be performed before

Pentecost, and that was to find a successor to Judas. Accordingly during the ten days between the ascension and the descent of the Holy Spirit Peter took the initiative in calling the Eleven together to fill up the vacancy. Accepting his authority and presidency, they adopted his criterion for selection, namely that the successful candidate must have been an eye-witness of all that Jesus had said and done from the baptism of John until his ascension; and after earnest prayer and casting lots they elected Matthias in Judas' place. All was now ready for the coming of the Holy Spirit who would be both the life, as well as the source of unity of the new organization, the Church, the assembly of those who accepted Christ as their Saviour, with the Apostles as his visible representatives.

10) *The Coming of the Holy Spirit (Ac 2:1f)*

The descent of the Holy Spirit on the Apostles and those gathered with them in the Upper Room was a public event in the sense that the mighty wind that accompanied it created such a sound that the whole of Jerusalem heard it; it was no hole-and-corner affair but was made known to all the inhabitants of the Holy City. That is to say, the inauguration of the Church was an historical event that was manifest to every one around and could not be hidden or denied. With the emergence of the Apostles from the Upper Room, inebriated with the joy and power of the Holy Spirit, the new era, the new dispensation foretold by Isaiah had begun. The whole group, some one hundred and twenty in all including the Mother of Jesus, were speaking in tongues and proclaiming to the inhabitants of the Holy City the mighty works of God and the fulfilment of all the ancient prophecies. This was indeed the great and manifest Day of the Lord, for Jesus Christ was fulfilling his promise to send the Holy Spirit, 'the promise of the Father', to remove the veil from the hearts of the nations and bring all into one.

11) *The Church of Christ in Action (Ac 2:37-47)*

On that first Pentecost, in response to Peter's call, about three thousand persons were baptized by the Apostles, the Church was founded in Jerusalem and the success of the work of Christ was secured.[50] This Church was to be the model for all the local Churches of which the One Church is made up, and in particular the pattern for the Churches that Paul was to establish a few years later. Luke, his disciple and companion, was to describe it in these words:

> All that believed were of one heart and soul and no one said that any of the things which he possessed was his own, but they had everything in common And they devoted themselves to the teaching of the Apostles, to the fellowship, to the breaking of the bread, and to the prayers (Ac 4:32; 2:42).

The Apostles and their disciples were now sure that Jesus Christ would also fulfil his final promise, namely to be with them until his return in glory with his angels at the end of time (Mt 28:20). He would be living with them now in a new way, in their hearts and souls and in his Sacraments, and his Church would be the living sacrament of his presence. The prophecy of Isaiah had at last been fulfilled which declared (Is 2:3):

> Out of Zion shall go forth the Law, and the Word of the Lord from Jerusalem.

12) *The New Outlook of the Apostles*

Luke has summed up the instructions given by Jesus to the

---

50 It is the Catholic faith that Christ himself is the founder of the Church, although modern theologians differ as to the amount of instruction about founding it that he gave to his disciples before his ascension. My own position is that the first two chapters of *The Acts* prove that the Church was fully viable from the day of Pentecost, though its main elements were not co-ordinated until that day. The Holy Spirit, promised by Jesus, was the catalyst at its birth. Nevertheless, all the main elements that were necessary for its springing to life on the day of Pentecost had first been thought through and then meticulously prepared by Jesus during his lifetime and during his resurrection appearances, and then shared with his Apostles in readiness for the unified vision that the Spirit would confer on them at Pentecost. From the day of Pentecost the Church has never ceased to develop as a living entity with respect to its organisation, liturgy and ritual in a way analogous to the development of the human body from the embryo to full maturity.

Apostles after the resurrection in the following terms:

> He was taken up after he had given injunctions to the Apostles he
> had chosen; to whom also he showed himself alive after his passion
> by many infallible proofs, being seen by them through forty days and
> speaking of the things pertaining to the Kingdom of God (Ac 1:2-3).

It would seem certain that the New Testament writers have
not given us a complete list of all the times that Jesus appeared; and it is likely that he appeared to the Twelve or to
some of them on other occasions. We know of the following
appearances:[51]

1) To Mary Magdalene and the other Mary (Mt 28:9-10),
2) To Mary Magdalene alone in the Garden (Jn 20:2f),
3) To two disciples on the road to Emmaus (Lk 24:13-33),
4) To Peter (Lk 24:34; 1 Cor 15:5),
5) To the Eleven, apart from Thomas (Lk 24:36-49; Jn 20:19-25),
6) To the Eleven, including Thomas (Jn 20:26-29),
7) To seven Apostles and disciples by the Lake (Jn 21:1-23),
8) To the Eleven on a mountain in Galilee (Mt 28:16-20),
9) To the Eleven at his ascension (Lk 24:50-53; Ac 14-11),
10) To James (1 Cor 15:5-7),
11) To five hundred brethren all at once (1 Cor: 15:5-7),
12) To Paul (Ac 9:1-19; 1 Cor 15:5-8).

Apart from the steps Jesus took to convince the Apostles that he
had the same body in which he had walked with them in
Galilee, an analysis of his post-resurrection instructions shows
that they included:

a) a careful instruction on the most important prophecies that
    he had fulfilled by his life, death and resurrection,

b) His injunction that he was sending them out with full

---

51 There is a very ancient Church tradition that he also appeared on Easter Day to
    his blessed mother.

authority to teach everything that he had taught them,[52]

c) the whole human race as the target of their apostolate,

d) the preaching of his resurrection from the dead (1 Cor 15:12f),

e) the baptism of everyone in the name of the Blessed Trinity,

f) the gift of the Holy Spirit (Lk 24:49),

g) the power to forgive sins and to withhold forgiveness,

h) the promise to be with them always until he returned in glory at a time unknown to all but his Father (Mt 28:20),

i) keep the first day of the week as the Lord's Day, i.e. our Sunday,

k) to continue to celebrate the Last Supper (the 'breaking of the bread') as a memorial (Jn 20:26; Ac 2:46; Ac 20:7).

They are therefore to be his infallible witnesses wherever they go and they will work signs as great or even greater than the ones he had already performed. St Mark writes:

> These signs will accompany those who believe. In my name they will cast our demons and will speak with new tongues; and in their hands they will pick up serpents; and if they drink something deadly it will not hurt them; they will lay hands on the sick and they will get well (Mk 16:17-18).

This tremendous battery of powers is obviously included in the phrase 'the things of the Kingdom'(Ac 1:3).

The Twelve had already received the most remarkable spiritual training. In the first place they had inherited from their forbears the whole Jewish way of life, the Torah of Moses, as developed and enriched century after century in the spiritual culture of the Chosen People. Despite the aberrations and folly of the priests, scribes and Pharisees, there existed all the time a quiet and unobtrusive minority of holy men and women in Israel, the counterpart of the seven thousand men who did not bow their heads to Baal (1 Kg 19:18), people like

---

52 However there is also the academic question how much of the material that we find on the lips of Jesus in the Gospels was uttered by him after the resurrection rather than during his earthly ministry. For instance, O. Cullman has suggested that the famous promise to Peter (Mt 16:18-19) was not spoken near Caesarea Philippi, but delivered to Peter during the forty days before his ascension (cf. note 24 above).

Simeon and Anna, Elizabeth and Zechariah, and Jesus chose his Apostles from this minority, some of whom had become disciples of John the Baptist and been trained by him. Jesus completed their preparation for their world mission with a final polishing up of their standards during the forty days to make them fully responsive to the outpouring of the Holy Spirit.

The excellence of their training is reflected in the prompt and workmanlike manner in which they coped, under the inspiration and leadership of Peter, with the enormous influx of neophytes on the day of Pentecost itself. They knew exactly what they had to do and did it efficiently and without fuss. The first converts were practising Jews from Palestine or the Diaspora (i.e. Jews living in other parts of the world), so that there was no problem as yet about admitting Gentiles. The Jewish way of life as modified by the words and behaviour of Jesus was their norm and their guide.

But the new Christian way of life differed from the start in certain important respects. The high priests had refused allegiance to Jesus, so that from the day of Pentecost Peter and the Apostles were unable to accept their authority and accordingly replaced the Torah with the worship of Jesus, their Way and Truth and Life. Having been expelled from the Synagogue the new Christians looked to the Apostles as rulers given them by Jesus himself. Baptism marked entrance into the new fellowship, and baptism signified belief that Jesus was truly God and equal to the Father and the Holy Spirit. Thus the Christians realised that they were an alien body in the midst of the Old Israel.

A further consequence of their separateness was that they could not participate any more in the Temple sacrifices which no longer had any meaning for them. The ancient animal offerings of the Temple era merely pre-figured in various ways the one Sacrifice of Christ who had been expelled from the Temple and the Holy City in order to offer his life outside it on the hillock of Calvary that overlooked it. Though they could continue to participate in the morning and evening prayer of the Temple, yet from the very first Lord's day they celebrated their new Passover rite, the Breaking of the Bread, in their own houses in the City. Thus the house-church was born on the day of Pentecost, and soon all twelve Apostles would have had their own house-churches to look after (Ac 2:46).

It is therefore clear that from the very beginning circumstances forced the Apostles to establish for all believers in Jesus a way of life that was quite independent of, though parallel to, that of the old Jewish regime which was to continue until the Temple and its rites and sacrifices were entirely destroyed by the Romans in AD 70, and its rites and sacrifices finally ceased.

22

The Mystery Hidden from Past Ages

In a final reflection on the earthly life of Jesus Christ, one cannot do better than take as one's guide the inspired reflections of St Paul writing some thirty years after the resurrection to the Churches of the Ephesians and Colossians and in the Letter to the Hebrews, which certainly also reflects his thought on the mystery of Christ.

In the first place, Christ can only be fully understood by those who have been given the gift of faith in him, a gift which is freely offered to all peoples in all ages by his heavenly Father, but which in every age is not accepted by some and is abused by others. The mystery is that the infinite God (invisible to human eyes because he is the supreme Spirit) created a world for human beings to live in, beings God-like because of endowed with free will; and, by allowing them to disobey and defy him, this God was able to show his love for them still more clearly by humbly entering into their world in order to win them back to himself. God, in the person of the Son of God, the divine Word, the Second Person of the Blessed Trinity, entered our world so quietly and unostentatiously that he had passed through it before the world at large got to hear about his coming into it. It was to be the privilege of his disciples to proclaim the Good News after his resurrection to his benighted and self-corrupted creatures.

The first Adam and Eve, though given idyllic surroundings in which to live, had knowingly disobeyed God's command through a sin of pride, lured on by Satan the leader of the fallen angels and our main but secret enemy. God's plan for the restoration of the human race to his grace was made known little by little to the Chosen People, the Jews, by steps which are recorded in the books of the Old Testament. With hindsight it is possible now to see the working out of God's great plan, but the final revelation, that the redemption of the human race was to be encapsulated in the person of Jesus, the son of Mary, was so astonishing that it took everyone by surprise, even those most intimately associated with its unfolding. Just as it was the woman, Eve, who had led Adam astray at the beginning of human history, so God chose to put things right by choosing another woman, Mary, who would through her perfect innocence, purity and humility be the instrument for bringing into the world the Son of God, the One who would undo the disobedience of Adam by a total obedience to his heavenly Father. In one of his Psalms king David evoked him in these words: 'Then I said, Lo, I come; in the roll of the book it is written of me; I delight to do thy will, O my God; thy law is in my heart' (Ps 39 [40]:8-9).

Although the portents at his birth were both striking and in keeping with his dignity, the divine plan arranged that the Messiah—for this is who he was—should remain anonymous and unrecognized until the moment of his manifestation, heralded so brilliantly by John the Baptist. The chief characteristic of his early manhood was his total self-effacement. He avoided acquiring any of the aids that men normally take to prepare themselves for high office and the world stage; that is to say, though of royal blood, he made no use of his connections, he made no attempt to acquire powerful friends, or to build up wealth and a following for public life as ambitious men always do. Nor did he seek a special education, but in fact at the request of his parents deliberately sacrificed his opportunity to undertake higher theological studies and returned to the humdrum life of Nazareth until God called him.

Whence then did Jesus draw all his strength and authority since he rejected all the normal aids to the acquisition of power and influence? He drew it from the grace of the Holy Spirit, coupled with his dedication to obeying the will of his heavenly Father, and from a perfect body received from the immaculately conceived Virgin Mary, who in her turn conceived him by the Holy Spirit. As the Second Adam he enjoyed the perfection of a human body and soul which had never been tainted with sin (i.e. opposition to and alienation from God) and which had fully responded to all the exigencies of human existence throughout his life as well as to the will of his Father. The first Adam in Paradise had of course possessed similar qualities, which made his sin all the more grievous and culpable. The Second Adam, however, would not fail, but he too would have to rely solely on the gifts with which his human nature had been endowed, coupled with the grace of God. And his life on earth, as recorded in the Gospels, reveals to us how he did so. In the private life of Jesus we see his total reliance on God's providence, his total trust in him and his absolute poverty, another word for his total detachment from everything terrestrial, though loving everyone and everything as God's creation and loving gift to men.

There is no need for us here to discuss the limitations, if any, of the knowledge that Jesus had of the total economy of salvation, that is, of God's over-all plan; for it is certain that he understood his own role in it perfectly. He knew himself to be 'the high priest of the good things to come' (Heb 9:11) and so 'the mediator of the New Covenant'; he knew too that by means of the voluntary sacrifice of himself on the Cross he would make available to all the world the gift of eternal life through membership of his body (Heb 9:15). By his life, death and resurrection he achieved all his aims, everything he set out to do in fulfilment of his Father's will; but precisely because he was a man and suffered the limitations of time and space, he had to act in such a way during his short life that he would also be able effectively to act upon all future generations of Christians until the end of time. This he did by means of the sacraments that he left to his

Church; for in these sacraments he continues to live on in the world in the breasts of all those who have been baptised into his name. For as St Paul says: 'He has chosen us in him before the foundation of the world... having predestined us unto the adoption of sons by Jesus Christ to himself, according to the good pleasure of his grace' (Eph 1:4-5).

The whole earthly life of Jesus was a preparation for his eternal role of Redeemer and Saviour of the world. For 'by delivering us from the power of darkness and translating us into the kingdom of his beloved Son, the Father has made us to be partakers of the inheritance of the saints in light'(Col 1:13,14). During his lifetime on earth, human eyes could not discern his glory (except the one glimpse that he gave Peter, James and John on the mountain), but in the light of the Holy Spirit St Paul was able to tell us that Jesus 'is the image of the invisible God, the firstborn of all creation', that is, of the new creation. Furthermore, although this fact too was hidden from the eyes of men, 'by him were all things created, those in heaven, and those on earth, visible and invisible.... And he is before all things, and by him all things consist. And he is the head of the body, the Church: who is the beginning, the first born from the dead... For it pleased the Father that in him should all fulness dwell' (Col 1:19). As Hans Urs von Balthasar wrote: 'Jesus was aware that he was God's final word of salvation to mankind'. Whilst on earth, he was a temporal subject of Herod Antipas and of the Roman emperor, but on the Last Day when he comes in power and glory with his angels and saints to judge the living and the dead, his fiat will decide the destiny for all eternity of those who ordered him around during his lifetime as well as those who followed him faithfully. He is indeed the head of all humanity; and all whose names are written in the Book of Life, including all those of good will who sought the truth but who were not granted to recognize him during their own lifetime, will then be duly purified and enlightened, and will finally be taken up with him into everlasting joy and the Kingdom prepared for them from the foundation of the world. Come, Lord Jesus, come!

Appendix

References to the Christ in Contemporary Jewish and Pagan Literature

1. The Roman historian Suetonius (69-140) in his *Vita Claudii*, 25, in discussing the foreign policy of Claudius, mentions in passing that 'because the Jews at Rome caused continuous disturbances at the instigation of Chrestus, he expelled them from the city' (*The Twelve Caesars*, Penguin Classics 1957). This is certainly a reference to Christ, but the historian mistakenly attributes to Christ the quarrels that had broken out in Rome between the Jews and the Christians during the year AD 51-52.

The same historian in his *Vita Neronis*, 16, when speaking of the control of civil order, refers to 'punishments inflicted on the Christians, a people addicted to a new and evil superstition'.

2. The Roman historian Tacitus (55-120), in his *Annales*, III, xv, 44, refers to the Christians as 'Chrestiani', and has this to say about them:

> Their name comes from Christ, who under the rule of Tiberius, was delivered up to punishment by the procurator Pontius Pilate. Though suppressed at the time, this detestable superstition broke out afresh, not only in Judea where this evil had taken birth, but also in Rome where everything horrible and shameful in the world gathered together and found numerous disciples.

Though Tacitus' attitude is prejudiced, his information is correct!

3. Pliny the Younger, when Legate in Bithynia, wrote a letter to the emperor Trajan about the Christians in that province (*Plinii Secundi Epistularum*, X, 96), in which he mentioned *inter alia* the following facts about them: Their lives were entirely innocent and blameless and no fault could be found with them except for their Christian 'superstitions'. Among their practices were their morning meetings on certain days, when they sang hymns to Christ whom they invoked as God; and they also had eve-

ning meetings when they had a common meal.

4. Flavius Josephus (37-100) was the name adopted by the Jew Joseph ben Matthias, when he came to live in Rome after the Jewish War of 67-70 under the patronage of Vespasian. He was a Pharisee and a priest by birthright and on his mother's side was of royal blood. When the aforesaid War ended he was able to retire to Rome on a pension provided by Vespasian and devoted the rest of his life to writing about the history of his nation and its conflict with Rome. For our present purpose we shall refer only to his *The Jewish War,* published before 79, and *The Antiquities of the Jews,* published about 95.

The *Jewish War* (cf. Loeb Classics, 1989 reprint) was originally written in Aramaic for the benefit of Josephus' compatriots between 67 and 72. After Josephus had come to Rome for Titus' Roman triumph in 72 he prepared a new edition in Greek, published between 75 and 79, dedicated to the emperor Vespasian, apparently omitting a large number of passages, some of which are now found only in the 13th cent Old Russian and Rumanian translations and are called by modern scholars 'Slavonic Additions'. However, scholars are still arguing whether they were part of the original Aramaic (cf. note 42).

The passage of interest to us in *The Antiquities of the Jews,* XVIII, 3, 3, (tr. G.A. Williamson) is as follows:

> Now there was about this time [during the procuratorship of Pontius Pilate], Jesus, a wise man, if it be lawful to call him a man, for he was a doer of wonderful works, a teacher of such men as receive the truth with pleasure. He drew over to him both many of the Jews and many of the Gentiles. He was the Christ; and when Pilate, at the suggestion of the principal men amongst us, had condemned him to the cross, those that loved him at the first did not forsake him, for he appeared to them alive again the third day, as the divine prophets had foretold these and ten thousand other wonderful things concerning him; and the tribe of Christians, so named from him, are not extinct at this day.

The above passage is in all the manuscripts and it is difficult to sustain the argument that it is a Christian interpolation as is often done by many Jewish scholars, some of whom seem to have been reluctant for ideological reasons to admit that Josephus could have written about Christ in these terms (cf. L.H. Feldman, *Josephus and Modern Scholarship,* Berlin 1984).

G.A. Williamson, editor of the Penguin Classics edition (1959) of *The Jewish War* holds that the 'Slavonic Additions' are not Christian interpolations but the genuine work of Josephus from an earlier Aramaic edition of our present Greek text for the following reasons: 1) because there would be no purpose for any Christian to go to the trouble of merely inserting such neutral and lack-lustre references as these with respect to the Christ, 2) the style is Josephus' style. Moreoever, out of the 22 alleged interpolations 15 are concerned with virulent attacks either on the Romans or on the high priestly families and the Herods, and this supports the view that they reflect Josephus' own true dislikes and feelings as a good Jew.

The following is the translation of the added passage about Jesus from Old Russian and Rumanian found after *Jewish War,* V.214 (pp. 657-8), one of the so-called Slavonic Additions:

> It was at this time that a man appeared—if man is the right word—who had all the attributes of a man but seemed to be something greater. His actions, certainly, were superhuman, for he worked such wonderful and amazing miracles that I for one cannot regard him as a man; yet in view of his likeness to ourselves I cannot regard him as an angel either. Everything that some hidden power enabled him to do he did by an authoritative word. Some people said that their first Lawgiver had risen from the dead and had effected many marvellous cures; others thought he was a messenger from heaven. However, in many ways he broke the Law—for instance, he did not observe the Sabbath in the traditional manner. At the same time his conduct was above reproach. He did not need to use his hands; a word sufficed to fulfil his every purpose.
>
> Many of the common people flocked after him and followed his teaching. There was a wave of excited expectation that he would enable the Jewish tribes to throw off the Roman yoke. As a rule he was to be found opposite the City on the Mount of Olives, where also he healed the sick. He gathered round him 150 assistants and masses of followers. When they saw his ability to do whatever he wished by a word, they told him that they wanted him to enter the City, destroy the Roman troops, and make himself king; but he took no notice.
>
> When the suggestion came to the ears of the Jewish authorities, they met under the chairmanship of the high priest and exclaimed: 'We are utterly incapable of resisting the Romans; but as the blow is about to fall we had better go and tell Pilate what we have heard, and steer clear of trouble, in case he gets to know from someone else and confiscates our property, puts us to death, and turns our children adrift'. So they went and told Pilate, who sent troops and butchered many of the common people. He then had the miracle-worker brought before him, held an inquiry, and expressed the opinion that he was a benefactor, not a criminal or agitator or a would-be king. Then he let him go, as he had cured Pilate's wife when she was at the point of death.

Returning to his usual haunts he resumed his normal work. When the crowds grew bigger than ever, he earned by his actions an incomparable reputation. The exponents of the Law were mad with jealousy, and gave Pilate 30 talents to have him executed. Accepting the bribe, he gave them permission to carry out their wishes themselves. So they seized him and crucified him in defiance of all Jewish tradition'.

It is clear from the above that the ministry of Jesus, brief though it was, must have made an enormous and unforgettable impact on the Jewish society of his time, and as a historian Josephus could not in honesty omit some sort of account of the man who changed the course of Jewish history. Joseph us however adopts the standpoint of a neutral observer and though unwilling to accept the claims of the Christ he remains deeply impressed by his integrity. From the fact that there are no less than seven of these Additions that relate to Jesus, it seems certain that he was a subject of great concern and interest to him; and when we inspect the contents of these passages it becomes clear that Josephus understood correctly the main facts about his life including the Gospel stories. Proof of this lies in the fact that he makes sure that the high priests are shown as bearing the chief responsibility for putting Jesus to death, in one account, and the Romans in the other.

CHRONOLOGICAL TABLE OF THE LIFE OF JESUS
(n.b.: The dates are approximate only)

CHURCH EVENTS	YEAR	STATE EVENTS
	BC 37	Herod the Great becomes king.
	31	Accession of Augustus Caesar.
	19-9	Rebuilding of the Temple.
Jesus is born in Bethlehem.	? 8	
Flight into Egypt.	? 6	
	4	Death of Herod the Great; Archelaus becomes tetrarch of Judea and Herod Antipas tetrarch of Galilee.
Holy Family returns to Nazareth.	? 2	
	AD 6	Deposition of Archelaus; Rebellion of Judas of Galilee.
	14	Death of Augustus; Tiberius becomes emperor.
	18	Caiaphas replaces his father-in-law Annas as high priest.
< See Table below >	26/27	Pontius Pilate prefect of Judea.
Conversion of St Paul.	28-30	
	? 32	
	36	Caiaphas and Pontius Pilate removed.
	38	Tiberius dies; Caligula succeeds.
	39	Death of Herod Antipas.
	41	Claudius becomes emperor; Herod Agrippa I king of Judea.
Peter's imprisonment and escape.	? 42	
Publication of St Matthew's Gospel.	? 43	
	44	Herod Agrippa I dies.
Famine prophesied by Agabus.	45/6	
Paul's First Missionary Journey.	46-48	
Council of Jerusalem.	49	

THE MAIN EVENTS OF THE MINISTRY OF JESUS

AD	
? 26/7	Beginning of Mission of John the Baptist.
28	
? Feb	Jesus comes to John for baptism.
? Apr	Passover (Jn 2): Jesus cleanses the Temple in Jerusalem - FIRST VISIT.
? Dec	Jesus leaves Judea for Galilee after John's imprisonment by Herod Antipas.
29	
? Feb	Feast of Purim - SECOND VISIT to Jerusalem (Jn 5).
Apr	Feeding of the Five Thousand.
Sep-Oct	Feast of Tents. Jesus preaches in Jerusalem (Jn 7-8) - THIRD VISIT.
Dec	Feast of the Dedication - FOURTH VISIT; Jesus leaves Galilee for Transjordan and Ephraim.
30	
? Feb	Raising of Lazarus in Bethany.
? Apr	Jesus enters Jerusalem to celebrate the Passover. His Passion. Crucifixion. Death. Resurrection.
May	Christ's Ascension.
May-Jun	Feast of Weeks (Pentecost). Descent of the Holy Spirit.

JERUSALEM IN THE TIME OF JESUS

Third Wall?

Pool of Bethzatha

BETHZATHA

Antonia

Sheep Gate

Calvary †

Second Wall

Court of the Israelites

Court of Women

TEMPLE

Solomon's Portico

Chamber of Hewn Stone

Gethsemane

Jaffa Gate

Court of Gentiles

Mt Olivet

Herod's Palace

Palace of Herod (?)

Xystus

Royal Portico

KIDRON VALLEY

UPPER CITY

TYROPOEON VALLEY

House of Caiaphas?

Cenacle

0 metres   300

LOWER CITY

N ↑

Gate of Essenes

Pool of Siloam

First Wall

GEHENNA

Hakeldama?

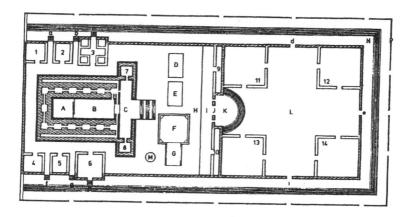

PLAN OF THE TEMPLE

(Courtesy of John Wilkinson, *Jerusalem as Jesus knew it*, London 1982)

100 metres

Plan of Herod's Temple as described by Josephus and in the Mishnah. Many details are not known in entirety and many of the following identifications are necessarily conjectural. Court of Gentiles and surrounding porticos are not shown here.

a	Gate of the Flame (or Jeconiah)
b	Gate of the Offering
c	(unknown)
d	Gate of the Women?
e	Gate of Singing?
f	Kindling Gate
g	Firstlings' Gate
h	Water Gate
i	(unknown)

A Holy of Holies *(Debir)*
B Holy Place *(Hekal)*
C Porch *(Olam)*
D&E Slaughtering places
F Altar
G Ramp
H East part, Court of the Priests
I Court of the Israelites
J Nicanor ('Beautiful'?) Gate
K Levites' place for singing
L Court of the Women
M Laver
N Terrace
O Fourteen steps
P Barrier at Court of Gentiles

1 Salt chamber
2 *Parwah* ('indeterminate') chamber
3 Chamber of the hearth
4 Wood chamber
5 *Golah* (cistern) chamber
6 'Chamber of Hewn Stone'
    (beneath chamber of Abtinas)
7&8 Chambers of the slaughter knives
9 Bakers' chambers
10 Custodian of the Robes' chamber
11 Lepers' chambers
12 Wood store
13 Oil store, also for wine
14 Nazirites' chamber

THE HOLY LAND AT THE TIME OF JESUS' MINISTRY

Index